T0359126

*The publication analyzes in a comprehensive way the characteristics and dynamics of innovation throughout the value chain and provides effective examples of how tourism businesses and destinations develop and implement innovative approaches. Innovation is at the heart of the 10YFP Programme on Sustainable Tourism (10YFP STP), led by UNWTO together with the Governments of France, Korea and Morocco, as it aims at accelerating the shift towards more sustainable consumption and production patters. Decoupling economic growth from resources use is not only needed in a tourism sector, which is continuously growing in importance and size, but it is also of pivotal importance for our nowadays societies. Innovation in tourism is of crucial importance for sustainable and resilient growth.*

Dirk Glaesser, Director, Sustainable Development of Tourism,
World Tourism Organization (UNWTO)

# Competence-Based Innovation in Hospitality and Tourism

Dr Pechlaner and Dr Innerhofer, the editors of *Competence-Based Innovation in Hospitality and Tourism*, argue that the industry operates within highly challenging and competitive environments. Changing environmental and market conditions continually force hotel businesses and service providers to offer their customers new and modified products and services, in order to remain competitive; those which respect value perceptions of markets and sustainable stakeholder reactions. This then raises the question of how innovations within this industry must be developed in order to achieve competitive differentiation.

The book demonstrates that the development and analysis of successful innovation strategies should integrate the resource-based view and its advancements, the competence-based view, as well as the dynamic capabilities approach and the relational view. Resource-based strategic management approaches view the firm as a bundle of resources and competences. They point to the importance of firm-specific resources and competences in explaining variations in competitive positions and performance differentiation between companies. The challenge of hospitality and tourism is to develop resources and competences that drive innovations.

This book will serve to advance the status quo of tourism research literature by combining innovation theories with network theories and tourism and destination development, by illustrating the development of cooperative competences and innovations in tourism and by showing, in a tailored way, how the challenge of the development of resources and competences that drive innovations in tourism can be managed.

**Dr Harald Pechlaner** is the Professor and holder of the Chair of Tourism, Catholic University of Eichstaett-Ingolstadt, Germany and Scientific Director of the Institute for Regional Development and Location Management at the European Academy of Bozen-Bolzano, Italy. He is the assessor for a number of scientific journals and he is a Member of several boards such as the Editorial Advisory Board of Tourism and Hospitality. He has been published in many English journals. Dr Elisa Innerhofer is a Senior researcher at the European Academy of Bozen-Bolzano, Italy, in the Institute for Regional Development and Location Management. Her book entitled *Strategic Innovation in the Hotel Industry* was published by Springer, in German in July 2012.

# Competence-Based Innovation in Hospitality and Tourism

Edited by
HARALD PECHLANER
ELISA INNERHOFER

Routledge
Taylor & Francis Group

LONDON AND NEW YORK

First published 2016 by Routledge

2 Park Square, Milton Park, Abingdon, Oxfordshire OX14 4RN

52 Vanderbilt Avenue, New York, NY 10017

*Routledge is an imprint of the Taylor & Francis Group, an informa business*

First issued in paperback 2020

*British Library Cataloguing in Publication Data*
A catalogue record for this book is available from the British Library

*Library of Congress Cataloging-in-Publication Data*
Names: Pechlaner, Harald, editor of compilation. | Innerhofer, Elisa.
Title: Competence-based innovation in hospitality and tourism /
    edited by Harald Pechlaner and Elisa Innerhofer.
Description: Farnham, Surrey, UK ; Burlington, VT : Gower, 2016. |
    Includes bibliographical references and index.
Identifiers: LCCN 2015029003 | ISBN 9781472463968 (hardback) |
    ISBN 9781472463975 (ebook) | ISBN 9781472463982 (epub)
Subjects: LCSH: Hospitality industry—Management. | Tourism—
    Management. | Strategic planning.
Classification: LCC TX911.3.M27 C636 2016 | DDC 647.94068—dc23
LC record available at http://lccn.loc.gov/2015029003

ISBN: 978-1-4724-6396-8 (hbk)
ISBN: 978-0-367-60602-2 (pbk)

Typeset in Palatino Linotype
by Apex CoVantage, LLC

# Contents

# List of Figures

# List of Tables

# Notes on the Editors

**Harald Pechlaner** (Prof. Dr) holds a Chair in Tourism and is Director of the Center for Entrepreneurship at the Catholic University Eichstaett–Ingolstadt in Germany. Harald Pechlaner is Adjunct Research Professor at Curtin University in Perth/WA (Curtin Business School). Since 2014 he is President of the International Association of Scientific Experts in Tourism (AIEST). He is Director of the Institute for Regional Development and Location Management at the European Academy of Bozen–Bolzano in Italy. His main areas of expertise include destination governance, resort and location management, and entrepreneurial management.

**Elisa Innerhofer** (Dr) is a senior researcher at the Institute for Regional Development and Location Management at the European Academy of Bozen–Bolzano in Italy. She studied International Economics and Business Studies and Political Science at the University of Innsbruck (Austria) and the Marquette University (US). She did her doctoral studies in Economic Science at the Catholic University Eichstaett–Ingolstadt (Germany). Her research interests are strategic innovation/product development in hospitality and tourism; transformation processes in regional development and culture as a locational factor.

# Notes on Contributors

**Monika Bachinger** (Dr) received her PhD from the Faculty of Economics at the Catholic University Eichstaett–Ingolstadt. In September 2013 she became a Professor of Tourism at the University of Applied Forest Science in Rottenburg, Germany. Her research centres on nature- based tourism and tourism product development with special focus on green value chains. She has carried out counselling projects on regional development processes, moderated panels of experts, and supported public participation processes.

**Tim Baird** is a PhD candidate at the University of Canterbury in Christchurch, New Zealand. He also holds a Master of Commerce with a First Class Honours degree from this institution. Tim has published in the areas of sustainability, biosecurity, innovation and wine tourism, with a particular focus on these issues within the New Zealand wine industry.

**Christian Buer** (Prof.) graduated from the University of St. Gallen (Hochschule St. Gallen – HSG) in 1992 in Business Administration and finished his PhD with Prof. Dr Claude Kaspar. His career began in the hospitality industry at Steigenberger Consulting, followed by responsibilities in Business Development and Marketing at Arabella Sheraton (Starwood) before he took responsibility for the hospitality real estates from Fundus Group. In 2004 Prof. Buer was appointed Chair of Business Administration and International Consulting at Heilbronn University; today he is responsible for the university's Department of Tourism and Hospitality. He is a member of the Travel Industry Club (TIC) and is the Advisor for Sciences. Prof. Buer is a member of the Association of Hotel Directors in Germany (HDV) and is active on the strategic advisory board of 'Education and Development'. He is Chairman of the Heilbronn Hospitality Symposium.

**Manuela De Carlo**, PhD in Business Administration and Management from Leuven University in Belgium, is full Professor at IULM University in Milan where she founded and directs the Masters course in Tourism Management. Her research focuses mainly on destination governance, on destination image formation and on the development of IT capabilities in tourism firms. Her research has been published in *Annals of Tourism Research, Current Issues in Tourism,* the *Journal of Place Management* and other journals.

**Fabienne Foss** (MA) is working as a marketing manager in the official tourism organization of Bavaria in Munich, Germany. She studied Entrepreneurship and Tourism at the Innsbruck, School of Management, Austria, and Business Management at the FH Kufstein University of Applied Sciences, Tyrol, Austria. During her study programme she spent a semester abroad at the Assumption University in Bangkok, Thailand, and gained practical experience in the fields of tourism, event management and marketing.

**Sarah Gardiner** is a lecturer in Tourism and Hotel Management at Griffith University, Gold Coast, Australia. Sarah holds a PhD in Marketing from Griffith University. She has worked in and acted as consultant on tourism and economic development to government and industry. Her current research interests are consumer behaviour, the design of experience and tourism destination marketing and development. She has published papers in leading tourism academic journals on these topics.

**C. Michael Hall** is Professor at the Department of Management, Marketing and Entrepreneurship at the University of Canterbury (New Zealand). He is Co-Editor of the journal *Current Issues in Tourism* and book review editor of the *Journal of Sustainable Tourism*. Michael Hall is Associate Editor for Asia and the Pacific, Tourism Geographies, and Editor of the Contemporary Geographies of Leisure, Tourism and Mobility book series. He is active as Co-Editor of the Aspects of Tourism book series, Editor of the Routledge Studies of Gastronomy, Food and Drink, and Co-Editor of the Routledge Critical Studies in Tourism, Business and Management. In addition, Michael Hall is Docent at the Department of Geography of the University of Oulu in Finland and Visiting Professor at the Linnaeus University School of Business and Economics in Kalmar (Sweden).

**Kir Kuščer** is a teaching assistant at the Faculty of Economics at the University of Ljubljana. He specializes in mountain tourism, innovativeness and development, and in the performance of the tourism sector in the Mediterranean countries. He has participated in numerous projects in Slovenia and on an international level. He was active in the development of foundations for the strategy of Slovenian tourism 2012–2016 and as a leader in the INTERREG IVC project (Digital Agenda for New Tourism Approach in European Rural and Mountain Areas).

**Cornelia Locher (Dr)** is an associate professor in Medicinal Chemistry in the School of Medicine and Pharmacology at the University of Western Australia. She is a member of the Australasian University Pharmacy Complementary Medicines Education (AUPCME) Group. Next to her expertise in natural product chemistry, she has developed a keen interest in alternative and complementary medicines, particularly phytomedicines, and their contribution to health and wellbeing.

**Tanja Mihalič** is a full Professor of Tourism and Head of the Tourism Institute at the Faculty of Economics, University of Ljubljana (FELU). At FELU she is also head of the Masters programmes in Tourism, including the joint international Erasmus Mundus EMTM (European Masters in Tourism Management). She is also a member of the European Commission's Tourism Sustainability Group and UNWTO's Education and Scientific Council. Tanja Mihalič has been involved in many research projects and has published a number of papers and books relating to tourism economics, development, competitiveness and policy and environmental management.

**Birgit Muskat** (Dr) is a senior lecturer at MCI Management Center Innsbruck, Austria. Currently she is an Adjunct Fellow at the School of Business at Notre Dame University in Australia. Birgit Muskat's research concentrates on overlapping areas in Organisational Behaviour and Tourism Management. She is involved in several funded international research projects. Her current research explores leadership, innovation and knowledge transfer in the context of tourism, events and services. Birgit Muskat has published a variety of high-quality peer-reviewed journal articles, book chapters, conference papers, and a book about tourism management. She has obtained researcher roles in academies in Australia and Germany. Prior to her academic career, she held a number of positions in the private industry sector with a particular focus on tourism and services.

**Matt Muskat** (Dr) is a senior lecturer at MCI Management Center Innsbruck, Austria, and currently an Adjunct Fellow at the School of Business at Notre Dame University in Australia. His research focuses on international marketing, consumer and travel behaviour, service experience and demographic change. Matt Muskat has a background in teaching and research in management and marketing in Australia, Germany, Singapore and Austria. His research has been published in various high-quality peer-reviewed journals and conference proceedings. He has published a book about demographic change in leisure and tourism.

**Mike Peters** (Dr) is full professor at the University of Innsbruck and holds the endowed Chair of SME and Tourism at the Department of Strategic Management, Marketing and Tourism. After finalizing his apprenticeship he worked for several years in the hotel industry in Germany before he studied social sciences at the Universities of Regensburg, Germany, and Innsbruck, Austria. He holds a PhD in Business Management. His research interests are small business' growth problems, innovation and entrepreneurship in small and family businesses.

**Christof Pforr (PhD)** is associate professor and course coordinator for Tourism and Hospitality and group leader of the Research Focus Area 'Sustainable and Health Tourism' with the School of Marketing at the Curtin Business School, Curtin University, Australia. He holds a PhD in Political Science from the Northern Territory University and a *Staatsexamen* in Geography and Political Science. He has a Teaching Certificate from the University of Tübingen, Germany. His main research interests include tourism policy and planning, sustainable (tourism) development, health tourism, coastal tourism and geotourism, as well as destination governance with a focus on network management and network analysis.

**Bettina Prukker-Losonczi** holds a BSc in Geography with minor subject Sociology and is currently working towards an MSc in Tourism and Regional Planning and Management and Geography at the Catholic University Eichstaett–Ingolstadt. Her academic interests include sustainable tourism, hospitality and destination governance. As a human geographer she is interested in the interrelationships between tourists and hosts and destinations and environments within a sustainable regional context.

**Hannes Rau** holds degrees in Tourism Management, Geography (BSc) and Forestry (BSc) and is currently working towards an MSc in Physical Geography at the University of Applied Forest Science in Rottenburg, Germany. His academic interests include sustainable forest management, natural conservation areas and large-scale protected areas. As a geographer, he is also concerned about the spatial interrelationships and implications within a regional context.

**Ruggero Sainaghi** received his PhD in Business Administration and Management from the St. Gallen University, Switzerland, and is full Professor at IULM University. His research interests are destination management (strategic positioning, archetypes, corporate governance, performance measurement) and competitive strategies of tourism firms (relationships between firm and destination strategy, firms' performance).

**Noel Scott** is Professor at the Griffith Institute for Tourism at Griffith University, Gold Coast, Australia. He has completed tourism consultancy projects in a number of countries, including Chile, China, Fiji, Saudi Arabia and Peru. He has published over 210 academic articles, including in 13 books. He has supervised 18 doctoral students to successful completion of their theses. His research interests include the study of tourism experiences, destination management and stakeholder organization.

**Cornelia Voigt** is an adjunct research fellow in the School of Marketing at Curtin University, Australia. She holds a Bachelor of Information Management from the Hochschule der Medien in Stuttgart, Germany, and a Master of Strategic Marketing from the University of Wollongong in Australia. In 2010 she was awarded with a PhD from the School of Management, University of South Australia. With her tourism research she has won several awards and has recently co-edited the book *Wellness Tourism: A Destination Perspective*. Her expertise in health tourism has led to the acquisition of competitive research grants and a number of invited speeches at international conferences. Her research expertise is in the areas of wellness tourism, medical tourism, strategic marketing and market research (consumer behaviour, motivation, segmentation), the relationship between tourism/leisure and well-being, positive psychology and health promotion.

**Michael Volgger** (Mag.) is a researcher at the Institute for Regional Development and Location Management at the European Academy of Bozen–Bolzano in Italy. He is studying for his doctorate at the Catholic University of Eichstaett–Ingolstadt in Germany. His main areas of expertise include destination governance and location management, innovation, and cooperation in tourism.

**Anita Zehrer** is deputy head and senior lecturer at MCI Tourism at the Management Center Innsbruck (MCI), deputy head of the MCI Academic Council, adjunct professor at the University of Canberra, Australia, and vice-president of the Deutsche Gesellschaft für Tourismuswissenschaft DGT e.V. (German Association for Tourism Research). She is a member of the Tourism Advisory Board of the Federal Ministry of Foreign Affairs and Energy, Germany. Her research interests are diverse and include consumer behaviour in tourism, service experiences and service design, social media in tourism, entrepreneurship and leadership in tourism, family business management in tourism, epistemology in tourism and tourism education. Anita Zehrer currently serves on several editorial boards such as the *Journal of Travel Research, Journal of Vacation Marketing, Tourism Analysis,* the *Tourism Review* and *the Journal of Hospitality and Tourism Management,* and is a reviewer for a range of tourism and hospitality journals.

# Foreword

New business models and distribution channels, together with evolving market conditions and changing needs and expectations from the consumer side, provide the momentum to reflect on how to take more innovative and strategic approaches to tourism planning and management.

This publication analyses in a comprehensive way the characteristics and dynamics of innovation throughout the value chain. It provides effective examples of how tourism businesses and destinations develop and implement innovative approaches and how they compete in dynamic markets.

Despite the slow economic recovery from the 2008 global financial crisis and subsequent rising geopolitical conflicts, tourism has regained a strong position: it represents 9 per cent of global GDP, 30 per cent of the world's export of services and one in every 11 jobs worldwide. With over 1.1 billion tourists travelling the world last year, the sector is one of the major economic and human activities of our time, benefiting many aspects of our lives – the economy, social progress, job creation and poverty alleviation. In addition, with an estimated six billion people travelling within their own countries, there are multiple opportunities to promote the right shift in our paradigm through innovation and the right vision.

The World Tourism Organization (UNWTO), as the United Nations specialized agency responsible for the promotion of sustainable, resilient and universally accessible tourism, is supporting the 10-Year Framework of Programmes on Sustainable Consumption and Production Patterns (10YFP), the United Nations framework of action designed to enhance international cooperation to accelerate the shift towards sustainable consumption and production in both developed and developing countries.

Among the programmes established under this global framework is the 10YFP Programme on Sustainable Tourism (10YFP STP), led by UNWTO together with the governments of France, Korea and Morocco. It envisages a sector that has globally adopted sustainable consumption and production practices through efficiency, innovation, new financing mechanisms and adaptability, resulting in enhanced environmental and social outcomes and improved economic performance within the framework of the Sustainable Development Goals (SDGs).

Innovation is at the heart of this Programme, as it aims at accelerating the shift towards more sustainable consumption and production patters. Decoupling economic growth from resources use is not only needed in a tourism sector which is continuously growing in importance and size but it is also of pivotal importance for today's societies. Tourism would thus not only lead this shift but would also inspire people's behaviour beyond their holidays in such a manner that they continue following these patterns during the rest of the year.

I therefore very much welcome the authors' efforts to focus on this important area of innovation, which is of crucial importance for sustainable and resilient growth.

Dr Dirk Glaesser
Director, Sustainable Development of Tourism
World Tourism Organization (UNWTO)

# Chapter 1

# Introduction: Innovation in Tourism and Strategic Management Approaches

ELISA INNERHOFER and HARALD PECHLANER

Increased social and economic change, the conditions of turbulence under which organizations and businesses have to be successful and the increased competition put pressure on all industries, also on tourism businesses and destinations. Creativity and innovation are needed to stay in business and in a competitive position. The dynamics of the external environment require destinations and hotel businesses to react proactively, to continually improve and renew their products and services and to adapt to changing market conditions and customer requirements. In the light of the above, this chapter opens the discussion of innovation and the need of specific competences related to innovation in tourism.

The purpose of this introductory chapter is twofold: First, it presents the tourism product with its peculiarities and specific features. Second, it gives an introduction to the theoretical background, which constitutes the common thread/ground of the book. Strategic management theories provide the framework against which the chapters that follow illustrate a wide range of innovation in tourism. The following introduction should provide a guide to the 13 chapters of the volume. It closes with some observations regarding innovations in tourism and competences needed to manage those innovations.

## Innovation in Tourism

Innovation and new service development are important strategic features to assure sustainable success of destinations and hospitality businesses. From a business perspective, innovation means modifications to existing offerings or the creation of new ones in order to stimulate performance and profits. Innovations are improvements and novel concepts that are valuable to existing and new customer segments and that facilitate differentiation, at least for a limited period of time (Brooker, 2014). The potential of differentiation through innovation mainly depends on two factors: Firstly, it is the ability of the innovator (for example, the tourism operator or the hotelier) to develop innovations whose development processes are difficult to follow and not transparent for the competitors. Secondly, it depends on the competitor's ability to gain insights into successful innovations occurring in other tourism businesses and to copy the idea developed by innovators. The more difficult it is for competitors to understand and imitate new products and services, the longer innovation based on differentiation of the first mover lasts (Brooker, 2014). But, what distinguishes innovative firms from those which primarily follow market trends and competitors? Why are some destinations or tourism businesses more innovative than others, even if they are competing in the same industry?

In order to understand performance differences between destinations or tourism businesses achieved through innovation, the next section starts with the illustration of the composition of the tourism product and its complexity. The section following presents the approaches for analysing competitive advantages through innovation in tourism from a strategic management perspective.

## The Complexity of the Tourist Product

An examination of the subject of innovation in tourism reveals that incremental innovations are the norm, while radical innovations are very rare (Peters and Pikkemaat, 2005). Innovations and innovation processes are very complex, especially in a service-dominated industry such as tourism. Besides the fact that services are intangible in nature and that the customer himself is involved in the production and implementation of services and thus strongly influences the quality of the service outcome (Corsten, 1985; Maleri, 1973; Hilke, 1989), it is the nature and composition of the tourism product which makes innovation highly complex. Products addressed to tourists are complex and heterogeneous (Bieger, 2000). The tourist product constitutes a combination of elements separated in time and space (Caccomo and Solonandrasana, 2001), often offered in the form of a package, including products, services and experience opportunities such as transportation, accommodation or leisure facilities (Smith, 1994; Middleton and Clarke, 2001). Several organizations and businesses are involved in bundling and packaging. They can be small and medium-sized enterprises, multinationals, hotel chains, tour operators, etc. The final tourism offer relies on the organizational complementarities and interdependences among actors and groups of actors involved in the development and planning of products and services (Tremblay, 1998; Aldebert, Dang and Longhi, 2011). Another characteristic feature of tourism is that goods are not produced and delivered to customers, but tourists have to organize their travels and to move to the resources (Maleri, 1973; Engelhardt, Kleinaltenkamp, and Reckenfelderbäumer, 1994; Innerhofer, 2012). While in many service processes the spatial proximity and synchronization of production and consumption can be avoided by using information and communications technologies, in the hospitality sector direct contact between provider and consumer is essential. Accommodation and hospitality services are tied to a specific location and reliant on the client's willingness to move. This is what makes the factor 'location' a crucial production factor for tourism service providers (Innerhofer, 2012).

Contrary to the production of industrial services, touristic products are experience goods (Decelle, 2006; Weiermair, 2001). Thus, from the customers' perspective innovation in tourism is perceived as a new psychological experience (Benkenstein, 2001). At the moment they purchase a service, like accommodation and board reservation, they act with uncertainty due to the intangible nature of most parts of the product. Services are performances, rather than objects, and cannot be seen, felt, tasted or touched in the same manner in which goods can be sensed. While goods are produced, sold and consumed, services are sold and then produced and consumed at the same time (Zeithamel, Parasuraman, and Berry, 1985). Their quality and utility are not known ex ante by consumers (Maleri, 1973; Tsai, Verma, and Schmidt, 2008; Aldebert, Dang and Longhi, 2011).

The special features of services in general and tourism services in particular increase the complexity of innovation processes. The critical point is the intangibility, from which challenges emerge for both customers and providers. Because of the risk customers must take when buying an outcome or an experience they cannot fully assess prior purchase, they are very sensitive to services that are highly innovative or completely new to the world. Service companies often provide a tangible representation of the service, incorporate physical clues or tightly relate the new service to the reputation or brand image (Brentani, 1991). Hotel businesses, for example, use the hotel infrastructure to make the service less abstract for the guest.

One of the main challenges service industries are confronted with is the protection of new ideas and innovations. Due to their intangibility, services cannot be protected through patents (Eiglier and Langeard, 1975). In tourism, product innovation is visible and can be imitated immediately. The same applies to the intangible parts of innovations, which can be experienced. Thus, innovation in tourism is unlikely to qualify for protection by intellectual property rights (Decelle, 2006). Decelle (2006) refers to this type of new knowledge as a 'public good'. New services are usually developed more easily and quickly than new goods. Producing and launching does not involve high investments in raw materials or prototypes. That is not the least of the reasons why innovation processes are often ongoing instead of formally planned and managed processes (Brentani, 1991). Changes and improvements are mainly in response to changes in client needs or offerings launched by competitors (Rushton and Carson, 1991).

The lack of protection against imitation prevents tourism businesses from undertaking costly and time-consuming pioneering actions, since achieving competitive advantages in the long run seems highly difficult (Wind, 1982). Being the first to introduce new concepts within the sector in which a business operates does not necessarily result in better performances and higher profits than those of competitors.

However, innovations in tourism still occur and some tourism businesses perform better than others. Following the definition of Malerba (2002) and his dynamic view of sectors, the tourism industry is a sectoral system of innovation and production, in which a set of products are produced and a set of agents carry out market and non-market interactions. The agents are individuals and organizations with specific resources, competences, learning processes and organizational structures and they interact with each other through processes of communication, cooperation or exchange. The system, its agents and products are subject to dynamic changes and transformations, which lead to the improvement of existing products and services and to the development of innovations (Hall and Williams, 2008; Aldebert, Dang and Longhi, 2011). This definition refers to the dynamics of external environments as well as to the resources and competences of agents and their interactions and combination efforts, which characterize the internal environment. These two factors are the central reference points for the strategic management approaches introduced in the following section.

## Strategic Management Approaches

Two essential paradigms of strategic management are the market-based view and the resource-based view. While the market-based approach pertains to the traditional understandings, the resource-based view began to emerge only in the 1980s/1990s and provides additional insights (Peteraf, 1993).

The essence of strategic management is the development and the maintenance of specific and strategically relevant assets and skills to achieve sustainable competitive advantages. In addition, the selection of strategic combinations and competitive markets is crucial (Aaker, 1989). According to the market-based view of strategic management, competitive advantage is related to external environments and market conditions, while the resource-based view relates a company's above-average performance to its internal characteristics. Osterloh and Frost (1996) describe the market-oriented strategy as the *idea of the fit*, and the resource-oriented strategy as the *idea of the stretch*. The *idea of the fit* postulates that a company's strengths and weaknesses have to be adjusted to the specific needs of customers, as well as to risks and opportunities of the environment. The *idea of the stretch* looks inside the company. Competences and resources should be stretched in order to exploit their potential and to obtain their maximum performance.

The market-based approach of strategic management takes a market-oriented view and assumes that a company's success mainly depends on the industry structure and its competitive position. The source of the informational advantages necessary to develop a strategy leading to above-average performances is the firm's competitive environment. Industry analysis is seen as a tool to develop competitive strategies (Porter, 1980; Henderson and Cockburn, 1994). Selecting the right industry and generic strategy within an industry is the key factor to success, because industry is the most significant predictor of a company's performance (Montgomery and Porter, 1991). According to this understanding, success is a function of the attractiveness of the industry in which the company competes, and of its relative position in that industry (Porter, 1991).

Focusing on the market and the competing environment to explain competitive advantages and performance differences among competitors leads, however, to some restrictions. The market-based view refers to the question of where a company competes, the selection of the competitive arena and the overall market environment. Competing the right way and in the right arena can be profitable, but only for a limited period of time and rarely in the long run. The way a business competes can be imitated relatively easily. Furthermore, the methodologies for the collection of information through industry analysis are in the public domain. Various companies can apply the same publicly available methodologies to the analysis of the same environment and thus gain the same insights. In addition, the skills of environmental analysis can be bought from consulting firms, and thus possible competitive advantages will only be temporary (Barney, 1986).

In this case firms may try to turn inwardly and analyse the resources and competences they already control. These can be a source of competitive advantage, if they are used to develop strategies leading to above-average performances. While information on competitive characteristics of the environment may be available to various firms in the market, information on company-specific assets are controlled only by the company itself. This conclusion leads to the basic assumption of the resource-based view, which considers the resource base of companies as the source of sustainable competitive advantages and long-term, above-average performances (Aaker, 1989; Rumelt, 1984; Wernerfelt, 1984; Barney, 1986). Notable authors and their contributions, as well as influential forces in the development of the resourced-based view and its developments, are cited in the following sections.

## THE RESOURCE-BASED VIEW AND ITS DEVELOPMENTS

The resource-based view postulates the notion that companies are fundamentally heterogeneous in terms of their resources and competences. Thus, the basic assumption is that resource and competence bundles underlying production are heterogeneous across companies, even if they belong to the same sector (Barney, 1991). Internal resources, competences and capabilities, which are distinctive and superior relative to those of competitors, can be the basis for competitive advantage. They may allow companies to produce more economically or to better satisfy customer requirements (Peteraf, 1993). These ideas are the basic principles of the resource-based view. The model has deepened the understanding as how resources are applied and combined, what makes competitive advantage sustainable and where company heterogeneity has its origin (Peteraf, 1993).

A strategically relevant asset or resource is something a company possesses such as a brand name, a good reputation, or even a special location, which is superior to the competition (Aaker, 1989). A skill or a competence is something that a company does better than competitors such as manufacturing, distributing or customer relationship management. The right combination of assets, resources, skills and competences can provide barriers to competitor thrusts (Aaker, 1989). But, in order to achieve sustainable competitive advantages the superior resources have to remain limited in supply, or the combination of these resources has to be opaque and thus inimitable by competitors (Peteraf, 1993; Foss 1997). Barney (1991) defines strategically relevant resources and competences as those which are valuable, rare, inimitable or not substitutable. Therefore, an asset which is homogeneous or can be easily bought and sold at an established price cannot be all that strategic (Barney, 1986). This assumption, called the 'VRIN-framework', is widely accepted in the literature.

The resource-based view of strategic management is the umbrella term for several sub-approaches. One of these approaches is the competence-based view (Freiling, 2001; Fischer, 2010), which sees the company as a bundle of tasks and knowledge (while the resource-based view defines the firm as a bundle of physical, organizational and human resources). The approach assumes that the existence of resources and competences is a necessary but not sufficient condition for the creation of sustainable competitive advantage. Competitive advantage is founded on understanding and managing the systems of knowledge and tasks. The term 'competence' embraces the ability to understand and manage these systems. The possession of these competences is a crucial key to success (Krogh and Roos, 1994; Sanchez, Heene, and Thomas, 1996). According to the competence-based view, the important point is the ability to develop and build competences (Freiling, Stephan, Matzler, and Stahl, 2002). Substitution or imitation gets more difficult if a product or a process is the result of an ongoing knowledge accumulation process. With a difficult-to-replicate advantage, profits will not be competed away (Teece and Pisano, 1994).

However, in responding to environmental and market changes, the development and adaptability of the resource base becomes crucial to enable innovation. Originally the resource-based view took a rather static view of the resource base. The continuously increasing dynamism of the environment led to the evolution of the theory. Researchers introduced a dynamic component in their analysis and explanations. In the context of innovation and innovation processes, integrating the shifting character of the environment in the analysis seems crucial and more expedient than following a static approach.

## THE DYNAMIC APPROACH OF THE RESOURCE-BASED VIEW

The pressure to be innovative and the conditions of turbulence under which organizations and businesses have to be successful lead to the assumption that a certain dynamic in managing internal resources, capabilities and competences is required. According to Teece and Pisano (1994) the winners in the global marketplace are firms that demonstrate rapid and flexible product innovations along with the management capability to coordinate and redeploy internal and external competences, called dynamic capabilities. In contrast to the resource-based view, the emphasis of the dynamic capabilities approach is on dynamics (Easterby-Smith, Lyles, and Peteraf, 2009). Dynamic capabilities refer to the ability to integrate, adapt, coordinate, develop, renew and reconfigure internal and external organizational skills, resources, assets, and competences towards changing environments (Teece, Pisano, and Shuen, 1997; Foss, 1997). Continuous improvement and organizational learning occurs. The patterns of behaviour and learning were established over a long period of time and are closely tied to the company and its human resources (Teece and Pisano, 1994). They cannot be replicated or traded on the market, but have to be built within the organization. This historicity or path dependence is the foundation of the creation of isolating mechanisms that prevent imitation (Rumelt, 1984; Cohen and Levinthal, 1990; Ossadnik, 2000). Due to the historicity of such development processes, innovative performances are history- or path-dependent too (Cohen and Levinthal, 1990). To imitate routines, processes and capabilities, first their complex dimensions need to be understood, then replication may follow (Teece, Pisano, and Shuen, 1997).

Due to its dynamic approach, instead of a merely static view, the dynamic capabilities approach with particular emphasis on company- or destination-specific resources and competences provides a coherent framework to explain competitive advantage through innovation. In order to be innovative and to maintain a competitive position, tourism organizations, hospitality businesses and destinations need the competence to develop, renew and reconfigure internal and external resources and competences in ways that create new or better value throughout the chain of services. Once internal assets are developed and superior to those of competitors, they have to be matched appropriately to environmental and market opportunities. Resource- and competence-based innovations have to meet customer needs and requirements. Organization and company capabilities as well as competition and market environment are important in shaping strategy and performance (Henderson and Mitchell, 1997).

## Conclusion and Organization of Chapters

The inwardly oriented approaches of strategic management define the conceptual and analytical framework of the book. The resource-based view and the market-based view are not perceived as contradictory theories, but as two interrelated approaches. It is ultimately for the customer to decide about success or failure of a new resource-based product or service. In addition, the evaluation and feedback of markets, as well as competitive actions, are important sources for innovative ideas. Market trends and developments are finally influencing which resources and competences have to be renewed, expanded or developed and which innovations are designed to achieve sustainable competitive advantage.

The understanding of innovation in tourism, on which this book is based, integrates resources and competences, as well as competitive market environment, as sources of performance and competitive advantages. Innovations are perceived as the result of the reconfiguration and the combination of resources and competences with market needs and requirements (Innerhofer, 2012). On the basis of the theoretical framework presented in this chapter, the book presents examples of how tourism businesses and destinations combine and reconfigure resources and competences to develop innovations and how they compete in dynamic markets.

The first two chapters are theory-based and give insights into innovation theories and the resource-based view of strategic management. Based on that, Chapter 2 presents results of a case study analysis focusing on resources and competences which are strategically relevant to develop successful innovation. Bachinger and Rau (Chapter 3) put the light on green entrepreneurship in tourism. Based on the assumption that green growth in tourism is needed, they describe green entrepreneurs, as well as green innovations, and discuss factors that are able to promote resource efficiency in tourism.

The second stream of chapters focuses on innovation activities in the hospitality industry. Volgger and Prukker-Losonczi (Chapter 4) discuss selected innovative hotel concepts within Europe. Their case study aims to identify current perspectives regarding innovations in the hospitality sector. By discussing selected innovation approaches, they illustrate what future paths in innovation in the hospitality industry may look like. From a theoretical perspective, the study integrates the market- and competence-based approaches into a comprehensive perspective. In Chapter 5 Zehrer, Muskat, and Muskat present a quantitative research study aimed at identifying the degree to which internal and external variables influence innovativeness and which factors stimulate innovativeness and innovative behaviour. The results address a gap in tourism research. Peters and Foss (Chapter 6) highlight innovation processes in small and family businesses and analyse how hoteliers attempt to implement innovation processes in their companies. They present the results of a qualitative survey, in which they investigated 4-star and 5-star hotels in Western Austria. Results show that formalization of innovation processes is a major success factor. Buer (Chapter 7) focuses his attention on alternative forecasting of economics for hotel investments and assumes that the economic power/strength of a region is positively correlated to the economic success of a hotel and that the economic power of the hotel is secondary for the overall economic success.

The third stream of chapters presents innovation at destination level. In Chapter 8 Kuščer and Mihalič introduce a theoretical model to understand and explore the relationships between tourism development, innovativeness and destination environments in mountain tourism destinations. Chapter 9 reproduces excerpts from an interview conducted by the two editors of the book. Innerhofer and Pechlaner discuss driving forces of innovation and the capability to imitate innovative ideas and create innovations through adaptation with the managing director of the Tyrolean Tourism Board. Gardiner and Scott (Chapter 10) present the results of an empirical qualitative study involving Australian and Chinese students. Due to the fact that there are only few case studies of successful examples of innovative experience design, they discuss the innovation process used to develop new beach experiences for Chinese visitors on the Gold Coast, Australia. The next chapter is about the generation of destination capabilities. Sainaghi and De Carlo (Chapter 11) present the development of a product introduced in an Italian resort, and analyse the destination capability behind and identify the key elements underlying this capability.

In Chapter 12 Baird and Hall discuss competence-based innovation in New Zealand's Wine Tourism and outline the relationships between different areas of innovation and different business strategies. They present results of a study in which they identified the extent to which internal and external competences are utilized by wine growers engaged in wine tourism.

Pforr, Voigt and Locher (Chapter 13) focus their attention on wellness tourism destinations and utilize a novel framework to assess wellness tourism destination competitiveness. Using the example of the Margaret River Wine Region of Western Australia, they assess the relevance of eight categories of wellness tourism resources and competences derived from the framework, which are considered to be crucial for competitiveness and success of wellness tourism destinations. The book concludes with Chapter 14, which is a summarizing overview of the editors.

## References

Aaker, D.A. (1989). Managing assets and skills: The key to a sustainable competitive advantage. *California Management Review*, 31(2), 91–106.

Aldebert, B., Dang, R.J., and Longhi, C. (2011). Innovation in the tourism industry: The case of Tourism@. *Tourism Management*, 32, 1204–1213.

Barney, J.B. (1986). Strategic factor markets: Expectations, luck, and business strategy. *Management Science*, 32, 1231–1241.

Barney, J.B. (1991). Firm resources and sustainable competitive advantage. *Journal of Management*, 17, 99–120.

Benkenstein, M. (2001). Besonderheiten des Innovationsmanagements in Dienstleistungsunternehmen. In M. Bruhn and H. Meffert (eds), *Handbuch Dienstleistungsmanagement. Von der strategischen Konzeption zur praktischen Umsetzung* (687–702). Wiesbaden: Gabler.

Bieger, T. (2000). *Management von Destinationen und Tourismusorganisationen*. München: Oldenbourg.

Brentani, Ulrike de (1991). Success factors in developing new business services. *European Journal of Marketing*, 25(2), 33–59.

Brooker, E. (2014). Developing a tourism innovation typology: Leveraging liminal insights. *Journal of Travel Research*, 53(4), 500–508.

Caccomo, J.L., and Solonandrasana, B. (2001). *L'Innovation dans le tourisme. Enjeux et strategies*. Tourismes et Sociétés. Paris: L'Harmattan.

Cohen, W.M., and Levinthal, D.A. (1990). Absorptive capacity: A new perspective on learning and innovation. *Administrative Science Quarterly*, 35(1), 128–152.

Corsten, H. (1985). *Die Produktion von Dienstleistungen. Grundzüge einer Produktionswirtschaftslehre des tertiären Sektors*. Berlin: Erich Schmidt.

Decelle, X. (2006). A dynamic conceptual approach to innovation in tourism. In OECD (Organisation for Economic Co-operation and Development) (ed.), *Innovation and Growth in Tourism* (85–106). Paris: OECD.

Easterby-Smith, M., Lyles, M.A., and Peteraf, M.A. (2009). Dynamic capabilities: Current debates and future directions. *British Journal of Management*, 20, 1–8.

Eiglier, P., and Langeard, E. (1975). Une approche nouvelle pour le marketing des services. *Revue Française de Gestion*, 2 (Spring), 97–114.

Engelhardt, W.H., Kleinaltenkamp, M., and Reckenfelderbäumer, M. (1994). Leistungsbündel als Absatzobjekte. Ein Ansatz zur Überwindung der Dichotomie von Sach – und Dienstleistungen. In H. Corsten (ed.), *Integratives Dienstleistungsmanagement. Grundlagen – Beschaffung – Produktion – Marketing – Qualität. Ein Reader* (31–69). Wiesbaden: Gabler,

Fischer, E. (2010). *Kooperative Kernkompetenzen: Management von Netzwerken in Regionen und Destinationen*. Wiesbaden: Gabler.

Foss, N.J. (1997). Resources and strategy: A brief overview of themes and contributions. In N.J. Foss (ed.), *Resources, Firms, and Strategies. A Reader in the Resource-Based Perspective* (3–18). Oxford: Oxford University Press.

Freiling, J. (2001). *Resource-based view und ökonomische Theorie. Grundlagen und Positionierung des Ressourcenansatzes*. Wiesbaden: Gabler.

Friedrich, S.A., Matzler, K., and Stahl, H.K. (2002). Quo vadis RBV? Stand und Entwicklungsmöglichkeiten des Ressourcenansatzes. In K. Bellmann, J. Freiling, P. Hammann, and U. Mildenberger (eds), *Aktionsfelder des Kompetenz-Managements* (29–58). Wiesbaden: Gabler.

Hall, M.C., and Williams, A.M. (eds) (2008). *Tourism and Innovation*. Bodmin: Routledge.

Henderson, R., and Cockburn, I. (1994). Measuring competence? Exploring firm effects in pharmaceutical research. *Strategic Management Journal*, 15 (Winter: Special Issue), 63–84.

Henderson, R., and Mitchell, W. (1997). The interactions of organizational and competitive influences on strategy and performance. *Strategic Management Journal*, 18(S1), 5–14.

Hilke, W. (1989). Grundprobleme und Entwicklungstendenzen des Dienstleistungs-Marketing. In W. Hilke (ed.), *Dienstleistungs-Marketing. Banken und Versicherungen – Freie Berufe – Handel und Transport – Nichterwerbswirtschaftlich orientierte Organisationen* (5–44). Wiesbaden: Gabler.

Innerhofer, E. (2012). *Strategische Innovationen in der Hotellerie. Eine ressourcenorientierte Fallstudienanalyse touristischer Dienstleistungsunternehmen.* Wiesbaden: Springer Gabler Verlag.

Krogh, G., and Roos, J. (1994). Corporate divestiture and the phantom limb effect. *European Management Journal*, 12(2), 171–178.

Malerba, F. (2002). Sectoral systems of innovation and production. *Research Policy*, 31, 247–264.

Maleri, R. (1973). *Grundzüge der Dienstleistungsproduktion.* Berlin, Heidelberg, New York: Springer.

Middleton, V.T.C., and Clarke, J. (2001). *Marketing in Travel and Tourism.* Oxford: Butterworth-Heinemann.

Montgomery, C.A., and Porter, M.E. (1991). *Strategy: Seeking and Securing Competitive Advantage.* Cambridge, Massachusetts: Harvard Business School Publishing.

Ossadnik, W. (2000). Markt – versus ressourcenorientiertes Management – alternative oder einander ergänzende Konzeptionen einer strategischen Unternehmensführung. *Die Unternehmung*, 54(4), 273–287.

Osterloh, M., and Frost, J. (1996). *Prozessmanagement als Kernkompetenz.* Wiesbaden: Gabler.

Peteraf, M.A. (1993). The cornerstone of competitive advantage: A resource-based view. *Strategic Management Journal*, 14, 179–191.

Peters, M., and Pikkemaat, B. (2005). Innovation in tourism, *Journal of Quality Assurance in Hospitality and Tourism*, 6(3/4), 1–6.

Porter, M.E. (1980). *Competitive Strategy. Techniques for Analyzing Industries and Competitors.* New York: Free Press.

Porter, M.E. (1991). Towards a dynamic theory of strategy. *Strategic Management Journal*, 12, 95–117.

Rumelt, R.P. (1984). Towards a strategic theory of the firm. In R. B. Lamb (ed.), *Competitive Strategic Management* (556–570). New Jersey: Prentice-Hall.

Rushton, A.M., and Carson, D.J. (1985). The Marketing of Services: Managing the Intangibles. *European Journal of Marketing*, 19(3), 19–40.

Sanchez, R., Heene, A., and Thomas, H. (1996). Introduction: Towards the theory and practice of competence-based competition. In R. Sanchez, A. Heene, and H. Thomas (eds), *Dynamics of Competence-Based Competition. Theory and Practice in the New Strategic Management* (1–35). Oxford, New York: Pergamon.

Smith, S.L.J. (1994). The tourism product. *Annals of Tourism Research*, 21(3), 582–595.

Teece, D.J., Pisano, G., and Shuen, A. (1997). Dynamic capabilities and strategic management. *Strategic Management Journal*, 18(7), 509–533.

Teece, D.J., and Pisano, G. (1994). The dynamic capabilities of firms: An introduction. *Industrial and Corporate Change*, 3(3), 537–556.

Tremblay, P. (1998). The economic organization of tourism. *Annals of Tourism Research*, 25(4), 837–859.

Tsai, W., Verma, R., and Schmidt, G. (2008). New service development. In C.H. Loch and S. Kavadias (eds), *Handbook of New Product Development Management* (495–526). Amsterdam: Butterworth-Heinemann.

Weiermair, K. (2001). Von der Dienstleistungsökonomie zur Erlebnisökonomie. In H.H. Hinterhuber, H. Pechlaner, and K. Matzler (eds), *IndustrieErlebnisWelten. Vom Standort zur Destination* (35–48). Berlin: Erich Schmidt.

Wernerfelt, B. (1984). A resource based view of the firm. *Strategic Management Journal*, 5, 171–180.

Wind, Y.J. (1982). *Product Policy: Concepts, Methods, and Strategy*. Boston, Massachusetts: Addison-Wesley.

Zeithaml, Valarie A., Parasuraman, A., and Berry, L.L. (1985). Problems and strategies in services marketing. *Journal of Marketing*, 43 (Spring), 33–46.

# PART I
# Innovation and Resource-based
# Approaches of Strategic Management

# A Resource-based Approach to Innovation in the Hospitality Industry – Case Study Analysis

ELISA INNERHOFER

Tourism service providers and the hospitality sector encounter challenges in the development of innovations resulting from the special features of service innovations. In order to guarantee a company's sustainable and long-term competitive position through the use of innovation, special isolation mechanisms must be established which protect innovations against imitation by competitors. If companies only pursue markets, competitors or short-term trends, tourism providers do not differentiate on the market. Differentiation potentials lie in the company's resources and competences, which are specific and unique and not readily accessible to competitors. Resource-based approaches to strategic management are inwardly oriented approaches that – in analysing competitive differences between companies – rely on existing intra-corporate resources and competences. From a resource-based view, innovations and hence generated competitive advantages are the visible expression of underlying strategically relevant resources and competences.

Based on the case study below, the author shows how innovations can be developed relying primarily on strategically relevant resources. The case study states that the imitation of new products and services by competitors is made more difficult and the expected success due to innovation becomes more steady and sustainable if strategically relevant, complex, and company-specific resources and competences provide the basis for the development of innovations. In tourism, which is a location-based service sector, the regional and local resources, as well as the competence to integrate the location in the business concept, are innovation-relevant resources and competences. They can lead to individuality and uniqueness and, consequently, generate competitive advantages.

## Background

In dynamic markets, companies are challenged not only to respond reactively to dynamic competitive situations but also to play strategically active and proactive in order to determine markets and recognize opportunities. Markets and industries impose pressure to which companies must respond. Innovations are one possible way to encounter this dynamic by initiative and action. Changed competitive conditions and increased pressure towards innovation activities also affect the tourism industry, apart from industrial enterprises and service providers (Tajeddini, 2010). In highly saturated markets such as the tourism market, innovations and innovation activities are necessary to ensure the survival and competitiveness of the acting companies (Keller, 2002; Peters and Weiermair, 2002; Weiermair, 2005; Klausegger and Salzberger, 2006). In the development of new products and services the tourism sector in terms of service industry is confronted with problems which significantly influence the innovation activities of the sector.

The intangibility of the service, as well as the need to integrate an external factor into the service production process, result in a heterogeneous service outcome and impede protection possibilities for innovations (Benkenstein, 2001; Meyer and Blümelhuber, 1994; Rück, 2000). Owing to their intangibility, service innovations cannot be patented (Tsai, Verma, and Schmidt, 2008). Difficulties in preventing imitation and protecting innovations can be encountered with strategic management. In order for innovations to be inimitable and hence be a source of competitive advantage, they must be made in a way that makes it difficult for competitors to understand the development process behind them. If company-specific and thus strategically relevant resources and competences precede the development of innovations, this bundle of resources and competences can develop protection against the imitation of innovations.

Resource-based approaches to strategic management try to explain and analyse the relationship between a company's resources and competences and its innovations, as well as the company's competitive advantage against other competitors in terms of innovations (see, for example, Wernerfelt, 1984; Oliver, 1997; Freiling, Gersch, and Goeke, 2008). For tourism as a service industry the resource 'location' and its associated natural and location-based (regional) resources are significantly important for the development of innovations.

In the following section, the resource-based view is introduced and the term 'innovation' defined. The characteristics of service innovations are subsequently explained. The final section presents the case study. In a first step, two service innovation concepts developed at a corporate level are demonstrated. In a second step, the concrete implementation of the innovation concepts in two hotel businesses is explained. The last section focuses on sustainability-related aspects of the company analysed in the case study. The outcome of this work is the result of a one-year research project carried out in the course of the author's doctoral dissertation.

## A Resource-based Approach to Innovation

The question of which innovations are created, what their development process looks like, and whether they actually lead to competitive advantages depends highly on the company's available potential, resources and competences.

These resources and potential are strategically relevant if they offer the potential for differentiation from competitors and at the same time meet customer requirements (Pechlaner and Fischer, 2006). In order to permanently retain achieved competitive advantages and thus to be sustainably positioned, uniqueness is required and imitation must be prevented. The durability and resistance of innovations depend on how easily they can be substituted, replicated or imitated.

Within the framework of strategic management, resource-based approaches (resource-based view – see Figure 2.1) link competitive differences between companies, as well as competitive advantages of one company against another, to the heterogeneous level of resources. In contrast to the market-based view, where competitive advantages are attributed to external factors, resource-based approaches understand competitive advantages as the result of a company's strategic assets. Competitive advantage is ascribed to idiosyncratic competences and resource-based deployments rather than to external characteristics (Lado, Boyd, and Wright, 1992).

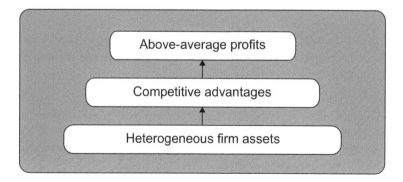

**Figure 2.1      Argumentation logic of the resource-based view**
*Source*: Based on Bamberger and Wrona, 1996 and Innerhofer, 2012.

Company heterogeneity in acquiring, deploying and developing resources and competences accounts for the generation of competitive advantages and economic rents. The resource-based view focuses on the characteristics of resources to explain company heterogeneity (Oliver, 1997). These approaches are based on an inside-out perspective, whereas the starting point of the analysis is the company's available resources and competences for the development of products and services. They influence the direction of diversification (Wernerfelt, 1984; Lado, Boyd, and Wright, 1992). The resources and competences of a company are characterized by time, historicity and experiences so that they are company-specific. Although every company is embedded in a business environment, there is still room for entrepreneurial actions and decision-making, which in turn shape environmental conditions according to the company's goals. These entrepreneurial actions and decision-making are influenced by the available resources and competences (Freiling, Gersch, and Goeke, 2008). In this case the future developments of a company are determined by the resource base, so that every company can be regarded as a unique, historically developed bundle of resources and competences (Penrose, 1959). Managers' past decisions and decision rules determine future actions. Hence, also sustainable advantages can be regarded as the result of history-dependent processes (Barney, 1991).

Owing to the immobility of company-specific resources which generate value only by application within the company (Figure 2.2), the heterogeneity of resources between companies is preserved (Dierickx and Cool, 1989; Barney, 1991; Amit and Schoemaker, 1993).[1] Company-specific resources are not commodities or products for which trade on the open market is technically possible or economically useful. These resources, representing a source with success potential, can be tangible and intangible factors contributing to added value (Thiele, 1997).

Wernerfelt (1984: 172) defines a resource as 'anything which could be thought of as a strength or weakness of a given firm'. The company's resources are the stock of available factors owned or controlled by the company (Amit and Schoemaker, 1993). These tangible and intangible resources allow companies to outperform competitors. In contrast, competences are necessary for the activation and reasonable use of resources; they are regarded as the performance of an organization and consist of individual and technical abilities, as well as explicit and implicit knowledge (Rasche, 1994; Hinterhuber and Friedrich, 1997; Innerhofer, 2012).

---

1    These resources are, for example, intangible resources like the brand image, the corporate reputation, or the corporate tradition.

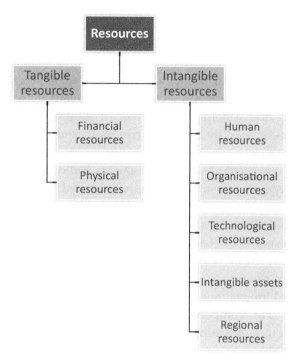

**Figure 2.2    Types of resources**
*Source*: Based on Innerhofer, 2012.


Innovative new products and services require investments in the existing portfolio of a company's resources and competences. A company's innovations are dependent upon its unique competence for acquiring, mobilizing, transforming and developing the bundle of resources and competences. Hence, innovative outputs depend on the acceptance of transformation processes (Lado, Boyd and Wright, 1992) necessary for the generation and implementation of new ideas.

Especially intangible resources and competences have an idiosyncratic nature, which ties them to the company and precludes their tradability on open markets, which might lead to sustainability. Intangible resources can be of different types and include intellectual property rights of patents, contracts, scientific works, a company's reputation and image, its know-how, networks and the organizational culture. Therefore, intangible resources can be people-dependent and people-independent (Hall, 1992). Resources and competences of these kinds have to be developed, accumulated and built up within a company over a long period of time.

According to Aaker (1989) the route to sustainable competitive advantage can be described as a process of managing assets and skills, i.e. tangible and intangible resources. In order to be a source of sustainable competitive advantage, resources and competences must be strategically relevant. Resources and competences are strategically relevant if they are valuable to the company and benefit the customer, if they cannot be imitated by competitors, can be used by the enterprise itself, and are scarcely available (Barney, 2011).

This means that the more difficult resources and competences are to buy, to sell, to imitate or to substitute the more enhanced is their strategic value (Amit and Schoemaker, 1993). They exhibit complex interrelationships, are intimately connected to the company and are characterized by taciturnity, complexity and specificity (Lado, Boyd and Wright, 1992). The characteristics of strategically relevant resources (Figure 2.3) and competences and the characteristics of the process by which resources and competences may be accumulated and innovations may be developed are related to the imitability of innovations. For competitors it is difficult to identify the relevant variables of the accumulation process, to specify which variables play a role in which stage of the process and to control variables and the process itself (Dierickx and Cool, 1989). Not least for this reason, the accumulation process is described as complex in nature. If strategically relevant, complex, and company-specific resources and competences provide the basis for the development of innovations and thus are upstream to innovations, the imitation of new products and services by competitors is made more difficult and the expected success due to innovation becomes more steady and sustainable.

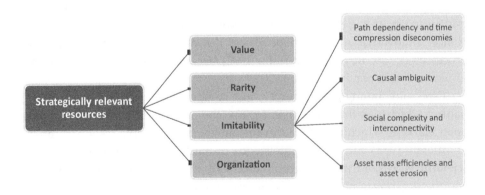

**Figure 2.3     VRIO characteristics of strategically relevant resources**
*Source*: Based on Innerhofer, 2012.

# Innovation – Identification and Definition

Innovation is derived from the Latin word *innovatio* and means 'renewal'. The root word indicates that an innovation does not necessarily have to be completely new but can also be a renewal of something that already exists (Thom, 1980; Hinterhuber, 1975; Weiermair, 2006). There has been no standardized and generally agreed definition of the word 'innovation' in the literature so far (Vahs and Burmester, 2005). Innovation in terms of renewal is interpreted and defined differently as far as content, target and purpose are concerned. One explanation for the different definitions of innovation is given by Corsten (1989), who argues that innovation researchers have different scientific backgrounds and come from different fields of study; and that the different underlying interests of the studies conducted lead to differing explanations of the term (Corsten, 1989; Innerhofer, 2012).

From the resource-based or competence-based view, innovation is perceived as a new combination of resources and competences. New services or new products are the results of a company's innovative use of existing resources and competences by recombining or further developing them (Innerhofer, 2012).

## DIMENSIONS OF INNOVATION

In order to define and identify the term 'innovation', Hauschildt created a catalogue of five dimensions (see Figure 2.4). Innovation can accordingly be defined in terms of content (What is new?), degree or intensity of newness (How new is it?), the perspective of the observer (For whom is it new?), time dimension (Where does an innovation begin and where does it end?), and the economic success of an innovation (new = successful?) (Hauschildt and Salomo, 2011). These definition levels of innovation are widely recognized in the literature.

In terms of content, innovation is seen as a result or an outcome. This result-oriented perspective is also referred to as 'innovation in the narrow sense'. A distinction is made between different types of innovation. Different fields or subject areas can be the objects of innovation. Depending on which object an innovation contains, a distinction can be made between product, service, marketing, sales, management and organizational innovations (Corsten, 1989; Herzhoff, 1991; Hjalager, 1997).

The dimension of intensity when describing innovation addresses the question of the extent of innovation and shows that the qualitative differences between an old and a new product can have different intensity levels (Reichwald and Schaller, 2006). In order to perform a gradual distinction of innovation, it will be distinguished between radical and incremental,

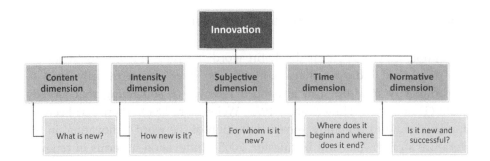

**Figure 2.4    The dimensions of innovation**
*Source*: Based on Innerhofer, 2012.

revolutionary and evolutionary or basic and enhanced innovations (Pleschak and Sabisch, 1996; Bierfelder, 1994; Johnson, Menor, Roth and Chase, 2000). Innovations can hardly be assigned clearly to one category, usually they are intermediate types between the two respective extremes (Thom, 1980).

The subjective dimension deals with the question, 'for whom is the innovation new' and refers to the perspective of the observer. As a point of reference to determine newness, a single economic subject, a company, a sector, a nation or the whole of mankind can be used. From a mere business point of view innovation exists, if the changed condition for the respective company, as a referential subject, is new (Hauschildt and Salomo, 2011; Vahs and Burmester, 2005).

The normative level addresses the question of the economic success of an innovation. The point of discussion is whether innovations should contribute to improving the previous state and subsequently achieve or exceed defined economic goals; or whether this is not strictly necessary. Thus, the aspect of newness is also linked with an aspect of progress, where it is not sufficient to change the existing state but it is necessary to enhance the current situation. Hinterhuber (1975), for example, describes innovation as the introduction or application of new or improved products, services or production processes. When talking about product innovation he refers to new, better or improved products; when talking about process innovation he refers to new, better and improved production processes. In the planning process of innovation, management is convinced of the success of and innovation, otherwise investments would turn out lower or would not be made. However, management is operating with an expected, not yet realized success (Hauschildt and Salomo, 2011).

The processual dimension realizes innovation as a temporal process of change (Busse, 2005). All stages of the innovation process – from searching for or generating ideas to market launch and the first economic use – are part of the term 'innovation' (Corsten, 1989).

## FEATURES OF INNOVATION

Regardless of how innovation is defined, innovations have certain features. Newness is the common feature of all approaches to definition. The degree of newness is therefore the constitutive characteristic that entails further special aspects.

Innovations are linked with uncertainty and risk, since their progression, process and characteristics are not known at the beginning (Thom, 1980; Mirow and Carsten, 2000; Gassmann and Granig, 2013; Noé, 2013). In this context, the results of innovations and the factors time, costs, expected return and economic use are insecure (Corsten, 1989). Another characteristic feature of innovation, and at the same time a source of uncertainty, is complexity (Thom, 1980; Pleschak and Sabisch, 1996). In general, innovations and their development process do not appear linear; they require division of labour and consist of complex problem structures, where known solution and action patterns often fail (Thom and Etienne, 2000). The high degree of complexity and the level of uncertainty increase the potential for conflict (Corsten, 1989; Herzhoff, 1991). Owing to the newness of innovations, implementing innovations means to dismiss well known familiar structures and to leave reliable paths. Uncertainty over the new condition results in the tendency to maintain the status quo (Witte, 1973). Employees often feel threatened by innovation and change and therefore refuse development.

The more radical the innovation is, the more it is refused and the more necessary it is to integrate, to support and to 'teach' employees and customers how to handle the new situation (Gallouj and Weinstein, 1997).

Since there is no accepted general and standardized definition of the term 'innovation', a working definition has been determined for this underlying research study. Accordingly, innovations are defined as novelties representing newness from the perspective of the regarding company. These innovations can be either radical and completely new, but also incremental and thus simply further developments or enhancements of existing products and services. The driving force behind innovation is the expected economic success (Innerhofer, 2012).

## Innovations in the Service Sector

Apart from the constitutive features of innovations, which significantly influence the generation of innovations and the innovation process, service innovations include the characteristics of services which make the development process even more complex.

Services differ from material assets first by intangibility and second by the necessity to integrate an external factor into the process of service providing (Hilke, 1989; Corsten, 2001; Maleri and Frietzsche, 2008). The intangible nature and the characteristics of services make it difficult to measure service innovations and improvements by methods normally used to measure product innovations or improvements. From the customer's point of view, intangibility makes it difficult to compare different service offers (Gallouj and Weinstein, 1997; Tsai, Verma, and Schmidt, 2008).

Process participation by the customer or guest leads to the synchronization of the service provision (or production) and its consumption (or transmission). Customers' participation and their role as co-producers in the production of a service is another major characteristic of service provision and makes the production process more complex and integrated (Gallouj and Weinstein, 1997). Additionally, intangible services cannot be stored, are not transportable and tradable, and are often location-based, like, for example, tourism services (Maleri, 1973; Corsten, 1985; Engelhardt, Kleinaltenkamp, and Reckenfelderbäumer, 1994).

With the integration of the customer as an external factor and with the synchronization of production and transmission, the difficulty of quality control for the service provider arises. So, for example, customers' satisfaction with the tourist service package largely depends on their participation (Corsten, 1985; Tsai, Verma, and Schmidt, 2008). The customer influences the quality of service performance. The consequence is that different guests imply very different service outcomes. The heterogeneity of service performance impedes quality control by the provider (Meyer and Blümelhuber, 1994). In addition, simultaneous service production and consumption implies direct contact, at least temporally. Direct contact is particularly important in the hospitality sector, where the service provider and the customer have to be at the same time in the same place. Regional contact necessity and location dependency of hospitality businesses turn the location into a central production factor. Whereas location dependency requires the mobility of customers and their motivation to overcome regional distances, providers can use destination-specific resources as attraction and input factors in the innovation process (Innerhofer, 2012).

The case study presented in the following section illustrates, among other factors, how the resource 'location' and the company's ability to use and to consider this resource in its daily business operations can influence the development of innovations.

## Case Study – Falkensteiner Michaeler Tourism Group

The findings and results of this study have been gathered by analysing the company Falkensteiner Michaeler Tourism Group (FMTG). This company was chosen for the case study analysis for the following reasons:

- The author was interested in analysing an Alpine hotel business. An implemented innovation with service-specific characteristics should be identifiable, so that interviewees may report on the innovation process. Furthermore, the innovativeness of the hotel chain had to be apparent, whereas the author had to rely on externally visible features (Lamnek and Krell, 2010). On the basis of an advance analysis of the literature, the author assumed that a systematic structure and concept of innovation processes are more likely to be identified in a hotel chain than in independent hotels (Orfila-Sintes, Crespi-Cladera, and Martinez-Ros, 2005). Last but not least, the chosen company had to agree to cooperate and agree on the use of the data and publication of the research results.[2]
- The Falkensteiner Michaeler Tourism Group provides and develops products and services in tourism and works in virtually all areas of tourism. As well as running hotels, the range of services offered by the company includes the development, planning and implementation of hotel facilities, consultancy services in the field of tourism property development, management and marketing, and the international monitoring and assessment of markets, developments and trends (FMTG – Markets, 2015).
- The holding company unites four business divisions: FMTG Service, FMTG Development, Michaeler and Partner, and FMTG Others (see FMTG – Business Divisions, 2015). The company has its roots in hotel management, which still constitutes its core business area and is carried out as part of FMTG Service. This area deals with operational leadership, as well as with the management and marketing of the hotels and residences. These

---

2   For further details see Innerhofer, 2012.

are company-owned hotels as well as management and lease businesses operating under the common brand Falkensteiner Hotels and Residences. They include 32 hotels and residences in 6 European countries, i.e. Austria, Italy, Slovakia, Czech Republic, Serbia and Croatia (as of January 2015) (Falkensteiner Hotels and Residences, 2015). The company's headquarters are in Vienna. FMTG Service as a core business area was the subject of the present study (Innerhofer, 2012).

- The company started as a family business in 1957, when Maria and Josef Falkensteiner opened the first guesthouse with seven beds in South Tyrol, Italy. In 1982, the second hotel followed in the same region. Finally, after the acquisition of further hotels in the region, the company entered the Austrian market in 1997. With the foundation of Michaeler and Partner as a tourism consultancy and with the establishment of a central purchasing company, the enterprise expanded its core business area and increased expansion abroad, whereas it focused on internationalization in the Eastern European area (Innerhofer, 2012; FMTG – Company history, 2015).

- The company's historical development and its rapid process of expansion reflect its value pyramid. FMTG adheres to its business tradition and tries to implement and develop this tradition by product and service innovations. Tradition and innovation form the guiding principles of the company. Human beings represent the focus of the company's activities; that is why the company describes itself as a dynamic enterprise. The company aims at result-oriented actions and at a courageous approach to developing and implementing new ideas, always taking into account that the measures taken should be sustainable. In this context, regional development and the integration of each location in the respective hotel concept is deliberately focused, while use is made of company-specific resources (FMTG – Values and aims, 2015). Taking regional location factors and resources into account, the infrastructure of the hotels is individual, which expresses each hotel's independence – despite homogeneous common elements. Hotel architecture and family tradition shape the company to such an extent that guests do not perceive it as a hotel chain. But due to its size and organizational structure, the company benefits from the realization of positive economies of scale by centralizing purchase, marketing and sales, as well as human resource management (Innerhofer, 2012).

- The company's differentiation potentials and competitive advantages against competitors result from the tradition and the historical development of the enterprise. They develop products by using historically grown resources and competences, which characterize the uniqueness of the company.
- The company's original area of operation was limited to the Alpine region. The hotel chain,[3] operating under the brand Falkensteiner Hotels and Residences, did not originate in the city hotel industry, later entering the resort hotel industry, but it emerged from the resort hotel industry. The individual hotels of the brand are characterized by individuality and location integration and, despite the size of the hotel facilities, they are family-run businesses. This is different from classic hotel chains, where hotels are marked by service standardization and similar infrastructures. The individuality of the hotel businesses is supported by the fact that in operational processes as well as in decision-making the company headquarters give enough flexibility to the hotel managers (e.g. implementation of innovations). The company sees one of its central strengths against competitors in individuality and thus in differentiation from classic hotel chains while realizing positive economies of scale (Innerhofer, 2012).
- FMTG Service has approximately 4,485 rooms (as of 2013). The hotels belong to the categories 3-star, 4-star, 4-star superior, and 5-star. The product portfolio of FMTG Service is divided into four strategic product lines and includes family hotels, wellness hotels, city hotels, and premium living residences, while each product line addresses different target groups (FMTG – We Live Tourism, 2015).

## INNOVATION BY FALKENSTEINER

The following section demonstrates two innovations identified within the framework of the study, representing combinations of product and service innovations. The customer can directly book these innovative services, which are included in several hotel offers of the three product lines (wellness, family, and city). The two innovations, which are the Acquapura Spa concept and the Alpe-Adria Culinary concept, are differently developed in the various product lines.

---

3   The company describes itself not as a hotel chain but as a hotel group (Innerhofer, 2012).

In order to emphasize the company-wide homogeneity of the wellness offer and to provide common ground for wellness holidays independently from the respective wellness hotels, the marketing department – located in the company headquarters – together with employees of the company, developed the Acquapura Spa concept. The marketing department's role was to determine a homogeneous strategic framework and the objectives for the concept. The water theme plays an important role in all destinations and all locations of the wellness hotels. That is why 'acqua pura' ('pure water') was chosen as a title for the homogeneous concept. Acquapura Spa is a company-specific and hotel-wide concept on the basis of which the individual spa areas and spa concepts of the hotel businesses are built. The company-wide concept primarily provides uniform standards and is based on three pillars. The first one represents an offer of classic massages, body and face treatments. Within the second pillar, Acquapura applications with special treatment ceremonies were developed which are company-specific and intended to differentiate the hotels from other wellness hotels. The third pillar emphasizes the unique character of the individual hotels, as each hotel focuses on a special wellness subject and accordingly adjusts its treatments (Falkensteiner Hotels and Residences, 2010). Depending on the hotel location and its prevailing geographical, historical, and natural conditions, the water theme and subsequently the hotel-specific spa concept are realized differently. Each hotel has its own philosophy according to regional traditions.

In particular, the second pillar – special treatments – is intended to implement elements and standards that clearly identify the company and differentiate it from competitors. In this context, differentiation from the competitor and the actual service innovation occur less by means of actual contents and treatments than by treatment ceremonies and their demonstration with certain rituals, emphasizing the experience for the guest (Innerhofer, 2012).

The Acquapura Spa concepts are individually interpreted in each hotel location and their labels refer to the region and the location, for example Steirische Natur-Wellness [Styrian nature wellness], Kneipp Pure Living, Kärnten Spa [Carinthia Spa], Südtiroler Bergwellness [South Tyrolean mountain wellness], Thalasso Spa and Marienbader Bäderkultur [Marienbad bathing culture] (Falkensteiner Hotels and Residences, 2010).

The Alpe-Adria Culinary concept pursues the same objective as the Acquapura Spa concept. With the establishment of homogeneous standards on the central level of the company, culinary in all hotels should be marked in line with a company-specific experience for the customer, allowing the company to differentiate from competitors. With the Alpe-Adria Culinary concept, the group wants to establish a homogeneous culinary hotel line. This idea is based on the history and tradition of the originally South Tyrolean family business. The innovative idea has come from the company founder himself, who aims to create a combination of Alpine and Mediterranean cuisine in terms of a homogeneous company-specific culinary philosophy based on South Tyrolean cuisine. Most of its hotels are situated in the Alpe-Adria area. Therefore, the culinary concept is characterized by the culinary tradition of this geographical area (Innerhofer, 2012).

Guidelines and qualitative standards form the framework concept without determining standardized cuisine. The flexibility granted in the implementation requires innovative and creative realization competences of the hotel businesses. Different location-specific theme days and subject corners form the actual contents of the concept.

Thus, enriching the cuisine with local specialties from the local area retains the identity and individuality of the hotels.

## CONCRETE EXAMPLES OF IMPLEMENTATION IN THE HOTEL BUSINESSES

Tourist services' dependence on location plays a major role in the design and implementation of innovation. In order to enable the integration of regional external resources, flexibility and scope for implementation are granted for all hotel businesses. This is intended to guarantee the individuality of all hotel businesses united under the common brand, despite standardization approaches.

In addition, due to location integration in innovation development, differentiation should be achieved in two ways: on the one hand, differentiation from other hotel chains and privately run hotel businesses of the same segment occurs by clear company positioning in the competitive market; on the other hand, the individual Falkensteiner hotels differentiate from each other and each refers to the region in which it is located.

Apart from location as a resource, location-based resources such as typical local products, cultural components, and regional influences, as well as the surrounding infrastructure, are applied in the innovations Alpe-Adria Culinary and Acquapura Spa. They serve as production factors (Innerhofer, 2012). The following section demonstrates the implementation of the innovative concepts by using two concrete examples.

The first hotel is the Hotel and Spa Bad Waltersdorf in the South Styrian thermal spa region. The hotel is situated next to one of Austria's most famous golf courses, which also plays a major role in the hotel offer. Cooperation takes place between the hotel and the golf operator in terms of special golf package offers. The Falkensteiner company can be recognized by the architecture of the hotel infrastructure, while at the same time the architecture reflects local characteristics. Location integration competence is first displayed by reflecting regional typical architecture and building materials; and second by integrating regional aspects such as regional cuisine, culture, customs, and traditions, as well as by cooperating with local actors in the development of products and offers.

The realization of innovative concepts includes the implementation of the standards given by the company headquarters while simultaneously using enough flexibility in terms of design in order to express individuality. Falkensteiner's individual wellness philosophy is the core element of the Acquapura Spa concept and can be found in all its wellness hotels. In this context, the focus is on the element water, which is thermal water in Bad Waltersdorf. The special Falkensteiner Acquapura treatments are dedicated to a local theme. Hotel Bad Waltersdorf focuses on Styrian nature wellness. Regional natural products and local traditions are part of the treatments. In Styria, local fruits are used for plant extracts, ointments, herbal teas, baths, and poultices. The hotel has adopted traditional healing knowledge and integrated it into its treatment methods. They hotel also offers special beauty treatments using its own cosmetic lines (Innerhofer, 2012; Falkensteiner Therme and Golf Hotel Bad Waltersdorf, 2015).

Competence in integrating the location also plays a major role when it comes to the implementation of the innovation concept Alpe-Adria Culinary. A certain degree of homogeneity and Falkensteiner's culinary philosophy should be visible in all hotels. Hotel Bad Waltersdorf refers to the Styrian thermal spa area, which is well known by gourmets, connoisseurs, and wine lovers. Typical Styrian dishes, with the addition of wines and specialities of the region, supplement the Alpe-Adria cuisine (Innerhofer, 2012; Falkensteiner Therme and Golf Hotel Bad Waltersdorf, 2015).

Another example of implementing the innovation concept is the Hotel and Spa Lamm Kastelruth in South Tyrol. Here, the location Kastelruth in the Dolomites, next to the ski and hiking resort Seiser Alm, plays a major role. When it comes to the implementation of the Acquapura Spa concept, Falkenstein's wellness philosophy and the element water are the centre of attention, as at the Hotel Bad Waltersdorf. The Hotel and Spa Lamm Kastelruth emphasizes mountain herbs and South Tyrolean mountain wellness, and tailors its treatments accordingly. The special wellness offer is called Kräuter-Wellness Aiuguana [herbal wellness Aiuguana]. Aiuguana are mentioned in the legends of Seiser Alm, where they represent Sciliar mountain witches who knew the healing powers of local water. Thus, old recipes are integrated into the wellness treatments. In addition to an indoor pool and whirlpool (standard wellness facilities also available in other Falkensteiner hotels), the hotel in

Kastelruth has a 'witch's grotto', a steam bath, and a Kneipp roundel. Another location-based element of wellness treatments is the traditional Kastelruth hay bath. Furthermore, the hotel features a herbal academy and a Kräuterplatzl [herbal corner] to give insights into typical local herbs.

Alpe-Adria Culinary, which unites the cuisine of all Falkensteiner hotels, i.e. the South Tyrolean, Croatian, and Austrian cuisine, also forms part of the Hotel and Spa Lamm Kastelruth offer. The individual feature in the implementation of innovation is the Alpine native South Tyrolean cuisine, which is prepared with local ingredients and enriched with herbs from the hotel garden. Furthermore, the hotel offers a typical South Tyrolean farmer's breakfast. The hotel restaurant is called Lammstube [lamb parlour] – and it is its cuisine is well regarded in the village of Kastelruth. The hotel's truly rustic atmosphere is strongly reminiscent of its location (Innerhofer, 2012; Falkensteiner Hotel and Spa Lamm Kastelruth, 2015).

## Sustainability and Ecology by Falkensteiner

Regional, location-based and natural resources have become an integral part of the innovation strategy of Falkensteiner. The same also applies to the concept of sustainability. Since guests ask for and are given information on sustainable products, the company tries to integrate and incorporate the concept of sustainability in its product and service offers. Its understanding of sustainable corporate responsibility is threefold: the company focuses on ecological, economic and sociocultural quality.

Sustainability has become a key corporate value (Figure 2.5). With regard to ecological sustainability, environmental protection, greywater reclamation, waste prevention and optimized energy use play a very important role in determining the hotel's actions (Falkensteiner Hotels and Residences – Sustainability, 2015). The hotel facility at Punta Skala (Croatia) is a good example to show the implementation and incorporation of ecological sustainability.

For this project the hotel management worked with international experts to implement a complex system that will minimize the ecological footprint in the long run. A water treatment plant supplies the hotel with the water needed for daily use on the holiday peninsula and generates energy for heating and cooling. In addition, a completely organic purification system helps to preserve the environment. The wastewater is cleaned and stored with the collected rainwater and with the greywater from the swimming pools. This water is then used for flushing toilets and to water the gardens. Water pumped from the sea is used for cooling in summer and for heating in winter.

Furthermore, a desalination system enables seawater to be used as drinking water. And besides that, the resort is free of cars. As a result of these measures, the hotel is advertised as 'a green resort directly at the sea' (Falkensteiner Hotel and Residences Punta Scala, 2015). Another ecologically sustainable hotel building is the Residence edel:Weiss at Katschberg, Austria. Here a 'class A' climate house has been constructed. The province of Bolzano has created an energy efficiency standard, according to which a 'class A' climate house has to be environmentally and climate-friendly, energy-conscious, comfortable and economically profitable (Falkensteiner Hotel and Residences – Sustainability, 2015).

**Figure 2.5    Sustainability as a key corporate value**
*Source*: The author.

The ÖGNI, the Austrian Association for a Sustainable Real Estate Industry, certifies sustainably built properties. The focus of the association is the support of solutions and ways for sustainable building, not only during the planning phase but also during the construction and operating phases. The first hotel in Austria certified by ÖGNI was the Falkensteiner Hotel and Spa Bad Leonfelden in Bad Leonfelden. Besides sustainable building, the integration of the local population – employed to provide the workforce – and the cooperation and collaboration with local producers are other important aspects of sustainability. The use of regional products contributes to local value creation and guided tours are offered on local farms. The company's profitability is sustained with regard to operating costs and to the company's reputation (Silvestre, 2012; Falkensteiner Hotel and Spa Bad Leonfelden, 2015).

## Conclusion

Despite the special features of service innovations and their challenges for tourism service providers, the research results demonstrate that successful innovations can still be identified. In this context, strategically relevant resources and competences as a starting point for innovations and thus as innovation potentials play a major role. Resources and competences are strategically relevant if they feature the characteristics described above, under 'Background'. The danger of imitation by competitors can be reduced if resources and competences form the basis for innovations. This strategic approach makes imitation attempts by competitors more difficult and can include a certain amount of protection.

As tourism in general and the hotel industry in particular relate to location-based services, the resource location's potential for innovation is particularly important. In the tourism industry especially the location is crucial and serves as a search field for the generation of ideas. It affects the attractiveness of the company and its innovations (Innerhofer, 2012). In the example chosen for the case study, the Alpine region is regarded as a starting destination and as a superior area linking all hotel businesses.

In addition, the case study shows that the topic of sustainability has become an integral part of tourism. Guests ask for sustainable products and services, while tourism providers take account of economic, ecological and sociocultural sustainability. From an economic point of view, sustainable innovations are a source of profits. The case study demonstrates that an innovative approach to sustainability can enhance tourism experiences, can protect natural resources and can maintain local and regional traditions.

## References

Aaker, D.A. (1989). Managing assets and skills: The key to a sustainable competitive advantage. *California Management Review*, Winter, 91–106.

Amit, R., and Schoemaker, P.J.H. (1993). Strategic assets and organizational rent. *Strategic Management Journal*, 14, 33–46.

Bamberger, I., and Wrona, Th. (1996). Der Ressourcenansatz und seine Bedeutung für die Strategische Unternehmerführung. *Zeitschrift für betriebswirtschaftliche Forschung*, 48(2), 130–153.

Barney, J.B. (1991). Firm resources and sustained competitive advantage. *Journal of Management*, 17(1), 99–120.

Barney, J.B. (2011). *Gaining and Sustaining Competitive Advantage*. Upper Saddle River, New Jersey: Prentice Hall.

Benkenstein, M. (2001). Besonderheiten des Innovationsmanagements in Dienstleistungsunternehmen. In M. Bruhn and H. Meffert (eds), *Handbuch Dienstleistungsmanagement. Von der strategischen Konzeption zur praktischen Umsetzung* (687–702). Wiesbaden: Springer Gabler Verlag.

Bierfelder, W.H. (1994). *Innovationsmanagement. Prozessorientierte Einführung*. München, Wien: Oldenbourg Verlag.

Busse, D. (2005). *Innovationsmanagement industrieller Dienstleistungen. Theoretische Grundlagen und praktische Gestaltungsmöglichkeiten*. Wiesbaden: Springer Gabler Verlag.

Corsten, H. (1985). *Die Produktion von Dienstleistungen. Grundzüge einer Produktionswirtschaftslehre des tertiären Sektors*. Berlin: Erich Schmidt Verlag.

Corsten, H. (1989). Überlegungen zu einem Innovationsmanagement – organisationale und personale Aspekte. In H. Corsten (ed.), *Die Gestaltung von Innovationsprozessen. Hindernisse und Erfolgsfaktoren im Organisations-, Finanz- und Informationsbereich* (1–56). Berlin: Erich Schmidt Verlag.

Corsten, H. (2001). Ansatzpunkte für ein integratives Dienstleistungs-management. In M. Bruhn and H. Meffert (eds), *Handbuch Dienstleistungs-management. Von der strategischen Konzeption zur praktischen Umsetzung* (51–71). Wiesbaden: Gabler Verlag.

Dierickx, I., and Cool, K. (1989). Asset stock accumulation and sustainability of competitive advantage. *Management Science*, 35(12), 1504–1511.

Engelhardt, W.H., Kleinaltenkamp, M., and Reckenfelderbäumer, M. (1994). Leistungsbündel als Absatzobjekte. Ein Ansatz zur Überwindung der Dichotomie von Sach- und Dienstleistungen. In H. Corsten (ed.), *Integratives Dienstleistungsmanagement. Grundlagen – Beschaffung – Produktion – Marketing – Qualität. Ein Reader* (31–69). Wiesbaden: Gabler Verlag.

Freiling, J., Gersch, M., and Goeke, C. (2008). On the path towards a competence-based theory of the firm. *Organization Studies*, 29, 1143–1164.

Gallouj, F., and Weinstein, O. (1997). Innovation in services. *Research Policy*, 26, 537–556.

Gassmann, O., and Granig, P. (2013). *Innovationsmanagement – 12 Erfolgsstrategien für KMU*. München: Carl Hanser Verlag.

Hall, R. (1992). The strategic analysis of intangible resources. *Strategic Management Journal*, 13, 135–144.

Hauschildt, J., and Salomo, S. (2011). *Innovationsmanagement*. München: Verlag Vahlen.

Herzhoff, S. (1991). *Innovations-Management. Gestaltung von Prozessen und Systemen zur Entwicklung und Verbesserung der Innovationsfähigkeit von Unternehmungen.* Köln: Eul.

Hilke, W. (1989). Grundprobleme und Entwicklungstendenzen des Dienstleistungs-Marketing. In W. Hilke (ed.), *Dienstleistungs-Marketing. Banken und Versicherungen – Freie Berufe – Handel und Transport – NichterwerbswirtschaftlichorientierteOrganisationen* (5–44). Wiesbaden: Gabler Verlag.

Hinterhuber, H.H. (1975). *Strategische Innovationsdynamik und Unternehmensführung.* Wien, New York: Springer Verlag.

Hinterhuber, H.H., and Friedrich, S.A. (1997). Markt- und ressourcenorientierte Sichtweise zur Steigerung des Unternehmenswertes. In D. Hahn and B. Taylor (eds), *Strategische Unternehmensplanung. Strategische Unternehmensführung. Stand und Entwicklungstendenzen* (988–1016). Heidelberg: Springer Verlag.

Hjalager, A.-M. (1997). Innovation patterns in sustainable tourism. An analytical typology. *Tourism Management,* 18(1), 35–41.

Innerhofer, E. (2012). *Strategische Innovationen in der Hotellerie. Eine ressourcenorientierte Fallstudienanalyse touristischer Dienstleistungsunternehmen.* Wiesbaden: Springer Gabler Verlag.

Johnson, S.P., Menor, L.J., Roth, A.V., and Chase, R.B. (2000). A critical evaluation of the new service development process. Integrating service innovation and service design. In J.A. Fitzsimmons and M.J. Fitzsimmons (eds), *New Service Development. Creating Memorable Experience* (1–32). Thousand Oaks, California: Sage.

Keller, P. (2002). Innovation und Tourismus. In T. Bieger and C. Laesser (eds), *Jahrbuch 2001/2002 Schweizer Tourismuswirtschaft* (179–194). St. Gallen: IDT-HSG.

Klausegger, C., and Salzberger, T. (2006). Innovationen und Unternehmenserfolg – untersucht am Beispiel ausgewählter Branchen im Tourismus. In B. Pikkemaat, M. Peters and K. Weiermair (eds), *Innovationen im Tourismus. Wettbewerbsvorteile durch neue Ideen und Angebote* (37–52). Berlin: Erich Schmidt Verlag.

Lado, A.A., Boyd, N.G., and Wright, P. (1992). A competency-based model of sustainable competitive advantage: Toward a conceptual integration. *Journal of Management,* 18(1), 77–91.

Lamnek, S., and Krell, C. (2010). *Qualitative Sozialforschung. Lehrbuch.* Weinheim, Basel: Beltz.

Maleri, R. (1973). *Grundzüge der Dienstleistungsproduktion.* Berlin, Heidelberg, New York: Springer Verlag.

Maleri, R., and Frietzsche, U. (2008). *Grundlagen der Dienstleistungsproduktion.* Berlin, Heidelberg: Springer Verlag.

Meyer, A., and Blümelhuber, C. (1994). Interdependenzen zwischen Absatz und Produktion in Dienstleistungsunternehmen und ihre Auswirkungen auf konzeptionelle Fragen des Absatzmarketing. In H. Corsten and W. Hilke (eds), *Dienstleistungsproduktion* (5–41). Wiesbaden: Betriebswirtschaftlicher Verlag Gabler.

Mirow, M., and Carsten, L. (2000). Planung und Organisation von Innovationen aus systemtheoretischer Perspektive. In G.E. Häfliger and J.D. Meier (eds), *Aktuelle Tendenzen im Innovationsmanagement* (249–268). Heidelberg: Physika Verlag.

Noé, M. (2013). *Innovation 2.0 – Unternehmenserfolg durch intelligentes und effizientes Innovieren.* Wiesbaden: Springer Gabler.

Oliver, C. (1997). Sustainable competitive advantage: combining institutional and resource-based views. *Strategic Management Journal,* 18(9), 697–713.

Orfila-Sintes, F., Crespi-Cladera, R., and Martinez-Ros, E. (2005). Innovation activity in the hotel industry. Evidence from Balearic Islands. *Tourism Management,* 26, 851–865.

Pechlaner, H., and Fischer, E. (2006). Alpine wellness: A resource-based view. *Tourism Recreation Research,* 31(1), 67–77.

Penrose, E. (1959). *The Theory of the Growth of the Firm.* Oxford: Oxford University Press.

Peters, M., and Weiermair, K. (2002). Innovationen und Innovationsverhalten im Tourismus. In T. Bieger and C. Laesser (eds), *Jahrbuch 2001/2002 Schweizer Tourismuswirtschaft* (157–178). St. Gallen: IDT-HSG.

Pleschak, F., and Sabisch, H. (1996). *Innovationsmanagement.* Stuttgart: UTB.

Rasche, C. (1994). *Wettbewerbsvorteile durch Kernkompetenzen. Ein ressourcenorientierter Ansatz.* Wiesbaden: Gabler Verlag.

Reichwald, R., and Schaller, C. (2006). Innovationsmanagement von Dienstleistungen – Herausforderungen und Erfolgsfaktoren in der Praxis. In H.-J. Bullinger and A.-W. Scheer (eds), *Service Engineering. Entwicklung und Gestaltung innovativer Dienstleistungen* (167–194). Berlin, Heidelberg: Springer Verlag.

Rück, H.R.G. (2000). *Dienstleistungen in der ökonomischen Theorie.* Wiesbaden: Gabler Verlag.

Tajeddini, K. (2010). Effect of customer orientation and entrepreneurial orientation on innovativeness: Evidence from the hotel industry in Switzerland. *Tourism Management,* 31(2), 221–231.

Thiele, M. (1997). *Kernkompetenzorientierte Unternehmensstrukturen. Ansätze zur Neugestaltung von Geschäftsbereichsorganisationen.* Wiesbaden: Gabler Verlag.

Thom, N. (1980). *Grundlagen des betrieblichen Innovationsmanagements.* Königstein/TS: Hanstein.

Thom, N., and Etienne, M. (2000). Organisatorische und personelle Ansatzpunkte zur Förderung eines Innovationsklimas im Unternehmen. In G.E. Häfliger and J.D. Meier (eds), *Aktuelle Tendenzen im Innovationsmanagement* (269–281). Heidelberg: Physika Verlag.

Tsai, W., Verma, R., and Schmidt, G. (2008). New service development. In: C.H. Loch and S. Kavadias (eds), *Handbook of New Product Development Management* (495–526). Amsterdam: Elsevier Butterworth-Heinemann.

Vahs, D., and Burmester, R. (2005). *Innovationsmanagement. Von der Produktidee zur erfolgreichen Vermarktung.* Stuttgart: Schäffer-Poeschel Verlag.

Weiermair, K. (2005). Prospects for Innovation in Tourism: Analyzing the Innovation Potential Throughout the Tourism Value Chain. *Journal of Quality Assurance in Hospitality and Tourism,* 6(3/4), 59–72.

Weiermair, K. (2006). Product Improvement or Innovation: What is the key to success in tourism? In OECD – Organisation for Economic Co-operation and Development (ed.), *Innovation and Growth in Tourism* (53–69). Paris: OECD.

Wernerfelt, B. (1984). A Resource Based View of the Firm. *Strategic Management Journal,* 5, 171–180.

Witte, E. (1973). *Organisation für Innovationsentscheidungen.* Göttingen: Schwartz.

## SOURCES

Falkensteiner Michaeler Tourism Group (FMTG):
Falkensteiner Hotel and Spa Bad Leonfelden (2015). Available at: http://www.falkensteiner.com/de/hotel/bad-leonfelden [accessed 7 January 2015].

Falkensteiner Hotel and Spa Lamm Kastelruth (2015). Available at: http://www.falkensteiner.com/en/hotel/kastelruth [accessed 7 January 2015].

Falkensteiner Hotels and Residences (2010). Acquapura Spa brochure, 2015. Available at: http://www.falkensteiner.com/12_web/hotels/iadera/web/files-14/wellness/acquapura-spa-brochure_en20012015.pdf [accessed 15 September 2015].

Falkensteiner Hotels and Residences (2015). Available at: http://www.falkensteiner.com/en [accessed 7 January 2015].

Falkensteiner Hotels and Residences Punta Skala (2015). Available at: http://www.falkensteiner.com/en/hotel/punta-skala/green-resort [accessed 7 January 2015].

Falkensteiner Hotels and Residences – Sustainability (2015). Available at: http://www.premiumliving.com/index3.html [accessed 7 January 2015].

Falkensteiner Therme and Golf Hotel Bad Waltersdorf (2015). Available at: http://www.falkensteiner.com/en/hotel/bad-waltersdorf [accessed 7 January 2015].

FMTG – Business divisions (2015). Available at: http://www.fmtg.com/en/ business-divisions/ [accessed 7 January 2015].

FMTG – Company history (2015). Available at: http://www.fmtg.com/en/ company-history/ [accessed 7 January 2015].

FMTG – Markets (2015). Available at: http://www.fmtg.com/en/markets/ [accessed 7 January 2015].

FMTG – Values and aims (2015). Available at: http://www.fmtg.com/en/values-aimes/ [accessed 7 January 2015].

FMTG – We Live Tourism (2015). Available at: http://www.fmtg.com/en/ [accessed 7 January 2015].

Silvestre, D. (2012). Falkensteiner Hotel mit ÖGNI Plakette zertifiziert. Österreichische Gesellschaft für Nachhaltige Immobilienwirtschaft (ÖGNI) setzt auf Nachhaltigkeit. *Observer*, (1542). Available at: http://www. michaeler-partner.com/App_Upload/news/6372_20120323_Medianet.pdf [accessed 29 January 2015].

## Chapter 3

# Green Entrepreneurship: What Drives Resource Efficiency in Tourism?

MONIKA BACHINGER and HANNES RAU

This study aims to identify drivers for green entrepreneurship in tourism, focusing on entrepreneurial resources and skills, as well as regional networks. Interviews conducted within the Northern Black Forest region show that the introduction of green innovations is made difficult. This is attributed to a lack of knowledge about natural resources and customer expectations among businesses, as well as their unwillingness to cooperate and share resources. This chapter contributes to the small body of literature on the view of tourism based on natural resources. Practical value is added by recommendations on how to foster green entrepreneurship as a tool for sustainable regional development in tourism.

The fifth IPCC report shows that climate change is progressing faster than projected and considers greenhouse gas emissions to be the main driver (IPCC, 2014). The OECD assumes that travel accounts for 5–6 per cent of global greenhouse gas emissions (OECD, 2012). This share will continue to rise as international arrivals increase (UNWTO, 2014). To end the cycle of growing demand and consumption of resources, we need green growth in tourism (Dean and McMullen, 2007; McEwan, 2013; Schaper, 2002). Travel must become more resource efficient (OECD, 2012). Within this context, this chapter discusses the question: Which factors are able to promote resource efficiency in tourism?

To answer this question, the concept of green entrepreneurship is presented (Anderson, 1998; Bennett, 1991; Dean and McMullen, 2007; Isaak, 2002; Schaltegger, 2002; Schaper, 2002). The following paragraphs describe who green entrepreneurs are and how green innovations differ from conventional innovations. Furthermore, different requirements for successful green entrepreneurship are discussed, considering internal qualities such as entrepreneurial resources and capabilities, as well as the external regional environment (see Kirkwood and Walton, 2010; Taylor and Walley, 2004).

## Green Innovation

Green innovations are based on the principle of ecological efficiency (Gibbs, 2009; McEwen, 2013; Melay and Kraus, 2012). Changes in supply or demand lead to a change in the relationship between resource input and product output. However, the term 'green innovation' does not necessarily imply a new product (Rennings, 2000; Taylor and Walley, 2004). Green innovation can also refer to production processes, for example if improved production techniques use less energy. Also, new organizational forms and processes can be considered green innovations, for example when a tourist resort invents a new organizational approach to guest mobility. In addition, sales and marketing innovations play a significant role (Rennings, 2000).

Two further considerations are relevant. Firstly, the difference between radical and incremental innovations (Isaak, 2002; Kenney, 2009): Radical innovations are 'game changing innovations that turn entire industries upside down' (OECD 2013: 16). Most innovations, however, are incremental and bring change in small steps (Kenney, 2009). Secondly, social and institutional innovations are relevant (Rennings, 2000). This means that entrepreneurs change the value system and the norms of society. Taking radical and institutional innovation together, we come to the concept of system innovations (Geels, 2005). Here, significant changes in the state of technology, knowledge, or business organization go along with significant changes in the behaviour of market actors. It is assumed that in terms of resource efficiency, the greatest potential is in system innovations (Gibbs, 2009; Kirkwood and Walton, 2010; Schaltegger, 2002, Taylor and Walley, 2004). Figure 3.1 summarises the concepts behind green innovation.

## Green Entrepreneurship

Green entrepreneurs are special because their understanding of success is not based on profit alone (McEwen, 2013). Their business goals and other characteristics are summarized in Figure 3.2 below. Not to be confused with non-profit enterprises, green entrepreneurs are profit-oriented and strive for profit maximization (Dean and McMullen, 2007; Melay and Kraus, 2012). Therefore they typically focus on larger markets instead of serving niche markets (Schaltegger, 2002). However, in addition to economic indicators such as turnover or profit, non-economic values, e.g., animal health, are indicators of success. Green entrepreneurs bridge the gap between the dynamics of

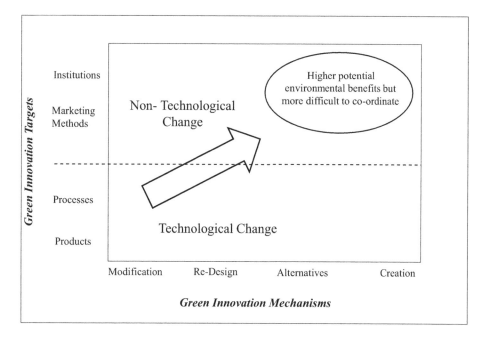

**Figure 3.1     Types of green innovation**
*Source*: OECD, 2013: 15.

sustainability and economy and consider their goals to be compatible (Gibbs, 2009; Gunawan, 2012; McEwan, 2013; Taylor and Walley, 2004).

Second, green entrepreneurs are 'change agents' (Allen and Malin, 2008; Isaak, 2002, Gibbs, 2009, McEwan, 2013). In line with the Schumpeterian concept of creative destruction, they displace existing products from the market and replace them with environmentally favourable solutions (Schumpeter, 1934). Resource efficiency is not merely an addition to the traditional business model. Resource efficiency is at the core of their business idea (McEwen, 2013). Thus, they distinguish themselves from other companies that foster environmental conservation for the purpose of saving costs or boosting their image (Taylor and Walley, 2004). Instead, green entrepreneurships evolve from original green ideas. They are highly value-oriented and strongly influenced by personal beliefs of the entrepreneur (Allen and Malin, 2008; Gibbs, 2009; Schaper, 2005; Schaltegger, 2002). Their market impact can be noticeable, especially if more than niche markets are targeted. They act as role models. Thus, green entrepreneurs promote green growth at the centre of an industry and bring about change (Gunawan, 2012; Schaltegger, 2002; Schaper, 2005).

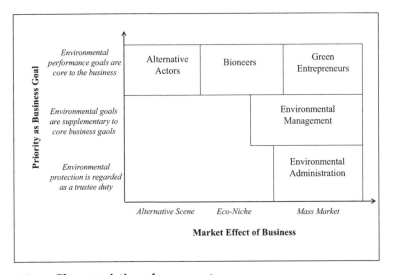

**Figure 3.2 Characteristics of green entrepreneurs**

*Source*: Schaltegger, 2002: 49 according to Schaltegger and Petersen, 2001. Reproduced with permission.

## Drivers of Green Entrepreneurship

In general, there are several drivers of green innovation (Gibbs, 2009; Kirkwood and Walton, 2010; Schick, Marxen and Freimann, 2002). First, the specific skills and expertise of the entrepreneurs determine their innovative capability. Second, market dynamics drive innovation: reacting to new customer needs (Dean and McMullen, 2007; Schaltegger, 2002). In order to identify market opportunities, the company requires specific competencies, which will be looked at in the next section. Third, technological trends lead to innovation. In order to recognize new trends, entrepreneurs rely on social networks, therefore, networks are considered the third driver of innovation in the following discussion (McEwan, 2013). Additionally, government may influence innovation by subsidies, taxation or regulatory measures. However, in this chapter, state intervention is not pursued further (Rennings, 2000; Shane, 2003).

### ENTREPRENEURIAL RESOURCES AND COMPETENCIES

Resources that are critical for success are scarce and valuable (Barney, 2002). Scarce resources are not procurable in markets. This is especially true for resources that have been refined within a company. An example of a refined resource is tacit knowledge, which is deeply rooted in the organizational structure (Grant, 1991). Also, a unique set or 'bundle' of several resources, i.e., a combination of knowledge and material inputs, is considered a refined resource. The second criterion of a critical resource is value. Valuable resources contribute to a higher efficiency in production processes (Teece, Pisano, and Shuen, 1997). In total, there are six types of critical resources: financial, physical, human, technological, social and organizational (Barney, 1991; Wernerfelt, 1984).

Tourism is unique in that not all resources are entirely owned by companies. Tourism relies on public goods, such as landscapes, plants and animal wildlife (Ritchie and Crouch, 2003; Vanhove, 2011). These public goods are combined with the resources of the company within the production process to create a refined resource (Blinnikka, Härkönen, Väisänen, and Tunkkari-Eskelinen, 2014). In this context, the quality of environmental and nature-related knowledge is important. This includes knowledge about the functioning of ecosystems, but also technical expertise in the management of natural resources. By combining this knowledge with natural resources green entrepreneurs develop specific, and thus scarce, resource bundles. These resource bundles are crucial for success. Therefore, tourism is based upon the relationship to the natural environment. A natural resource based view of the firm may be applied (Hart, 1995; Rodriguez, Ricart, and Sanchez, 2002).

## MARKETING COMPETENCY OF THE FIRM

Competencies can be understood as 'repeatable patterns of action in the use of assets' (Sanchez, 2004: 519). Competencies determine how companies use their resources to place products or services on the market (Dosi, Faillo, and Marengo, 2008; Freiling, Gersch, and Goeke, 2008; Sanchez, 2004). Competencies may appear on three levels (Freiling, 2004; Pechlaner, Bachinger, Volgger, and Anzengruber-Fischer, 2014). First, they may direct the refining process from normal input goods to success-related resources. Second, competencies determine how these resources are shaped into products and services. Last but not least, competencies are key to a company's ability to perceive market demands and react accordingly. However, not all of these competencies are equally important. Most significant are core competencies, which are characterized by a high degree of relevance to customers, uniqueness in competition and applicability in different market segments (Freiling, Gersch, and Goeke, 2008; Freiling, 2004; Hamel and Prahalad, 1994).

For these reasons, a company's market observation and penetration skills are a crucial requirement for environmental innovations (Pechlaner, Bachinger, Volgger, and Anzengruber-Fischer, 2014). However, marketing innovations in tourism often fail because these skills are lacking (Peters and Buhalis, 2004). Small businesses, which dominate tourism, have little opportunity to conduct market research. They find it difficult to accurately estimate the potential of green markets, have little information about potential customers, and often their business ideas lack economic viability. Market demand and business ideas do not align (Tunkkari-Eskelinen, Matilainen, and Asunta, 2014).

## REGIONAL NETWORKS

Networks and their role in supporting innovation has become the subject of a major research field related to green innovation (Audretsch, 2003; Pechlaner and Bachinger, 2010). The concept of open innovation seems to be of particular relevance here (Chesbrough, 2003). Open innovation involves the opening of the innovative process of a company. The aim is to use the external business environment in terms of customers or suppliers to increase the innovative potential. This requires specific skills (Doepfer, 2013; Duschek, 2004; Lavie, 2006).

Central to these skills is the ability to cooperate (Gulati, Nohria, and Zaheer, 2000). This requires the ability to identify potential areas for networking, to address suitable partners and to define the content of the cooperation (Teece, 2007; Pihkala, Harmaakorpi, and Pekkarinen, 2007). Secondly, the cooperation process has to be organized. In order to exchange ideas and knowledge between companies, contact points for sharing knowledge have to be defined. This process is as efficient as the absorptive capacity of the partners (Cohen and Levinthal, 1990). Last but not least cooperation requires a normative foundation, in terms of shared beliefs and interests. Thus, mutual trust necessary for sharing knowledge can be established (Pechlaner and Bachinger, 2014; Pihkala, Harmaakorpi, and Pekkarinen, 2007).

It is specific to tourism that the consumed good is not only a product or a service. Instead, guests consume a service chain. This service chain is made up of transport companies, hoteliers, and sports and cultural facilities, and includes local, municipal or regional tourism organizations (Ritchie and Crouch, 2003). While each stakeholder within the service chain may be involved on a different level and fulfil a different role, a common point of reference has to be shared to ensure the chain of services is consistent in itself. Therefore, they must share knowledge (McLeod and Vaughan, 2015).

# Green Entrepreneurship in the Northern Black Forest

The Black Forest is located in the southwest of Germany. The following study focuses on the northern part of the Black Forest. From an administrative point of view it encompasses the four counties Calw, Freudenstadt, Pforzheim and Enz (RNSW, 2015). Overall, the region has a population of about 590,000, with 180,000 employees (RNSW, 2015). In the region there are about 580 accommodation establishments, which recorded almost 2.4 million overnight stays in 2013 (StaLa, 2015). The overnight tourism contributed to a value generation of around €295 million in 2011. A similar amount is reported for day trips (PWC, 2013).

From a tourist's point of view, the Northern Black Forest is marketed as a sub-region of the destination Black Forest. Since the mid-1990s, the destination has had to struggle with an ageing guest structure. In addition, there have been image and price problems, as well as massive investment backlogs (Krull, 2011). While today, tourism in the Black Forest is recovering and overnight stays are rising, the sub-region of the Northern Black Forest still struggles with economic recession (PWC, 2013: 16). Against this background, the Black Forest National Park was established in January 2014. It covers an area of approximately 10,000 hectares (NLP, 2015).

## SAMPLING AND RESEARCH DESIGN

Applying a qualitative research design, data was collected by conducting expert interviews (Flick, 2014; Mayring, 2014). The interviews took place in September 2014. A total of nine interviews were held with hoteliers, local tourism experts and representatives of the National Park. The interviewees were selected according to their expert status and by the following criteria: first, interviewees should be able to speak on behalf of a larger group; secondly interviewees should be known for being visionary. The interviews were conducted using a semi-structured guideline. The answers were evaluated using qualitative content analysis (Kohlbacher, 2006; Mayring, 2014).

The interview guideline addressed three topics. First, respondents were asked to describe the importance of resource efficiency within their organization. The aim was to identify specific entrepreneurial skills related to resource efficiency. The second part of the questionnaire was concerned with the relationship between the companies and the market. It examined whether market opportunities for resource efficiency are recognized and prioritized by the entrepreneurs. Finally, the role of regional networks for tourism businesses was evaluated.

## MAIN RESULTS

The first part of the following paragraph focuses on the internal resources and competencies of tourism service providers in the Northern Black Forest. The importance of resource efficiency for their products is discussed. Furthermore the specific skills which were necessary to create these resource-efficient products are investigated and the question of whether these skills develop a regional reach is evaluated.

The results of the study are discussed in the following sections, and at the end, Table 3.1 summarizes the main results.

## THE RELEVANCE OF RESOURCE EFFICIENCY IN THE NORTHERN BLACK FOREST

There already are a number of positive examples in the Northern Black Forest related to resource efficiency. Into this context may be placed the KONUS card, a guest pass for free use of public transport. Additionally, there is a catering initiative which aims to use local products with low $CO_2$ emissions ('30-kilometre menus'). There are efforts to use woods from trees grown in the region for hotel furniture and fittings. Furthermore, some travel deals in the field of nature-based tourism incorporate and address their guests' consciousness of efficient resource use and nature conservation. In this context the 'culinary hiking heaven' tourism product of the city of Baiersbronn has gained attention.

To most companies, however, resource efficiency is not a central concern. Economic success in terms of a solid income is a priority. Environmental protection is pursued only if it connects to economic objectives. Therefore, resource efficiency is not considered an entrepreneurial opportunity. Rather, companies try to deal with the task of environmental protection in an administrative manner, mainly by acquiring eco-certificates like Viabono or EMAS. The requirements of certification are commonly considered a burden that is too demanding and comes with little economic advantage. Most companies do not see the business case for resource efficiency.

## ENTREPRENEURIAL RESOURCES AND THE NATIONAL PARK

Two types of resources are critical when creating attractive products and services in the field of ecotourism. The first is nature itself. Interviewed respondents noted, however, that the Black Forest lacks a real unique selling proposition at the moment. The landscape is not unique, since time is needed for the appearance of the forests to return from commercially managed to wild and natural. Animal wildlife is also not particularly spectacular; species such as lynx or wolves, which exist in other national parks, are missing. In addition, a great number of attractions are not recognized for their value or are not easily accessible. Without the necessary infrastructure, nature is not part of the tourist experience.

The second critical resource is knowledge about nature. For the National Park to yield positive economic effects, service providers need creativity. However, creativity needs a knowledge base. Currently only a small part of the population and very few touristic entrepreneurs know about the purpose of the national park. There is a lack of understanding about ecological processes. Moreover, there is a lack of knowledge regarding the expectations of National Park tourists. Thus, there is no basis to create attractive travel products. The background for this lack of knowledge is the traditional relationship between man and nature in the region. Conservation of natural resources was considered a luxury.

## MARKET OPPORTUNITIES BASED ON THE NATIONAL PARK

The interviews suggest that the establishment of the National Park provides several market opportunities. First, the perception of national parks is positive worldwide. They represent authenticity and the love of nature. These connotations, however, raise certain expectations of national parks. For example, guests and visitors want to experience old forests. Knowledge of customer expectations would facilitate the development of new business opportunities. However, interviewees did not demonstrate a clear picture of potential target groups.

Second, the National Park provides the opportunity to cater to high-quality standards. The park itself conveys a quality statement. Due to this, a multiplication effect can arise and trigger quality enhancement in other segments of the touristic chain. By living up to the high standard of the National Park's natural environment, the region may become a quality tourism destination. Since quality tourist products may result in higher prices, a higher return on investment may be realized.

Third, the philosophy of the National Park is resource efficiency. Since it is a place where nature can develop according to its own rules, the National Park educates visitors about the natural environment and the finiteness of its resources. If this philosophy is introduced into economic value chains, resource efficiency may become a catalyst for economic development. Some promising developments are already taking place in the energy sector. A number of communities and companies now satisfy most of their energy demand by renewable energy sources. New technologies are being developed to store energy more efficiently or save water.

## REGIONAL NETWORKING IN THE NORTHERN BLACK FOREST

The designation of the National Park has divided the population in the Northern Black Forest. There are opponents and proponents. A large part of the population regrets that the resources of the forest cannot be used as they were in the past, especially since the forest was often the livelihood for many local residents. At the same time, there are different expectations of tourist enterprises in the National Park. Some hope the park will spur tourism development. Others primarily consider the National Park a conservation project with limited economic effects. Overall, many tour operators want to profit without having to invest much. Expectations of the park administration are high: it is expected to finance infrastructure improvements as well as marketing.

### Table 3.1    Summary of main results

| Topic | Main content | Key statement |
|---|---|---|
| Resource efficiency relevance | To most companies resource efficiency is not a central concern. Economic success in terms of a solid income is a priority. Environmental protection is pursued only if it connects to economic objectives. | Restaurant guests appreciate being informed that portions are small, but may be enlarged if necessary. This signals resource efficiency and is economically sustainable (Interview 1, 47: 10–47: 46). |
| Entrepreneurial resources | Only a small part of the population and very few touristic entrepreneurs know about the purpose of the national park. There is a lack of understanding about ecological processes. | It would be important for the development of new services or value chains that touristic partners are curious and eager to learn more about the processes and developments in the national park (Interview 2, 20:05 – 20:13). |
| Market opportunities | The interviews suggest that the establishment of the National Park is seen as a market opportunity. However, interviewees did not demonstrate a clear picture of potential target groups. | The national park provides an opportunity for tourism, because the region can occupy a market niche and attract special guests and target groups (Interview 3, 22:56 – 23:03). |
| Regional networking | The designation of the National Park has divided the population in Northern Black Forest. There are opponents and proponents. This situation makes cooperation difficult. | For some partners the national park and the common marketing of the park is not the objective … they want profit without bringing in their own resources (Interview 4, 54:58 – 55:13) |

This situation makes cooperation difficult. The interviewees suspect that there is a lack of coordination and unwillingness to share information. However, in order to capitalize on opportunities represented by the National Park, a cooperative effort of all involved stakeholders along the service chain is necessary. Beyond that, interviewees also recommended cooperation with non-tourism businesses from manufacturing or the timber industry. Cooperation requires that stakeholders share common values, interests and ideas about the National Park. However, the current public dissent makes cooperative efforts difficult.

## Conclusion

Overall, there is a close relationship between the people within the Northern Black Forest region and nature. However, this relationship is currently characterized by economic use, rather than conservation of natural resources. The recent establishment of the National Park fundamentally changes this relationship. Nonetheless, the region and its businesses could profit from the park in terms of an increase in tourism. Entrepreneurs could create products around customers' emotions and expectations of the National Park. As a result, this might lead to higher-quality products and generate more regional value.

Furthermore, the National Park puts nature conservation and thus resource efficiency at the centre. The notion of resource efficiency as a guiding theme could support green innovations in various industries. With some promising examples in the region, innovations concerning energy efficiency are considered to hold great potential. Apart from that, new organizational forms of cooperation in traffic, energy production or food consumption could arise. For instance, a region-wide e-mobility concept could allow tourists to conveniently switch between different means of transportation. Because of the large market size affected by the tourism industry of the Northern Black Forest, the potential impact on market dynamics is considerable – a precondition for real green entrepreneurship.

So far, few companies capitalize on these opportunities. This can be explained in part by the fact that the state of nature and wildlife in the National Park does not yet conform to associations with wilderness. Additionally, companies lack knowledge about utilizing natural resources in green production processes. The traditional knowledge is based around consuming natural resources rather than conserving nature. Therefore, there is a clear need for entrepreneurs to become educated about basic natural processes and the underlying ideas of a national park.

Furthermore, companies also lack knowledge in terms of market expertise. Many tourism entrepreneurs in the Northern Black Forest only vaguely know their potential target groups. Moreover, there is often no understanding of guests' expectations and motivations when visiting the National Park. This is not a sufficient condition for developing successful products. In addition, tourism enterprises and other businesses send contradictory messages to potential customers. This is due to the fact that there are still bitter rivals in the region who reject the park and communicate their disapproval to guests, creating a clear challenge for tourism marketing.

Finally, the implementation of resource efficiency in the tourism service chain needs the support of all partners involved. However, networking requires a shared basic understanding. And it requires trust. Neither currently exists in the Northern Black Forest: stakeholders' expectations of the National Park vary greatly. The heated debate prior to the establishment of the park has led to a great level of mistrust and division. In addition, not everyone involved understands the principles of a service chain. Therefore, they hardly recognize the opportunities of cooperation and share little interest in collaborative efforts.

At the moment, it is primarily the local tourism offices, regional tourism organizations and tour operators who recognize the business opportunities of resource efficiency. Hoteliers, transport operators and most of the local authorities do not see these opportunities. Therefore, the interests of green entrepreneurship are currently represented by tourism organizations. These entities, however, do not do business commercially. Therefore, value-creation opportunities remain unused.

## MANAGEMENT IMPLICATIONS

Based on the experience in the Northern Black Forest recommendations for the promotion of green entrepreneurship can be formulated. Green entrepreneurship can succeed at the crossroads of natural resources and sound ecological and technological knowledge. The first task of a regional management strategy should therefore be to provide the tourism stakeholders with relevant knowledge. The flow of knowledge between knowledge institutions such as governments or universities and companies should be intensified. Beyond that, not only tourism service providers but also enterprises in industry, commerce and agriculture should be integrated into this knowledge-sharing process.

Second, successful entrepreneurship requires an accurate knowledge of customer preferences. Small and medium-sized enterprises in the tourism market lack this knowledge because they cannot afford to conduct marketing analysis. Furthermore, they often lack the financial means for larger investments, often due to the part-time nature of their businesses or because they are unable to borrow capital. This will make it difficult for them to meet the implicit quality statements and expected standards of the National Park. They will not be able to participate in the aforementioned multiplication effect of quality, price and value generation in the region. A regional development strategy could therefore supply tourism service providers, especially hotels and restaurants, with current market information on green target groups. In addition, the training and education of stakeholders is an essential component in order to increase quality standards across all levels of the service chain.

Finally, tourism requires businesses to be willing to cooperate and capable of cooperating. Cooperation is possible if there is a strong normative foundation, a shared value system, and common beliefs. If these are not present, the priority of any regional development strategy should be to work with stakeholders towards such a common baseline and build trust.

Furthermore, it has become apparent that green entrepreneurship is not represented equally across all parts of the service chain. While hoteliers and restaurateurs are hesitant to take on the business opportunities provided by resource efficiency, others understand the trend. These are primarily tourist offices and regional tourism organizations. They develop products that represent the philosophy of the National Park, which is resource efficiency. This raises the question whether tourist offices should operate as for-profit businesses so that the value potential of this market niche can be realized.

## References

Allen, J.C., and Malin, S. (2008). Green entrepreneurship: A method for managing natural resources? *Society and Natural Resources*, 21(8), 828–844.

Anderson, A.R. (1998). Cultivating the Garden of Eden: Environmental entrepreneuring. *Journal of Organisational Change Management*, 11(2), 135–144.

Audretsch, D.B. (2003). *Entrepreneurship: A Survey of the Literature* (European Commission Enterprise Papers No. 14). European Commission. Retrieved from website: http://ec.europa.eu/enterprise/newsroom/cf/_getdocument. cfm?doc_id=1837

Barney, J.B. (1991). Firm resources and sustained competitive advantage. *Journal of Management*, 17(1), 99–120.

Barney, J.B. (2002). *Gaining and Sustaining Competitive Advantage.* Upper Saddle River, New Jersey: Prentice Hall.

Bennett, S. (1991). *Ecopreneurship: The Complete Guide to Small Business Opportunities from the Environmental Revolution*. New York: Wiley.

Blinnikka, P., Härkönen, A., Väisänen, H.M., and Tunkkari-Eskelinen, M. (2014). Finnish micro entrepreneurs' perceptions of sustainability issues in rural tourism. In J. Suni and R. Komppula (eds), *International Conference on Rural Tourism and Regional Development Proceedings – Rural Tourism as a Facilitator of Regional Development* (13–26). Retrieved from: http://epublications.uef.fi/pub/urn_isbn_978–952–61–1416–3/urn_isbn_978–952–61–1416–3.pdf

Chesbrough, H.W. (2003). The era of open innovation. *Sloan Management Review*, 44(3), 35–41.

Cohen, W.M., and Levinthal, D.A. (1990). Absorptive capacity. A new perspective on learning and innovation. *Administrative Science Quarterly*, 35(1), 128–153.

Dean, J.T., and McMullen, J.S. (2007). Toward a theory of sustainable entrepreneurship: Reducing environmental degradation through entrepreneurial action. *Journal of Business Venturing*, 22, 50–76.

Doepfer, B. (2013). *Co-innovation Competence: A Strategic Approach to Entrepreneurship in Regional Innovation Structures*. Wiesbaden: Springer Gabler.

Dosi, G., Faillo, M., and Marengo, L. (2008). Organizational capabilities, patterns of knowledge accumulation and governance structures in business firms: An introduction. *Organization Studies*, 29(8 and 9), 1165–1185.

Duschek, S. (2004). Inter-firm resources and sustainable competitive advantage. *Management Review*, 15(1), 53–73.

Flick, U. (2014). *An Introduction to Qualitative Research*. London: Sage Publications.

Freiling, J. (2004). A competence-based theory of the firm. *Management Review*, 15(1), 27–52.

Freiling, J., Gersch, M., and Goeke, C. (2008). On the path towards a competence-based theory of the firm. *Organization Studies*, 29. 1143–1164.

Geels, F.W. (2005). *Technological Transitions and Systems Innovations: A Co-evolutionary and Socio-technical Analysis*. Cheltenham, UK: Edward Elgar.

Gibbs, D. (2009). Sustainability entrepreneurs, ecopreneurs, and the development of a sustainable economy. *Greener Management International*, 55. 63–78.

Grant, R.M. (1991). The resource-based theory of competitive advantage: Implications for strategy formulation. *California Management Review*, 33(3), 114–135.

Gulati, R., Nohria, N., and Zaheer, A. (2000). Strategic networks. *Strategic Management Journal*, 21(3), 203–215.

Gunawan, A.A. (2012). *Ecopreneurship Concept and its Barriers: A Literature Review*. Paper presented at the National Seminar on Business Ethics at the Institut Teknologi Bandung. Retrieved from: http://share.ciputra.ac.id/

Department/Staffs/iba/Laura/Umum/Pak    per    cent20Eko/Prosiding    per cent20Call per cent20For per cent20Papers per cent20and per cent20Seminar per cent20Nasional/IX.ESME2.pdf

Hamel, G., and Prahalad, C.K. (1994). Competing for the future. *Harvard Business Review*, 72(4), 122–128.

Hart, S.L. (1995). A natural-resource-based view of the firm. *Academy of Management Review*, 20(4), 986–1014.

IPCC (2014). *Climate Change 2014: Synthesis Report*. Contribution of Working Groups I, II and III to the Fifth Assessment Report of the Intergovernmental Panel on Climate Change, edited by R.K. Pachauri and L.A. Meyer. Geneva, Switzerland: IPCC. Retrieved from: http://www.ipcc.ch/pdf/assessment-report/ar5/syr/AR5_SYR_FINAL_SPM.pdf

Isaak, R. (2002). The making of the ecopreneur. *Greener Management International*, 38. 81–92.

Kenny, M. (2009). *Venture Capital Investment in the Greentech Industries: A Provocative Essay*. BRIE Working Paper 185. Retrieved from: http://brie.berkeley.edu/publications/wp185.pdf

Kirkwood, J., and Walton, S. (2010). What motivates ecopreneurs to start business? *International Journal of Entrepreneurial Behavior and Research*, 16(3), 204–228.

Kohlbacher, F. (2006). The use of qualitative content analysis in case study research. *Forum Qualitative Social Research*, 7(1). Retrieved from: http://www.qualitative-research.net/index.php/fqs/article/view/75/153

Krull, (2011). *Tourismus im ländlichen Raum – am Beispiel Schwarzwald* [Tourism in rural areas – the case of the Black Forest]. Paper presented at the conference Unser Dorf hat Zukunft [The future of our village] held on 15 March 2011. Retrieved from: http://www.gartenakademie.info/pdf/Dorfwettbewerb_2011/Sasbachwalden/4_Vortrag_    per    cent20Krull_Tourismus_laendl_Raum.pdf

Lavie, D. (2006). The competitive advantage of interconnected firms: An extension of the resource-based view. *The Academy of Management Review*, 31(3), 638–658.

Mayring, Ph. (2014). *Qualitative Content Analysis. Theoretical Foundation, Basic Procedures and Software Solution*. Retrieved from: http://nbn-resolving.de/urn:nbn:de:0168-ssoar-395173.

McEwan, T. (2013). Ecopreneurship as a solution to environmental problems: Implications for college level entrepreneurship education. *International Journal of Academic Research in Business and Social Sciences*, 3(5), 264–288.

McLeod, M., and Vaughan, R. (2015). Introduction. In M. McLeod and R. Vaughan (eds), *Knowledge Networks and Tourism* (1–8). New York: Routledge.

Melay, I., and Kraus, S. (2012). Green entrepreneurship: Definitions of related concepts. *International Journal of Strategic Management*, 12(2), 1–12.

NLP (2015). *Nationalpark Nordschwarzwald* [Website of the Black Forest National Park]. Retrieved from: http://www.nordschwarzwald-nationalpark.de/index.php?id=1

OECD (2012). *OECD Tourism Papers: Green Innovation in Tourism Services.* [Online – Organisation for Economic Co-operation and Development.] Retrieved from: http://www.oecd-ilibrary.org/docserver/download/5k4bxkt1cjd2.pdf?expires=1427581495andid=idandaccname=guestandchecksum=69C7438FECF3449855DBAB15519BB8F9

OECD (2013). *Working Party on SMEs and Entrepreneurship (WPSMEE): Green Entrepreneurship, Eco-innovation and SMEs Final Report.* [Online – Organisation for Economic Co-operation and Development.] Retrieved from: http://www.oecd.org/officialdocuments/publicdisplaydocumentpdf/?cote=CFE/SME per cent282011 per cent299/FINALanddocLanguage=En

Pechlaner, H., and Bachinger, M. (2010). Knowledge networks of innovative businesses: An explorative study in the region of Ingolstadt. *The Service Industries Journal*, 30(10), 1737–1756.

Pechlaner, H., and Bachinger, M. (2014). Regional core competencies as a basis for entrepreneurship? The German hop-growing area of the Hallertau. *Entrepreneurship and Innovation*, 15(1), 41–50.

Pechlaner, H., Bachinger, M., Volgger, M., and Anzengruber-Fischer, E. (2014). Cooperative core competencies in tourism: Combining resource-based and relational approaches in destination governance. *European Journal of Tourism Research*, 8. 5–19.

Peters, M., and Buhalis, D. (2004). Family hotel business: Strategic planning and the need for education and training. *Education and Training*, 46(8–9), 406–415.

Pihkala, T., Harmaakorpi, V., and Pekkarinen, S. (2007). The role of dynamic capabilities and social capital in breaking socio-institutional inertia in regional development. *International Journal of Urban and Regional Research*, 31(4), 836–852.

PWC (2013). PricewatherhouseCooper. *Gutachten zum potenziellen Nationalpark im Nordschwarzwald. Zusammenfassung der wesentlichen Ergebnisse* [Expertise on a potential national park in the Northern Black Forest. Summary of main results]. Berlin: Tridix.

Rennings, K. (2000). Redefining innovation: Eco-innovation research and the contribution from ecological economics. *Ecological Economics*, 32. 319–332.

Ritchie, J.R.B., and Crouch, G. (2003). *The Competitive Destination: A Sustainable Tourism Perspective*. Wallingford: C.A.B. International.

RNSW (2015). *Regionalverband Nordschwarzwald* [Website of the regional planning office of Northern Black Forest]. Retrieved from: http://www. nordschwarzwald-region.de/regionalverband/

Rodriguez, M.A., Ricart, J.E., and Sanchez, J.P. (2002). Sustainable development and the sustainability of competitive advantage: A dynamic sustainable view of the firm. *Creativity and Innovation Management,* 11(3), 135–146.

Sanchez, R. (2004). Understanding competence-based management: Identifying and managing five models of competence. *Journal of Business Research,* 57. 518–532.

Schaltegger, S. (2002). A framework for ecopreneurship: Leading bioneers and environmental managers to ecopreneurship. *Greener Management International,* 38. 45–58.

Schaltegger, S. and Petersen, H. (2001). *Ecopreneurship: Konzept und Typologie* [Ecopreneurship: Concept and Typology]. Lüneburg, Germany: Centre for Sustainability Management; Lucerne, Switzerland: Rio Management Forum.

Schaper, M. (2002). The essence of ecopreneurship. *Greener Management International,* 38. 26–30.

Schaper, M. (2005). Understanding the green entrepreneur. In M. Schaper (ed.), *Making Ecopreneurs: Developing Sustainable Entrepreneurship* (3–12). Farnham, UK: Ashgate.

Schick, H., Marxen, S., and Freimann, J. (2002). Sustainability issues for start-up entrepreneurs. *Greener Management International,* 38. 59–70.

Schumpeter, J. (1934). *The Theory of Economic Development.* Cambridge, MA: Harvard University Press.

Shane, S. (2003). *A General Theory of Entrepreneurship.* Cheltenham: Edward Elgar.

StaLa (2015). *Statistisches Landesamt* [Statistical Data from the federal bureau of statistics of Baden-Wuerttemberg]. Retrieved from: http://www.statistik. baden-wuerttemberg.de/SRDB/home.asp?H=HandelBeherb

Taylor D.W., and Walley E.E. (2004). The green entrepreneur: Opportunist, maverick or visionary? *International Journal of Entrepreneurship and Small Business,* 1(1–2), 56–69.

Teece, D.J. (2007). Explicating dynamic capabilities: The nature and microfoundations of (sustainable) enterprise performance. *Strategic Management Journal,* 28(13), 1319–1350.

Teece, D.J., Pisano, G., and Shuen, A. (1997). Dynamic capabilities and strategic management. *Strategic Management Journal,* 18(7), 509–533.

Tunkkari-Eskelinen, M., Matilainen, A., and Asunta, J. (2014). Customer insight as a driving force for development of sustainability elements in rural tourism. In J. Suni and R. Komppula (eds), *International Conference on Rural Tourism and Regional Development Proceedings – Rural Tourism as a Facilitator of*

*Regional Development* (56–66). Retrieved from http://epublications.uef.fi/pub/urn_isbn_978-952-61-1416-3/urn_isbn_978-952-61-1416-3.pdf

UNWTO (2014). *Tourism Highlights.* Retrieved from NGO website: http://mkt.unwto.org/publication/unwto-tourism-highlights-2014-edition

Vanhove, N. (2011): *The Economics of Tourism Destinations.* London and New York: Routledge.

Wernerfelt, B. (1984). A resource based view of the firm. *Strategic Management Journal,* 5, 171–80.

# PART II
# Innovation in the Hospitality Industry

PART II

Innovation in the Hospitality Industry

# Chapter 4

# Current Innovation Perspectives in the European Hotel Industry: An Exploratory Analysis

MICHAEL VOLGGER and BETTINA PRUKKER-LOSONCZI

This chapter presents an exploratory study of current innovation perspectives in the European hotel and accommodation industry. Its aim is to capture current opinions and discourses about innovation, and (to a lesser extent) about practices, and to disentangle the thinking (and acting) about types and sources of innovation. To achieve this aim, the chapter introduces nine cases of innovation in the European accommodation sector, interprets selected statements taken from qualitative interviews with managers and owners of these accommodation cases and critically overviews a set of innovation awards in the hospitality industry. First, results suggest that systemic, institutional and social innovation perspectives are emphasized, as compared to product, management and communications innovation perspectives. Second, results indicate that current innovation perspectives in the European accommodation industry intensively combine resource-based and market-driven considerations.

## Current Trends

The European hospitality sector in general and the accommodation industry in particular are facing a turbulent environment. This has resulted, on the one hand in some traditional accommodation models struggling with the phenomena of maturity and stagnating or decreasing key performance indicators, even in tourism-intensive areas (Dominici, 2014; Ganzer, 2015); and booming alternative concepts such as Airbnb™ on the other hand (Nasr, 2015). Therefore we may suppose that the accommodation and hotel industry is faced with even stronger pressure to innovate than before and, consequently, accommodation providers are currently considering or already have implemented adjustments. The purpose of this chapter is to investigate the types of current thinking on innovation and (to a lesser extent) innovative action that can be found among selected managers and owners in the European hotel and accommodation industry and in international hotel innovation awarding practice over recent years.

Innovation may be understood as an (implemented) process or an (implemented) outcome of a process that is *perceived as new* by the individuals involved (Rogers, 1982; Van de Ven, 1986). Following this premise, stepwise innovation and even phenomena that others might consider to be imitation can be innovations, as long as the individuals perceive them as new. Specifically in the hotel industry innovation is assumed to be mainly a stepwise process often resulting in minor adjustments (Jones, 1996; Peters and Weiermair, 2002; Volo, 2004). The question is whether this allegation can still be maintained for the near future, or will we assist in more radical and fundamental changes in the hotel and accommodation industry under substantially varying framework conditions?

Scholars request research on innovation in hospitality, which is still rather scant, to understand the nature of innovation practice and innovation thinking, monitor their development and register any major changes (Ottenbacher, 2007; Orfila-Sintes and Mattsson, 2009). Based on a review of hotel innovation awards and an exploratory qualitative interview study of the European hotel industry, this chapter explores (1) which types of innovation and (2) which major drivers and sources of innovation are currently emphasized and considered. The chapter closes by highlighting potential touch points to the discussion on strategic management concerning determinants of firm performance, which has become known as the debate between market-based and resource-based approaches (see Innerhofer, 2012).

## Literature Review

### TYPES OF INNOVATION

Innovations tend to be diverse in nature. Differing and complementary approaches have been established to classify innovations and are part of the canon of innovation research and practice today. By differentiating innovations in the hotel industry based on their type, Ottenbacher and Gnoth (2005) and Orfila-Sintes and Mattsson (2009) propose four main types of innovations: product innovation (*service scope*), process innovation (*back-office innovation*), management innovation (including business models and organizational aspects), and communications innovation. In accordance with other authors (Hjalager, 1997; Elzen, Geels and Green, 2004; Novelli, Schmitz and Spencer,

2006; Enz and Harrison, 2008; Phills, Deiglmeier and Miller, 2008), we may add a further category, system innovation (or institutional innovation, which also comprises, for the purpose of this chapter, instances of social innovation) as an additional type tends to have more wide-ranging socio-cultural implications.

Empirical studies on innovation types in the hotel and accommodation sector are rare. An exception is provided by Vila, Enz and Costa (2011), who find that Spain's largest hotel chains devote their energies mainly to management innovations followed by product innovations. However, considering only implemented innovations, respondents mentioned most frequently the innovation category of an enhanced knowledge of the market, including sales channels and communications, followed by product innovation. Management innovations played a less important role in this context, which indicates discrepancies between innovation efforts and innovation implementation regarding different innovation types.

## SOURCES AND DRIVERS OF INNOVATION

Regarding the innovation sources, we may distinguish market-driven innovations and resource- or competence-driven innovations. Based on the idea that adaptation to the market and its development significantly determines the success of a firm, the market-based view suggests that innovation should closely observe and react to *given* market and contextual developments (Porter, 1980; 1985). By contrast, following the ideas of the resource-based view (Penrose, 1959; Barney, 1991; Wernerfelt, 1995), an above-average performance of firms may depend on their access to and application of distinct resources and capabilities that are difficult to imitate. Hence, innovation should focus on developing inimitable, internal resources and capabilities in an inside-out type of process. Innovation success would be a consequence of building new competences or exploiting them in novel, non-erodible ways. In an extended resource-based perspective (also known as the 'relational view'), these resources and capabilities might be additionally rooted at the inter-organizational network level (Pechlaner et al., 2014) and, thus, innovation can imply significant changes at this network level (Pforr et al., 2014).

Within the existing literature on drivers and sources of (successful) hospitality and hotel innovations, two major approaches can be found (see also Hagel and Singer, 1999): one that underscores the role of market screening and market responsiveness (focus on market) and one that emphasizes the importance of human resource management and leadership (focus on employees) in order to establish efficient and effective innovation processes in hotels and accommodation businesses. This second, employee- and leadership-oriented approach relates to resource-based perspectives (see Pechlaner,

Fisher, and Hammann, 2006). However, it has some additional links to the market-focused approach, since employees are perceived to be important in part exactly because they can identify consumer needs and convince customers of the benefits of new services and thereby significantly help in implementation (Ottenbacher, 2007).

An example of the market-oriented approach is the study of Vila, Enz and Costa (2011), which reports cases of innovation in the Spanish hotel industry that were characterized by a clear audience targeting. The study of Ottenbacher, Gnoth and Jones (2006) emphasizes the critical role of market responsiveness when considering hospitality innovations. Ottenbacher (2007) points in the same direction and suggests that understanding the customer and the market is a prerequisite for successful service innovation in hospitality: 'Successful hospitality innovations are customer-driven. Hence, to succeed requires managers first to focus on getting an in-depth knowledge and appreciation of the customer's needs, wants, and behaviors' (Ottenbacher, 2007: 445).

Located within the second, employee-centred research stream, Enz and Siguaw (2003) underline the role of individuals and leadership in hospitality innovation. Moving in a similar direction, Ottenbacher and Gnoth (2005) find that resources and their organization are considered to be important drivers of service innovation success in the German hotel industry. In particular, employee training and involvement, as well as human resource management, even seem to be, in some instances, relatively more important than market orientation and market communications. Tajeddini (2010) confirms that entrepreneurial orientation and fostering an innovation promoting corporate culture are positively associated with innovativeness. In contrast, customer orientation does not appear to be unambiguously related to an increased innovativeness. Tseng, Kuo and Chou (2008) and Chen (2011) confirm the crucial role of organizational culture and human resource management in driving hotel innovativeness.

A somewhat broader but predominantly resource-based perspective on drivers of innovations is adopted by Orfila-Sintes and Mattsson (2009). They present evidence that supports the importance of service providers' competences and resources (such as information and knowledge generation and interpretation) as drivers of innovation in the hotel industry. The size of the establishment is found to play an important role as well. Bigger hotels tend to have a higher tendency to innovate, especially as far as management and process innovations are concerned. Additionally, different customer segments may also imply different impulses to innovation, with some stimulating the hotelier to be innovative and others less.

Jacob et al. (2003) find similar patterns regarding firm size and geographical scope of hospitality enterprises. Both seem to foster innovativeness. Martínez-Ros and Orfila-Sintes (2009) present data that indicates that non-owner managers are more likely to engage in radical innovation than owner-managed hotels, which might be related to an attitude of managers that is characterized by a considerable openness to change (compared to more conservative attitudes of owners).

## Innovation Awards in the Hotel Industry

For a first glance in the direction that innovative thinking and acting in the hospitality sector are heading, innovation awards may be a relevant study object. A variety of hotel innovation awards exist. Most of these reward particular features such as special hotel design or hotel architecture (e.g. the European / Asian Hotel Design Awards, the Hospitality Design Awards, the International Hotel and Property Awards and the International Hotel Awards), a hotel's attention to environmental and sustainability issues (the Blue Hotel Award), or special interest themes (Fodor's 100 Hotel Awards). Other awards tend to adopt a more comprehensive assessment of innovation and the degree of innovativeness in the overall accommodation concept integrating different perspectives, such as architecture and service design, formation and education of staff, and social aspects such as the promotion of social and environmental responsibility (the Hospitality Innovation Award, Hotelimmobilie des Jahres, MKG's Worldwide Hospitality Awards). Interestingly, the Hospitality Innovation Award does not reward a hotel property, but rather an outstanding figure or organization. In 2014 the Dean of Cornell University School of Hotel Administration and the general manager of Ecole hôtelière de Lausanne received the prize for their research and training performance (Hotelforum, 2015).

The Radical Innovation Award challenges the hotel industry to elevate the guest experience using new thinking in design and operations. An existing hotel establishment or a new concept can be rewarded. The criteria consist of concept, design, creativity and potential impact on the industry (Radical Innovation Award, 2015a). Recently, award-winning hotel concepts have focused on promoting the symbiosis of iconic architecture and urban landscape (Koi Bridge Hotel concept, Winner 2012), repurposing existing spaces (Pop-Up Hotel concept, Winner 2013), or proposing greenhouse gardens that act as air filters to remove harmful toxins in the air (Green Air Hotel concept, Winner 2014). These examples of recent award winners indicate a search for new ideas within the hotel industry to contribute to tackling wider societal problems like rural exodus, vacancy rates and climate change. The questions whether and how hotels can engage with social issues seems to gain in importance (Radical Innovation Award, 2015b).

Last but not least, another important focus reflected in innovation awards is technology-driven service innovation. The TechOvation Award from the Hotel Technology Next Generation (HTNG) is designed to reward the most innovative hospitality technology of the year (HTNG, 2015a). Looking at the winners over the last few years, the importance of technology-aided guest entertainment is striking. Among the award-winning innovations were a so-called smart TV (Winner 2011), which offers guests a world of online apps, a personal media network app (Winner 2012) and a wireless streaming device (Winner 2013), which enable guests to more efficiently stream content to the in-room TV (HTNG, 2015b).

These briefly outlined examples of hotel innovation awards indicate that besides new products and services (e.g., innovative architecture or entertainment experiences driven by new technologies), setting the basics for innovation by establishing a sophisticated human relationship management and leadership style, and promoting social innovations are considered important to innovativeness in the hotel sector. Overall, it seems that these awards increasingly favour an out-of-the-box mentality, which does not fear to engage in radical and systemic changes with a potentially profound impact on the hotel and accommodation sector.

## Interviews with European Hotel Owners and Managers

In order to gather ideas on current innovation perspectives ('innovation thinking') in the European hotel and accommodation industry, we conducted nine semi-structured qualitative interviews with European hotel owners and managers who have implemented innovative concepts that won significant media coverage. These innovations range from radical to substantial and thus should cover the range of more extended innovation activities in the sector. We did not consider very incremental innovation projects. Interviewees were asked to discuss their own hotel and accommodation concept with regard to innovation, to comment on its potential impact on the hotel industry and to express their opinion about potential future developments in the accommodation sector. The interviews lasted between 15 minutes and 45 minutes and were conducted on the phone between March and June 2015. The interviewees were recorded, transcribed and analysed for major categories.

The first part of this section briefly introduces the selected case studies. The second part presents selected statements taken from the qualitative interviews with the hotel managers and interprets them concerning the innovation perspectives they manifest. We took these statements directly from the interviews and categorized them according to whether they offer insight into the type of innovation or into sources and drivers of innovativeness in the accommodation sector.

## THE CASES

### Culture- and art-driven hotel innovation

The *Pixel Hotel* in Austria and the *Null Stern Hotel* in Switzerland are both concepts inspired by broader social issues such as vacancy rates and abandoned properties. The *Pixel Hotel* concept is anchored in a cultural and urban development perspective and is driven by architects who had no previous connection to the hospitality industry. The concept consists of scattering the hotel's rooms throughout the city or destination. This innovative approach led them to winning the Radical Innovation Award in 2009 (Radical Innovation Award, 2015b). The idea is to reuse abandoned properties by implementing a way of lodging into them. It builds on and modifies existing resources and thus seems driven by assumptions akin to the resource-based view.

The Null Stern Hotel is a hybrid between an art installation and an accommodation establishment. The hotel, which is a museum by now, has been established in an abandoned Swiss bunker. Thus, like the Pixel Hotel it devotes attention to the issue of abandoned properties. However, the purpose of this reuse is meant to be a radical criticism of today's hotel system. Its concept includes a new definition of luxury and the creation of new values. In sum, it may be regarded as a resource-based driven innovation that aims to combine art, social criticism and the accommodation system to create something new.

### Hotel innovation to foster community orientation

The 25hours Hotel, operating in Germany, Austria and Switzerland, The Student Hotel in the Netherlands and Belgium and the CUBE Hotel, operating in Austria and Switzerland, are accommodation approaches that try to foster community access and/or community building. While the 25hours Hotel strives to bring the city's specific urban lifestyle into the hotel by being an attractive spot also for locals (community access), The Student Hotel and the CUBE Hotel try to target a specific market segment and, in part, proactively shape its dynamics (community building).

The 25hours Hotel is an approach that leverages regional resources in order to create an authentic and regionally rooted experience (despite the hotel's presence in several cities). Within the 25hours Hotel concept, authenticity is mainly ensured by attracting locals into the hotel bar, restaurant or shop. The Student Hotel is a concept that follows current market trends and covers some so far uncovered niches. It is a mix of student dormitory and boutique hotel, and provides a hybrid offer to a target group that is in search of affordable accommodation for flexible periods. An important trait of the target group is that its members like being in a community of individuals that help each other to master problems in a new city. In this way it somehow breaks with one of the core principles of the hotel industry, namely a duration of stay that is limited to a maximum of a couple of weeks. In 2014, The Student Hotel won the Worldwide Hospitality Award in the category Best Innovation Hotel (Hospitality Awards, 2015).

The CUBE Hotel is a targeted accommodation offer designed for active and sporty guests who often bring their own sports equipment. The concept is based on extensive market research and implements the findings obtained in a rather straightforward manner. Based on the assumption that community and sharing are important issues for today's guests, the CUBE Hotel provides extensive open spaces, where people can gather around and share their experiences in an open community setting. Additionally, it closely integrates the destination into its offer. An all-in-one concept provides packages that include tickets for ski slopes and other destination offers located outside the hotel.

### Innovation towards luxurious versions of ecotourism accommodation

Almdorf Seinerzeit, operating in Austria, Whitepod in Switzerland and Attrap'Rêves in France offer experiences that combine ecotourism experiences with upmarket facilities. Again, this innovation aims at valorizing regional resources (mostly nature, partly culture) by adjusting them to current market and market segment dynamics.

Almdorf Seinerzeit is an Alpine interpretation of a resort hotel. It seeks to offer traditional life in an Alpine mountain village adjusted to the needs and wants of the modern guest. This innovation is rooted in an appreciation of regional competences while trying to modify them according to the preferences of a luxury market segment. Thereby it seems able to cater to guests having nostalgia for nature and traditional ways of life, but not wanting to renounce the benefits of modern society.

The Whitepod is an eco-luxury lodging site in the mountains. The concept aims to combine closeness to nature with luxury amenities, and hospitality establishments with eco-friendliness and regionality. In particular, Whitepod takes the first steps beyond the physically stable nature of hotels by relying on a light and easily removable infrastructure. Attrap'Rêves moves even further towards mobile accommodation concepts as a means of moving into unspoiled areas. Guests sleep in transparent and inflatable plastic bubble domes, which can be placed virtually everywhere. At the end of the season, the bubbles are deflated. The idea behind this concept was to build a lodge that can provide a genuine natural experience without sacrificing the services of a hotel, but also leaving the surrounding nature intact after moving the bubbles.

### Social innovation in the hotel industry

The Grandhotel Cosmopolis in Germany is a social project which addresses parallelisms between tourists and refugees. Paying hotel guests and asylum seekers are both housed in the same building – a former retirement home. This setup should encourage encounters between these different groups of guests. The concept utilizes previously unused resources and provides an answer to an up-to-date social problem. Not least, it may be able to make a thought-provoking contribution to the value set of hospitality.

## SELECTED INTERVIEW STATEMENTS

### Types of innovation

> *It is very much about the mentality, the attitude of an entrepreneur and hotelier. [...] We create experiences within the meaning of real encounters; it is not about faking it. The friendliness is an attitude, therefore you have to go deep inside and create a new mentality. [...] Well, that does not mean that you must create a huge framework programme, but it is about the warmth. However, you really must be able to feel it. This is precisely the source of energy for people who have an establishment. The guest is the central element. People who have no fun with their guests are in the wrong profession. Many hotels have fun with the concept but not with the guest. As soon as a guest arrives, it is work and this has a negative connotation. This mentality has to change. (Interviewee A, 2015, translated by the authors)*

The interviewee underlines the need to innovate or re-establish the basics of hospitality, i.e. hospitality in the sense of a welcoming culture and as a value system. He regards the core elements of the host–guest encounter ('liking the guest') such as friendliness and kindness as more important than other peripheral service attributes. In sum, the innovation perspective that is presented here is systemic and/or social in type ('institutional'). It is a perspective that regards the creation of true encounters in the host–guest context as the central issue in innovation efforts in the accommodation sector.

> *I think that the principle of Airbnb™ will intensify even more in the next 15 years. The concept of Airbnb™ is also about encounters, not just overnight stays. It is about much more. You not only select the bed but also the owner. Completely different from a hotel, which is anonymous. [–] Yes, I think accommodation concepts such as family businesses will survive. Hotel establishments intended for business people will also survive. But all the hotels in between will have a difficult time, because they are too expensive or no longer able to offer what the guest wants to experience. (Interviewee A, 2015, translated by the authors)*

The same interviewee in a second statement confirms and expands on his affirmation of systemic innovation requirements around the idea of facilitating 'real' encounters in the accommodation sector. Starting from this assumption, the interviewee sees Airbnb™ as being in a good position to meet social requirements for accommodation that go beyond just selling a bed to include exchanging stories and fostering tangible interactions between human beings. Therefore, according to this interviewee, future accommodation approaches need to either enable real social encounters (Airbnb™ and family-managed hotels seem to be in a good position), or cater for business travellers (and their specific requirements, including budget). In contrast, those hotel concepts that are stuck in between might encounter severe problems.

> *We will experience two cases. On the one hand, we will see that where brands are not very strong yet, standardized or international brands will increase in importance. This will happen. In the past, we did not see this process in typical rural or resort areas. They just knew the individual hotel. In contrast, in future, there will be a high degree of fragmentation. Many people will say that this is too much and they will be looking for more individual offers. [...] In addition, I noticed that 90–95 per cent of the hotels in Europe have no brand. This will probably decrease. [This does] not necessarily mean that only four or five big brands may work, but certainly, small new brands as well. Today's customer and the next generation are very brand-aware. However, the individual hotels must try to create something special for themselves. You can use a special product emphasis very differently from someone who does the same up to 50 times. (Interviewee D, 2015, translated by the authors)*

This statement points in a direction that is similar to the one expressed in the previous statement. However, the underlying innovation perspectives seem to be two in this case: on the one hand, owing to a lack of economies of scale in the current setting, the European accommodation industry, which is to a significant extent dominated by small-sized and/or family-led enterprises, offers opportunities for innovations in management and communications. On the other hand, however, differentiation based on historically established organizational and regional competences and capabilities remains a valid development direction.

> *I think if there is a lesson that needs to be learned in the tourism sector, that is that there is on the one hand a growing degree of economic skills, a bigger stream of people and bigger companies. The question is how do we create the personal experience, the unique environment under these premises? That's a difficult job. For example, in the Alpine regions where the family hotels offer great personal experience and even know the guests by name, guests return. If that is replaced by chain hotels it is hard to create this situation again. Through our concept of creating a community, this experience can be offered again and we can create more meaningful tourism. [...] I would say, our unique selling point is the focus on community: the idea of a group of guests, which share things and therefore form a community. [...] Getting together within the community and the possibility of longer or shorter stays are the most important aspects of the innovative concept. (Interviewee E, 2015)*

Again, starting from the idea of two major future development paths for the accommodation sector, this interviewee proposes the idea of a middle path between the supposed need to generate scales and synergies, and the individualization requested by guests. The interviewee proposes that by clearly targeting customer segments and creating communities, chain hotels might be able to come closer to the uniqueness or advantage of experience that smaller hotels possess. Such a community creation approach goes far beyond pure innovation in the immediate 'service-scape' and entails features of a systemic innovation that require accommodation suppliers to look beyond the walls of their establishments and to intensively and even proactively engage with dynamics in the broader society.

> *We build restaurants, which are not perceived as hotel restaurants [...] We cater mainly for local people. We try to offer things that we think will work in a specific city. [...] In Berlin, we managed to attract locals and for hotel guests this is interesting as well, because they want contact*

*with locals. This mixture is an interesting approach. [This is based on] a social development – that guests are interested in getting to know the city and its people. With gastronomy we can bring together both. (Interviewee B, 2015, translated by the authors)*

This statement from another interviewee points in a direction that is similar to those manifested in previous statements. The underlying idea of a requirement for innovation in the accommodation sector is again that of enabling encounters in this specific sense of encounters between guests and residents. This perspective on innovation transcends the direct level of immediate product innovations, process innovation or even technological innovation; it is full of references to broader social dynamics and thus has systemic and institutional implications. The interviewee underscores that by saying that the hotel restaurant (which would be the product or service innovation as such) needs to be conceptualized as a means to a specific social or systemic end, i.e. as a means to bring locals into the hotel, because in his view that is what guests are looking for.

*I believe that it is [...] moving in a direction where everything is much more open. Where there is not just a room and a table where you are entertained and where you can sleep, but one where you can get in touch with other people, where you simply have plenty of options to do things, away from this 'in the back is the service provider and in the front the customer'. That could also mean that reception desks disappear and that everything will run in a more fluid way. I do not think that we will need reception desks, because you can already check in online anyway. Then you will have people on site who will help you with all sorts of things, which you will still need. But the whole thing will probably proceed in a way that is a bit more relaxed. (Interviewee C, 2015, translated by the authors)*

This interviewee predicts innovations in the accommodation sector that may lead to more open and flexible, and to some extent more 'natural' and fluid settings, fostering the encounter between the accommodation supplier and guests. At first glance this may seem to be a process innovation (renouncing traditionally structured reception desks). However, such procedural change as it is presented here can be a specific instance of a more profound and comprehensive change in settings and even values that increasingly emphasize openness, social interaction and human contact, as well as fluidity.

*The digitalization allows you to get almost as close as going there by yourself. What people will look for is to create a story. The story can happen either by doing something off the beaten track, having a personal connection with a local community, etc. The main way that you can facilitate and organize that I think you see is in the area of Airbnb™. People are able to share information and you also see it in the popularity of our hotel, or even the hostels. People make new connections, so hostels are places for younger and older people. It is basically breaking down barriers. I think the next years will be an opportunity for non-traditional hospitality companies and concepts. I think that it is where innovation will come from. (Interviewee E, 2015)*

This interview statement highlights that the experience economies of tourism in general and the accommodation sector in particular need to engage in more profound innovation activities that may go beyond simplistic service adaptations. These extensive innovation activities are required because the 'service-scape' offered by new information and communications technologies challenges tourism and hospitality. The interviewee suggests that guests are increasingly looking for experiences that they do not encounter at home. However, what they do encounter at home is expanding due to the extending range of virtual experience opportunities. Higher-order experiences potentially offered by the accommodation sector (and tourism) may include getting in direct touch with the local community and moving off the beaten track. In any case, such development paths for accommodation may imply significant deviations from some past developments and in particular a need to remove barriers. Assuming the need to engage in systemic changes, the claim that non-traditional hospitality companies and concepts will play an increasingly important role as innovation promoters seems tenable.

## Sources and drivers of innovation

*I believe that our approach is innovative because we are trying to break new ground and to continuously question ourselves. […] If there was a simple formula [for our success], then everyone would imitate it. There are many factors […] It starts with the company. We are a private company with four private shareholders and therefore we do not have the pressure to grow rapidly. […] We can take our time to discover interesting hotels. I think that our shareholder structure is promoting innovation. There are also the different people who we work with, who also shape and form the hotel. The basis, to have no excessive expansion pressure and the personalities who are working here, is the reason for our success. (Interviewee B, 2015, translated by the authors)*

This interviewee identifies a number of drivers of innovativeness in his hotel business. He underscores the importance of reflexivity and self-criticism and the impact of the corporate and shareholder structure on innovativeness. Having fewer shareholders may facilitate the creation of freedom, free space and time for innovation that, on the contrary, a publicly listed company may not have. In this sense, the logic that underlies a publicly listed company with the growth pressures that translate into time pressures may become harmful for innovation in some instances. Finally, the interviewee emphasizes the role of staff and creative people in fostering innovativeness.

*We analysed guests and tourism trends a little before we started, and looked at what the new generations in tourism actually expect from their vacations. What do you need to do differently so that you still have many guests in the future? We found that guests would prefer to take their mountain bikes into their rooms and don't want to leave them unlocked in a basement, as is often required in accommodation small and large. And they want flexible opening times and a lot of space – space to share experiences with friends sitting at a table. (Interviewee C, 2015, translated by the authors)*

Another interviewee argued that analysing the market, understanding customer interests and their dynamics in detail, have been crucial to successful innovation. In particular, what seems critical is extrapolating current consumer expectations into the future and anticipating changes involved in that development. Again, this interviewee affirms the increasing importance of the social element ('community') in the accommodation offer.

*I would say it [our accommodation concept] is a reinvention. [...] The Austrians, the Italians, the German and the Swiss have this connection [to their mountains] and can do something with it. These countries, with their connections to the Alps, always had self-catering groups that, for instance, had their own hut. Now, we combine this with a hotel concept. The reinvention has been more extensive, in that we thought of dusting off certain things, for example, life in the Alpine hut. You just have to do certain things differently to make it work for a hotel guest. We thought about how it used to be on a mountain*

*pasture and how we can reinterpret that today without distorting it.*
*(Interviewee D, 2015, translated by the authors)*

Taking the Alps as an example, this interviewee points out that successful innovations may depend on the close match of customer segments with (traditional) regional competences. Thus, the central challenge for innovation may be to appreciate existing (regional) resources and to reinterpret them in a manner that matches current customer demand without losing authenticity and appearing artificial or faked. In sum, this statement entails considerations that are close to the assumptions of the resource-based perspective.

## Conclusion

This chapter has explored current perspectives on, opinions of and practices affected by innovation (innovation thinking and acting) in the European hotel industry by looking at statements presented by European hotel managers who have implemented innovative accommodation concepts and by scanning some recent international innovation awards in hospitality. Being exploratory in nature, the study has limitations and its findings cannot be generalized without significant restrictions. For instance, the study did not consider cases of very incremental innovations, or hoteliers who did not engage in innovation activities at all. However, both exploratory data sources (interviews and awards) seem to point in similar directions, which increases the validity of the findings.

Overall, the findings indicate that developments in information and communications technologies (ICT) severely affect the European hotel and accommodation industry. This change in circumstances seems to provide a window of opportunity for more fundamental and even radical innovation initiatives. In particular, today's information and communications technologies can guarantee an enlarged 'experience-scape' 'at home', which challenges the experience economies of tourism in general and the accommodation sector in particular. Tourism and hospitality are challenged to provide unique experiences that cannot be provided through the use of ICT at home. In other words, the ability for hotels to offer added experience value is becoming more contested.

This situation seems to push the innovation agenda of some hotels and accommodation establishments towards a type of innovation that is more systemic than only directly focusing on the immediate 'service-scape' or processes, management approaches and means of communication. Considering the interviewees' statements, it appears that institutional, social and systemic innovations that valorize the host–guest encounter and are able to reduce the barriers around it are in vogue. As is indicated also by the overview of some innovation awards, accommodation establishments are increasingly required to interact with broader societal issues and developments (and may be rewarded for doing so). However, it is quite straightforward that an industry that sees part of its offer challenged tries to expand its unique features. In this regard, real encounters and tangible communities that cannot be realized through the digital world might be a relevant option. Additionally, being stages in the enjoyment of nature and (traditional) cultural experiences could be the means to strengthen the uniqueness of the hospitality offer.

The exploratory analysis indicates that two major streams are expected to increasingly dominate innovation activities in the accommodation sector. On one side we may see cost- and scale-driven innovations in management and communications that could lead to bigger (cooperative) units in the European hotel sector and reduce the number of stand-alone hotel businesses. On the other side, establishments might consider novel ways to offer unique and individualized experiences. As is indicated by the interviewees, systemic and social innovations in combination with the preservation and further development of established core competences may play a role in this regard. Interviewees also indicated a third path between the two extremes. This third way might consist in strong community-building coupled with a clear targeting of audiences and/or a customization of local cultural traits. In general, hotels that appear stuck in the middle between the two or three paths are believed to encounter insecurities and troubles.

Concerning the major sources of innovativeness, this exploratory study indicates that none of the ideal typical perspectives present in theory (a market-based view, a resource-based view, or – when extended to inter-firm relations – a relational view) seem to fully and completely match the practices and opinions of hotel managers and innovation awarding that were encountered. In contrast, most of the innovation thinking and acting that was encountered manifests the idea that it might be necessary to intertwine resource-based and market-based considerations in order to adapt unique resources and capabilities to current market dynamics. This relates to a particular emphasis that interviewees and awards are given on leadership and staff development. It is probably staff where the two perspectives of the resource- and market-based views are most easily and naturally interconnected. Looking at the alleged need for systemic changes in the accommodation sector, we might even argue that only when innovations are based on the interface of resource-based and market-driven considerations they could achieve the required systemic character.

Maybe European hotels have effected superficial adaptations to minor market development for long periods, while their basic offer has remained the same. However, we might see in the near future (which is, indeed, already part of the present) a remarkable degree of radical innovation in hospitality and accommodation. Whether this hypothesis holds true, it is, as one interviewee outlined, a time when self-reflection and good staff might be crucial capabilities to ensure sustainable success – in order, we may add, to overcome restrictive focus on resources or markets. Thus, this may be the right time to look beyond established categories in (innovation) theory as well. And staff is definitely a good point to start from.

## References

Barney, J. (1991). Firm resources and sustained competitive advantage. *Journal of Management* 17, 99–120.

Chen, W.J. (2011). Innovation in hotel services: Culture and personality. *International Journal of Hospitality Management*, 30(1), 64–72.

Dominici, L. (2014). Gli hotel rivedono la redditività. *Il Sole 24 Ore*, 31 January, 46.

Elzen, B., Geels, F.W., and Green, K. (eds), (2004). *System Innovation and the Transition to Sustainability: Theory, Evidence and Policy*. Cheltenham, UK: Edward Elgar Publishing.

Enz, C., and Siguaw, J. (2003). Revisiting the best of the best: Innovations in hotel practice. *Cornell Hotel and Restaurant Administration Quarterly*, 44(5/6), 115–123.

Enz, C., and Harrison, J. (2008). Innovation and entrepreneurship in the hospitality industry. In R. Wood and B. Brotherton (eds), *The SAGE Handbook of Hospitality Management* (213–228). London: Sage.

Ganzer, D. (2015). *Multi-ownership: Finanzierungsmodell der Hotellerie*. Hamburg: Igel Verlag.

Hagel, J., and Singer, M. (1999). Unbundling the corporation. *Harvard Business Review*, 77, 133–144.

Hjalager, A.M. (1997). Innovation patterns in sustainable tourism. An analytical typology. *Tourism Management*, 18(1), 35–41.

Hospitality Awards (2015). Available at: http://hospitalityawards.com/en/the-winners/hospitality-awards/2014/the-student-hotel/ [accessed 29 June 2015].

Hotelforum (2015). Available at: http://www.hotelforum.org/en/awards/hospitality-innovation-award.html [accessed 29 June 2015].

HTNG (2015a). Available at: http://www.htng.org/techovation-award [accessed 29 June 2015].

HTNG (2015b). Available at: http://www.htng.org/techovation-award/ innovation-award, [accessed 29 June 2015].

Innerhofer, E. (2012). *Strategische Innovationen in der Hotellerie: Eine ressourcenorientierte Fallstudienanalyse touristischer Dienstleistungsunternehmen.* Wiesbaden: Springer Verlag:.

Jacob, M., Tintoré, J., Aguiló, E., Bravo, A., and Mulet, J. (2003). Innovation in the tourism sector: Results from a pilot study in the Balearic Islands. *Tourism Economics*, 9(3), 279–295.

Jones, P.A. (1996). Managing hospitality innovation. *The Cornell Hotel and Restaurant Administration Quarterly*, 37(5): 86–95.

Martínez-Ros, E., and Orfila-Sintes, F. (2009). Innovation activity in the hotel industry. *Technovation*, 29, 632–641.

Nasr, R. (2015). Airbnb[TM] is now bigger in Europe than US: Exec. CNBC Online. Available at: http://www.cnbc.com/id/102637142 [accessed 25 June 2015].

Novelli, M., Schmitz, B. and Spencer, T. (2006). Networks, clusters and innovation in tourism: A UK experience. *Tourism Management*, 27(6), 1141–1152.

Orfila-Sintes, F., and Mattsson, J. (2009). Innovation behavior in the hotel industry. *Omega*, 37(2), 380–394.

Ottenbacher, M.C. (2007). Innovation management in the hospitality industry: Different strategies for achieving success. *Journal of Hospitality and Tourism Research*, 31(4), 431–454.

Ottenbacher, M.C., and Gnoth, J. (2005). How to develop successful hospitality innovation. *Cornell Hotel and Restaurant Administration Quarterly*, 46(2), 205–222.

Ottenbacher, M., Gnoth, J., and Jones, P. (2006). Identifying determinants of success in development of new high-contact services: Insight from the hospitality industry. *International Journal of Service Industry Management*, 17(3), 344–363.

Pechlaner, H., Bachinger, M., Volgger, M., and Anzengruber-Fischer, E. (2014). Cooperative core competencies in tourism: Combining resource-based and relational approaches in destination governance. *European Journal of Tourism Research*, 8, 5–19.

Pechlaner, H., Fischer, E., and Hammann, E.M. (2006). Leadership and innovation processes – development of products and services based on core competencies. *Journal of Quality Assurance in Hospitality and Tourism*, 6(3–4), 31–57.

Penrose, E. (1959). *The Theory of the Growth of the Firm.* New York: John Wiley.

Peters, M., and Weiermair, K. (2002). Innovationen und Innovationsverhalten im Tourismus, In Bieger, T. and Laesser, C. (eds), *Schweizer Jahrbuch für Tourismus 2001/2002*, 157–178. Switzerland: St. Gallen.

Pforr, C., Pechlaner, H., Volgger, M., and Thompson, G. (2014). Overcoming the limits to change and adapting to future challenges governing the transformation of destination networks in Western Australia. *Journal of Travel Research*, 53(6), 760–777.

Phills, J.A., Deiglmeier, K., and Miller, D.T. (2008). Rediscovering social innovation. *Stanford Social Innovation Review*, 6(4), 34–43.

Porter, M.E. (1980). *Competitive Strategy: Techniques for Analyzing Industries and Competitors*. New York: Free Press.

Porter, M.E. (1985). *Competitive Advantage: Creating and Sustaining Superior Performance*. New York: Free Press.

Radical Innovation Award (2015a). Available at: http://www.radicalinnovationaward.com/#about [accessed 29 June 2015].

Radical Innovation Award (2015b). Available at: http://radicalinnovation inhospitality.blogspot.it/p/2011-winners.html [accessed 29 June 2015].

Rogers, E. (1982). *Diffusion of Innovations*. 3rd Edition. New York: The Free Press.

Tajeddini, K. (2010). Effect of customer orientation and entrepreneurial orientation on innovativeness: Evidence from the hotel industry in Switzerland. *Tourism Management*, 31(2), 221–231.

Tseng, C.Y., Kuo, H.Y., and Chou, S.S. (2008). Configuration of innovation and performance in the service industry: Evidence from the Taiwanese hotel industry. *The Service Industries Journal*, 28(7), 1015–1028.

Van de Ven, A.H. (1986). Central problems in the management of innovation. *Management Science*, 32(5), 590–607.

Vila, M., Enz, C., and Costa, G. (2011). Innovative practices in the Spanish hotel industry. *Cornell Hospitality Quarterly*, 53(1), 75–85.

Volo, S. (2004). Foundation for an innovation indicator for tourism: An application to SME. In Keller, P. and Bieger, T. (eds), *Proceedings of the 54th AIEST Congress* (361–376). St. Gallen: AIEST.

Wernerfelt, B. (1995). The resource-based view of the firm: ten years after. *Strategic Management Journal*, 16, 171 ff.

# Chapter 5

# Innovation in Tourism Firms

ANITA ZEHRER, BIRGIT MUSKAT and MATT MUSKAT

The aim of this research was to identify the degree to which internal and external variables influence innovativeness. With this objective we address a significant gap in tourism research as, although the importance of innovation is widely recognized, open questions remain about measurement for services and, in particular, for the tourism industry. With data from a comparative study of Australia, Germany, Austria, and Switzerland we identify factors that enable innovation outputs and processes for tourism providers. We review the relevant literature and analyse quantitative data of survey respondents to our international questionnaire. Results determine those internal and external factors that stimulate innovativeness and innovative behaviour.

## Innovation Defined

Innovation is the driver of tourism businesses' success, leading to a competitive edge for operators and entire destinations (Danneels, 2007; Semlinger, 2007; Nordin, 2003). Specifically, innovation is defined as 'an idea, practice, or object that is perceived as new by an individual or other unit of adoption' (Rogers, 1995: 11). A distinction is typically made between 'invention', 'innovation', 'diffusion' and 'imitation'. Hence, while the term 'invention' stands for creating something new in general, 'innovation' means to successfully establish a new product on the market or to implement a new process in the production cycle of a company (Galbraith, 2004). 'Diffusion' and 'imitation' essentially mean that competitors start to adapt and copy new products and processes (Brockhoff, 1999; Pechlaner, Fischer, and Priglinger, 2006; Hauschildt and Salomo, 2007). Gallouj and Savona (2010) suggest that the aim of an innovation in the service sector should be twofold: innovation should foster economic growth and at the same time foster the well-being of involved people.

Nowadays, little doubt remains about the importance of innovation for the tourism industry (Tschurtschenthaler, 2005; Pechlaner, Fischer, and Priglinger, 2006; Walder, 2006; Keller, 2006), with single tourism businesses as well as destinations competing for new product innovation to gain strategic advantages.

However, tourism still lags behind in creating innovative solutions, which might be due to the low number of licences and patents in tourism, as well as problems of free-riding among the large number of tourism stakeholders within a destination (Hjalagar, 2002; Wöhler, 2006).

## Innovation Research

Innovation research is a very complex research area and various research domains contribute to innovation theory and practice, such as the innovation process (Drucker, 1984), disruptive innovation (Christensen and Overdorf, 2000) and open innovation (Chesbrough, 2003). Theories of innovation consider various levels of analysis, e.g. single-firm level or entire economies, societies or specific industry sectors. The two major research domains from which innovation theories are derived are: economics and sociology (Sundbo, 1998).

Economic theory, for example, suggests that innovation is an activity that creates economic growth (Schumpeter, 1934), whereas sociology historically understands innovation rather as a contributing factor to the renewal of social behaviour (McClelland, 1961) leading to social change (Zollschan and Hirsch, 1964). As a synthesis of both research domains Sundbo deduces the definition: 'Innovation is thus a macrophenomena, a matter of socioeconomic growth' (Sundbo, 1998: 1).

Related to those different levels of analysis, there are three perspectives on innovation that management research can take: micro-, macro- and meso-perspectives. Micro-level perspectives on innovation consider innovation taking place within a firm, Kay 1979; Tushman and Moore, 1988; Twiss, 1976); macro-level perspectives take a societal approach and encompass society in general; while meso levels regard the processes in between – firms and society. Even if innovation happens at a micro level, it still influences society at a macro level (Sundbo, 1998). This chapter looks at micro-level, as well as the tourism industry sector as a unit of analysis. Here, the significance of innovation and the ability to innovate is essential to a firm's success. Hence knowledge about innovation is a key component of the managerial role, skills and competencies.

With regard to the micro-level firm perspective, previous studies have singled out several internal and external factors that contribute to tourism providers' abilities to be innovative. Internal, or 'organizational factors', are discussed by Tidd, Bessant, and Pavitt, 2007; Freeman and Soete, 1997; Kleer, 2008; Malerba and Brusoni, 2007; Mattsson, Sundbo and Fussing-Jensen, 2005; Porter, 1990; Prahalad and Hamel, 1990; Sarkar, 2007; and Talke, 2007. External, or 'market and demand-driven factors', were researched by Asheim and Isaksen, 2000; Falk, 2007; Gallouj and Weinstein, 1997; Goldstein et al. 2008; Kleer, 2008; Mattsson, Sundbo and Fussing-Jensen, 2005; Scotchmer, 2004; Sundbo, 1998; and Sundbo, Orfila-Sintes, and Sørensen, 2007.

In tourism most studies argue from an economics stance and conceptualize innovation using Schumpeter's five innovation categories (Walder, 2006; Hall and Williams, 2008): product innovations, process innovations, the utilization of new resource markets, new suppliers, and the change of market structures (Schumpeter, 1965). For tourism, Hjalager (2010) extended this classification, further adding three additional types of innovation: 'managerial', 'marketing' and 'institutional service'.

Those existing frameworks are well accepted and offer suitable explanations for tourism innovation categories. In particular, they offer explanations on innovation output categories that result from the creation and implementation of new ideas and services, as well as processes and products.

However, there has been criticism that the established approaches are not comprehensive and integrative enough and, further, that those categories do not provide solutions to understanding the firm as a whole. Instead, existing research into single categories of innovation do not consider the firm's entire ability to innovate. Research conducted by den Hertog, van der Aa, and de Jong (2010), for example, shows that there is an overemphasis on technology as the single driving force of innovation; Hjalagar (2010) and Camison and Monfort-Mir (2012) identify a high concentration on tourism research related to product and process innovation.

As a result, there are increasingly claims that a more integrated, systems-based and holistic approach to understanding innovation is needed. Scholars highlight the need for research that is necessary to combine knowledge of organizational and technological factors of innovation (den Hertog, van der Aa, and de Jong, 2010).

Thus, the research gap relates to the overall lack of tourism-specific studies on innovation (Pikkemaat, 2005). While, overall, innovation and innovativeness is considered as highly important and researched in other industries (Pechlaner, Reuter, and Zehrer, 2010), innovation in tourism remains an under-researched topic and innovation underestimated in tourism (Hall, 2009; Hall and Williams, 2008; Hjalager, 2010; Sundbo, Orfila-Sintes, and Sørensen, 2007). Even if innovation is under-researched in the tourism field, 'until now […] [it] has mainly been examined in a piecemeal case-by-case manner' (Hjalager, 2010: 9). Furthermore, there is a need for more quantitative studies to determine which factors of innovativeness determine innovativeness most (Hall, 2009; Hjalager, 2010; Pechlaner, Reuter, and Zehrer, 2010), since there is still a lack of understanding of the essential elements of tourism businesses innovation.

## Innovation Research in the Tourism Sector

There are specific elements that constitute the structure of the tourism sector, which consists largely of small and medium-sized enterprises (SMEs). Based on a synthesis of the literature, those characteristics can be grouped into three clusters:

a)   *external constituencies of tourism within the world economy:* changing global markets, consumer preferences, technology, organization factors of production, new sources of workers and new forms of investment put the tourism industry into a challenging situation (Hall and Williams, 2008). Thus, products and processes in tourism are continuously changed and modified (Hall and Williams, 2008);

b)   *the overall small-sized structure of the sector:* as Pechlaner, Raich, Zehrer, and Peters (2004: 9) observe, 'in most parts of the world, but notably in many regions of Europe, tourism has developed into [...] a *fragmented industry'*. The significant competitive disadvantages faced by SMEs in tourism include: (i) little scope for economies of scale; (ii) limited potential for diversification; (iii) lack of access to capital markets; (iv) inadequate information about the market; and (v) high debt-to-capital ratios as a result of past mis-investments in facilities that now have low utilization rates and poor operating returns. For these reasons, many tourism SMEs face an insecure future (Freel, 2000; Hjalager, 2010). As most research concentrates on large-sized firms (Salavou, Baltas, and Lioukas, 2004) there is a lack of overall knowledge about innovation in small firms, especially as there is an issue with most SMEs being too operational at the expense of being strategic (Mumford, Gold, and Thorpe, 2012).

c)   *behavioural issues:* besides the perceived structural issues there are specific behavioural issues that hinder innovation in tourism businesses and lead to little knowledge transfer in SMEs (Hjalager, 2010). One structural issue relates to SME innovation depending on managerial structure and competencies (Wynarczyk, 2013). Hence, 'there is limited awareness of such mechanisms within the entrepreneurial context' (Kempster and Cope, 2010: 12). Furthermore, SMEs fail to create a business culture that promotes creativity. Leadership has been identified as a barrier to SME innovation (McAdam, McConvery, and Armstrong, 2004).

Morrison (2003) found that in the UK training needs of SME owner-managers in tourism are not met; SMEs rely upon external learning culture, facilitated by the government, however this external learning culture is often not being provided.

Table 5.1 presents results of those findings which identified internal and external innovation factors that have been found to influence innovativeness of firms.

The aim of this research is to identify the degree to which internal and external factors influence innovativeness in a tourism context. At the same time, we propose that both external and internal factors of organization might need to be considered. With this aim we align with previous research that a more integrated, systems-based and holistic approach to understanding innovation is needed, as currently there is too much emphasis on single driving forces of innovation, such as technology (den Hertog, van der Aa, and de Jong, 2010), and research needs to consider more systemic views (Ahmed and Shepherd, 2010).

## Empirical Study

This chapter reports the results of a quantitative study among tourism-related innovation award winners in Australia, Austria, Switzerland and Germany. A self-administered questionnaire was designed based on theoretical and empirical literature. Respondents were asked to rate the importance of internal and external influencing factors using a five-point interval scale with 1 being important and 5 being unimportant. The order of the factors was randomized to reduce the possibility of bias associated with the order of items. Data for the study was collected by an online survey administered to 519 former winners or finalists of tourism-related innovation awards in Germany, Austria, Switzerland and Australia between November 2013 and April 2014. The award winners were directly and personally contacted via email, which included a link to the questionnaire; a reminder was sent out in December 2013 and in March 2014.

Altogether 174 people answered the questionnaire, which equals a response rate of 33.52 per cent. The socio-demographic results are shown in Table 5.2. The table shows that the majority of the respondents represent SME tourism businesses and that the majority of them provide industry experience of more than ten years.

**Table 5.1    Factors influencing a firm's ability to innovate**

| Variable | Influencing factor | References |
|---|---|---|
| **Internal variables** | | |
| Entrepreneur | – methodological skills and general know-how in the industry<br>– expertise from other industries<br>– international experience<br>– personality | e.g. Kleer, 2008; Peters and Pikkemaat 2008; Sundbo, Orfila-Sintes and Sørensen, 2007; Walder, 2006; Mattsson, Sundbo and Fussing-Jensen, 2005; Asheim and Isaksen, 2000; Freeman and Soete, 1997; Porter, 1990; Schumpeter, 1939 |
| Organizational culture | – innovativeness is part of the organizational culture<br>– vision and strategy includes innovation<br>– commitment to learning and adaptation<br>– being open towards new developments | e.g. Conway and Steward, 2009; Peters and Pikkemaat 2008; Koellinger, 2008; Falk, 2007; Bessant and Tidd, 2007; Talke, 2007; Mattsson, Sundbo and Fussing-Jensen, 2005; Prahalad and Hamel, 1990 |
| Employees | – level of qualifications of manager/s<br>– staff receive training<br>– management systems / quality systems<br>– intrapreneurship<br>– incentives for employees | e.g. Malerba and Brusoni, 2007; Bouncken, Koch and Teichert, 2007; Hipp and Grupp, 2005; Hjalager, 2002; Freeman and Soete, 1997 |
| Resources | – size of organization<br>– investment into research<br>– access to investment capital | e.g. Kleer, 2008; Sundbo, Orfila-Sintes and Sørensen, 2007; Malerba and Brusoni, 2007; Sundbo, Orfila-Sintes and Sørensen, 2007; Sarkar, 2007; Peters, Weiermair and Katawandee, 2006; Scotchmer, 2004; Gallouj and Weinstein, 1997; Schumpeter, 1939 |
| **External variables** | | |
| Customer | – awareness of customers' needs<br>– integrating customers through surveys<br>– meeting needs of target groups | e.g. Goldstein et al. 2008; Wöhler, 2005; Pikkemaat and Peters, 2005; Porter, 1990 |
| Market | – technological advance<br>– collaboration with other tourism companies<br>– cooperating with other companies – outside tourism<br>– patent protection and trademark rights<br>– uncertainty of external environment<br>– market structure and competitiveness | e.g. den Hertog, van der Aa and de Jong 2010; Koellinger, 2008; Kleer, 2008; Sundbo, Orfila-Sintes and Sørensen, 2007; Pikkemaat and Holzapfel, 2007; Bouncken, Koch and Teichert, 2007; Buhalis and Egger, 2006; Hauschildt and Salomo, 2007; Mattsson, Sundbo and Fussing-Jensen, 2005; Pikkemaat, 2005; Pechlaner, Fischer, and Hammann, 2005; Porter, 1990 |
| Incentives | – receiving subsidies<br>– access to public support programmes for innovations<br>– winning awards<br>– incentives from destinations | e.g. Conway and Steward, 2009; Kleer, 2008; Sarkar, 2007; Scotchmer, 2004; Keller, 2002; Falk, 2007; Mattsson, Sundbo and Fussing-Jensen, 2005; Scotchmer, 2004 |

Table 5.2    Profile of respondents

|  | Characteristic | Frequency | Percentage |
|---|---|---|---|
| Gender |  |  |  |
|  | Male | 94 | 54.0% |
|  | Female | 79 | 45.5% |
| Company Size |  |  |  |
|  | 1–9 employees | 72 | 41.4% |
|  | 10–49 employees | 62 | 35.6% |
|  | 50–249 employees | 31 | 17.8% |
|  | >250 employees | 9 | 5.2% |
| Industry Experience |  |  |  |
|  | Less than a year | 1 | 0.6% |
|  | 1 to 3 years | 7 | 4.0% |
|  | 3 to 5 years | 20 | 11.5% |
|  | 5 to 10 years | 37 | 21.3% |
|  | More than 10 years | 109 | 62.6% |

The aim of this research was to identify the degree to which internal and external factors influence innovativeness. In order to address these results respondents were invited to indicate the importance of each factor. Tables 5.3 and 5.4 provide the mean values of the top and bottom internal and external enabling factors.

Table 5.3    Internal enabling factors

| TOP | BOTTOM |
|---|---|
| **Learning** (1.47)<br>Commitment to learning and adaptation | **Size** (3.50)<br>Size of organization |
| **Being open** (1.43)<br>Being open towards new developments | **Experience** (3.09)<br>The senior management has international experience (over 6 months abroad) |
| **Skills** (1.55)<br>The senior management has methodological skills and general know-how of the industry | **Participation** (2.56)<br>Employees participate in the development of the company |

**Table 5.4    External enabling factors**

| TOP | BOTTOM |
| --- | --- |
| **Awareness** (1.21)<br>Awareness for customers' needs | **Subsidies** (2.75)<br>Receiving subsidies |
| **Meeting needs** (1.63)<br>Meeting needs of target groups | **Patent** (2.69)<br>Patent protection and trademark rights |
| **Collaboration** (1.90)<br>Collaborating with other industries | **Uncertainty** (2.66)<br>Uncertainty of external environment |

Table 5.3 shows that work experience seems to be less important for the respondents, who in general showed a high amount of industry experience themselves. Table 5.4 depicts that awareness of customers' needs is essential, which raises the question of how co-creation might work in a tourism context. Interestingly also, that uncertainty is perceived to be less important.

## Conclusion

The study produces a number of findings that we believe will be noteworthy. Based on the resource-based view, there are factors which relate to employees, factors which include knowledge items, factors which relate to strategic issues and factors which comprise entrepreneurial areas. As regards the dynamic capabilities of a company and its external influencing factors (Grant, 1991), we assume to identify factors comprising incentives for innovativeness, factors representing customer-related issues and factors relating to the market.

Both external and internal factors that influence innovativeness need to be connected, managed, and implemented into the culture of a company. Both factors are constituents of a company's competitiveness. Following the strategic approach favoured for services by Sundbo (1997) innovations are market-driven, i.e. ideas for innovations come from all parts of a company inside and outside. This study might confirm that external factors – especially the customer and his needs – influence innovativeness more than factors which relate to the company itself. This underlines the customer focus within the service-dominant logic (S-D logic), where the customer is co-creating the service experiences, making it a holistic process (Vargo and Lusch, 2004). This seems also to be true as regards innovation; the integration of the customer seems to be an important variable for the innovativeness of the company. The internal factor which seems to be of utmost importance for innovativeness according to our preliminary findings is the qualification of the employees, as tourism is heavily reliant on its employees, who must have the competencies and skills to reply to the growing worldwide competition, changing demand patterns, the claim for better products and offers, the decreasing attractiveness and increasing uniformity of offers, and other developments related to tourism (Zehrer and Mössenlechner, 2008).

In summary, the study shows that both external and internal factors need to be considered when understanding innovation and innovativeness. Consequently, a more integrated, systems-based and holistic approach is needed; currently there is too much emphasis on single driving forces of innovation, such as technology (den Hertog, van der Aa, and de Jong, 2010), thus we conclude that research needs to consider more systemic views (Ahmed and Shepherd, 2010).

# References

Ahmed, P.K., and Shepherd, C. (2010). *Innovation Management: Context, Strategies, Systems, and Processes*. Harlow, UK: Pearson Prentice Hall.

Asheim, B., and Isaksen, A. (2000). Localised knowledge, interactive learning and innovation: between regional networks and global corporations. In M. Taylor and E. Vatne (eds), *The Networked Firm in a Global World* (163–198). Farnham, UK: Ashgate.

Bessant, J., and Tidd, J. (2007). *Innovation and Entrepreneurship*. Hoboken: John Wiley.

Bouncken, R., Koch, M., and Teichert, T. (2007). Innovation Strategy Explored: Innovation Orientation's Strategy Preconditions and Market Performance Outcomes, *Zeitschrift für Betriebswirtschaftslehre*, Special Issue 2007(2), 71–95.

Brockhoff, K. (1999). *Forschung und Entwicklung: Planung und Kontrolle*. 5th Edition. München/Wien: Oldenbourg Wissenschaftsverlag.

Buhalis, D., and Egger, R. (2006). Informations- und Kommunikationstechnologien als Mittel zur Prozess- und Produktinnovation für den Unternehmer. In B. Pikkemaat and M. Peters (eds), *Innovationen im Tourismus* (163–176), Berlin: ESV-Verlag.

Camison, C., and Monfort-Mir, V.M. (2012). Measuring innovation in tourism from the Schumpeterian and the dynamic-capabilities perspectives. *Tourism Management*, 33(4), 776–789.

Chesbrough, H. (2003). The logic of open innovation: Managing intellectual property. *California Management Review*, 45(3), 33–58.

Christensen, C.M., and Overdorf, M. (2000). Meeting the challenge of disruptive change. *Harvard Business Review*, 78(2), 66–77.

Conway, S., and Steward, F. (2009). *Managing and Shaping Innovation*. Oxford: Oxford University Press.

Danneels, E. (2007). The process of technological competence leveraging. *Strategic Management Journal*, 28(5), 511–533.

Den Hertog, P., van der Aa, W., and de Jong, M.W. (2010). Capabilities for managing service innovation: Towards a conceptual framework. *Journal of Service Management*, 21(4), 490–514.

Drucker, P.F. (1984). The discipline of innovation. *Harvard Business Review*, 63(3), 67–72.

Falk, R. (2007). Measuring the effects of public support schemes on firms' innovation activities: Survey evidence from Austria. *Research Policy*, 36(5), 665–679.

Freel, M.S. (2000). Barriers to product innovation in small manufacturing firms. *International Small Business Journal*, 18(2), 60–80.

Freeman, C., and Soete, L. (1997). *The Economics of Industrial Revolution*. London: Pinter.

Galbraith, J. (2004). Designing the innovating organization. In K. Starkey, S. Tempest and A. McKinlay (eds), *How Organizations Learn: Managing the Search for Knowledge* (202–223). Hampshire UK: Cengage Learning EMEA.

Gallouj, F., and Savona, M. (2010). Towards a theory of innovation in services. In F. Gallouj and F. Djellal (eds), *The Handbook of Innovation and Services* (27–48). Cheltenham, UK: Elgar.

Gallouj, F., and Weinstein, O. (1997). Innovation in services. *Research Policy*, 26(4), 537–556.

Goldstein, D.G., Johnson, E.J., Herrmann, A., and Heitmann, M. (2008). Nudge your customers toward better choices. *Harvard Business Review*, 86(12), 99–105.

Grant, R. (1991). The resource-based theory of competitive advantage: Implications for strategy formulation. *California Management Review*, 33(1), 114–135.

Hall, C.M. (2009). Innovation and tourism policy in Australia and New Zealand: Never the twain shall meet? *Journal of Policy Research in Tourism, Leisure and Events*, 1(1), 2–18.

Hall, C.M., and Williams, A.M. (2008). *Tourism and Innovation*. London: Routledge.

Hauschildt, J., and Salomo, S. (2007). *Innovationsmanagement*. Munich: Vahlen.

Hipp, C., and Grupp, H. (2005). Innovation in the service sector: The demand for service-specific innovation measurement concepts and typologies. *Research Policy*, 34(4), 517–535.

Hjalagar, A.-M. (2002). Repairing innovation defectiveness in tourism. *Tourism Management* 23(5), 465–474.

Hjalager, A.-M. (2010). A review of innovation research in tourism. *Tourism Management*, 31(1), 1–12.

Kay, N.M. (1979). *The Innovating Firm: A Behavioural Theory of Corporate R and D*. London: MacMillan Press.

Keller, P. (2002). Innovation und Tourismus. In T. Bieger and C. Laesser (eds), *Jahrbuch 2001/2002 Schweizer Tourismuswirtschaft* (179–194). St. Gallen: IDT-HSG.

Keller, P. (2006). Towards an innovation-orientated tourism policy. In B. Walder, K. Weiermair, and A. Sancho Perez (eds), *Innovation and Product Development in Tourism* (55–70). Berlin: ESV Verlag.

Kempster, S., and Cope, J. (2010). Learning to lead in the entrepreneurial context. *International Journal of Entrepreneurial Behavior and Research*, 16(1), 5–34.

Kleer, R. (2008). *Three Essays on Competition Policy and Innovation Incentives.* Würzburg: Julius-Maximilian-Universität.

Koellinger, P. (2008). Why are some entrepreneurs more innovative than others? *Small Business Economics*, 31, 21–37.

Malerba, F., and Brusoni, S. (eds), (2007). *Perspectives on Innovation.* Cambridge, UK: Cambridge University Press.

Mattsson, J., Sundbo, J., and Fussing-Jensen, C. (2005). Innovation systems in tourism: The roles of attractors and scene-takers. *Industry and Innovation*, 12(3), 357–381.

McAdam, R., McConvery, T., and Armstrong, G. (2004). Barriers to innovation within small firms in a peripheral location. *International Journal of Entrepreneurial Behaviour and Research*, 10(3), 206–221.

McClelland, D.C. (1961). *The Achieving Society.* Princeton, NJ: Van Nostrand.

Morrison, A. (2003). SME management and leadership development: market reorientation. *Journal of Management Development*, 22(9), 796–808.

Mumford, M.A., Gold, M.J., and Thorpe, M.R. (eds) (2012). *Gower Handbook of Leadership and Management Development.* Aldershot, UK: Gower Publishing.

Nordin, S. (2003). *Tourism Clustering and Innovation: Paths to Economic Growth and Development.* Härnösand, Sweden: The European Tourism Research Institute, Mid-Sweden University.

Pechlaner, H., Fischer, E., and Hammann, E.-M. (2005). Leadership and innovation processes – Development of products and services based on core competencies. *Journal of Quality Assurance in Hospitality & Tourism*, 6(3/4), 31–57.

Pechlaner, H., Fischer, E., and Priglinger, P. (2006). Die Entwicklung von Innovationen in Destinationen – Die Rolle der Tourismusorganisationen. In B. Pikkemaat, M. Peters, and K. Weiermair (eds), *Innovationen im Tourismus. Wettbewerbsvorteile durch neue Ideen und Angebote* (121–136). Berlin: ESV Verlag.

Pechlaner, H., Raich, F., Zehrer, A., and Peters, M. (2004). Growth perceptions of small and medium-sized enterprises (SMEs) – the case of South Tyrol. *Tourism Review*, 59(4), 7–13.

Pechlaner, H., Reuter, C., and Zehrer, A. (2010). Innovation awards in the German tourism industry. In K. Weiermaier, P. Keller, H. Pechlaner and

F. Go (eds), *Innovation and Entrepreneurship – Strategies and Processes for Success in Tourism* (81–96). Berlin: Erich Schmidt Verlag.

Peters, M., and Pikkemaat, B. (2006). Innovation in tourism. *Journal of Quality Assurance in Hospitality & Tourism*, 6(3–4), 1–6.

Peters, M., Weiermair, K., and Katawandee, P. (2006). Strategic brand management of tourism destination. In P. Keller and T. Bieger (eds), *Marketing Efficiency in Tourism* (65–79). Berlin: Schmidt.Pikkemaat, B. (2005). Zur empirischen Erforschung von Innovationen im Tourismus. In H. Pechlaner, P. Tschurtschenthaler, M. Peters, B. Pikkemaat, and M. Fuchs (eds), *Erfolg durch Innovation. Perspektiven für den Tourismus- und Dienstleistungssektor* (87–102). Wiesbaden: Gabler Verlag.

Pikkemaat, B., and Holzapfel, E.M. (2007). Innovationsverhalten touristischer Unternehmer: Triebkräfte und Hemmnisse. In R. Egger and T. Herdin (eds), *Tourismus, Herausforderung, Zukunft* (241–258), Wien: LIT Verlag.

Pikkemaat, B., and Peters, M. (2005). Towards the measurement of innovation – A pilot study in the small and medium sized tourism industry. *Journal of Quality Assurance in Hospitality and Tourism*, 6(3/4), 89–112.

Porter, M.E. (1990). *The Competitive Advantage of Nations*. New York, NY: Free Press.

Prahalad, C.K., and Hamel, G. (1990). The core competence of the corporation. *Harvard Business Review*, May–June, 79–91.

Rogers, E.M. (1995). *Diffusion of Innovations*. New York, NY: Simon & Schuster.

Salavou, H., Baltas, G., and Lioukas, S. (2004). Organisational innovation in SMEs: The importance of strategic orientation and competitive structure. *European Journal of Marketing*, 38(9/10), 1091–1112.

Sarkar, S. (2007). *Innovation, Market Archetypes and Outcome: An Integrated Framework*. Heidelberg, New York: Physica.

Schumpeter, J.A. (1934). *The Theory of Economic Development: An Inquiry into Profit, Credit, Interest, and the Business Cycle*. Oxford, UK: Oxford University Press.

Schumpeter, J. A. (1939. *Business Cycles: A Theoretical, Historical, and Statistical Analysis of the Capitalist Process*. 2 volumes. New York: McGraw-Hill.

Schumpeter, J.A. (1965). Economic Theory and Entrepreneurial History. In E.C.J. Aiken (ed.), *Explorations in Enterprise*. Cambridge, MA: Harvard University Press.

Scotchmer, S. (2004). *Innovation and Incentives*. Cambridge, MA: MIT Press.

Semlinger, K. (2007). Innovationshemmnis 'Kundennähe'? – Zur Notwendigkeit einer nachfrageseitigen Ergänzung der kleinbetriebsorientierten Innovationsförderung. *Zeitschrift für KMU und Entrepreneurship* 55(3), 147–166.

Sundbo, J. (1997). Management of innovation in services. *The Service Industries Journal*, 17(3), 432–455.

Sundbo, J. (1998). *The Theory of Innovation: Entrepreneurs, Technology and Strategy. New Horizons in the Economics of Innovation.* Northhampton, MA: Edward Elgar.

Sundbo, J., Orfila-Sintes, F., and Sørensen, F. (2007). The innovative behaviour of tourism firms – Comparative studies of Denmark and Spain. *Research Policy*, 36(1), 88–106.

Talke, K. (2007). Corporate mindset of innovating firms: Influences on new product performance. *Journal of Engineering and Technology Management*, 24(1), 76–91.

Tidd, J., Bessant, J., and Pavitt, K. (1997). *Managing Innovation: Integrating Technological, Market and Organisational Change.* Chichester, UK: Wiley.

Tschurtschenthaler, P. (2005). Die gesamtwirtschaftliche Perspektive von touristischen Innovationen. In H. Pechlaner, P. Tschurtschenthaler, M. Peters, B. Pikkemaat, and M. Fuchs (eds), *Erfolg durch Innovation. Perspektiven für den Tourismus- und Dienstleistungssektor* (3–22). Wiesbaden: Gabler Verlag.

Tushman, M., and Moore, W.L. (1988). *Readings in the Management of Innovation.* Pensacola, FL: Ballinger.

Twiss, B. (1976). Economic perspectives of technological progress: New dimensions for forecasting technology. *Futures*, 8(1), 52–63.

Vargo, S.L., and Lusch, R.F. (2004). Evolving to a new dominant logic for marketing. *Journal of Marketing*, 68(1), 1–17.

Walder, B. (2006). Sources and determinants of innovations – The role of market forces. In B. Walder, K. Weiermaier, and A. Sancho Pérez (eds), *Innovation and Product Development in Tourism* (7–24). Berlin: Erich Schmidt Verlag.

Wöhler, K. (2005). Der Kunde als Innovationsquelle. In H. Pechlaner, P. Tschurtschenthaler, M. Peters, B. Pikkemaat, and M. Fuchs (Hrsg.), *Erfolg durch Innovation. Perspektiven für den Tourismus- und Dienstleistungssektor* (243–259). Wiesbaden: Gabler.

Wöhler, K. (2006). Wahrnehmung von Innovationen: soziale und kulturelle Aspekte. In B. Pikkemaat, M. Peters, and K. Weiermair (eds), *Innovationen im Tourismus. Wettbewerbsvorteile durch neue Ideen und Angebote* (85–95). Berlin: Erich Schmidt Verlag.

Wynarczyk, P. (2013). Open innovation in SMEs. *Journal of Small Business and Enterprise Development*, 20(2), 258–278.

Zehrer, A., and Mössenlechner, C. (2008). Industry relations and curricula design in Austrian tourism Master programs: A comparative analysis. *Journal of Teaching in Travel and Tourism*, 8(1), 73–95.

Zollschan, G.K., and Hirsch, W. (1964). *Explorations in Social Change.* Boston, MA: Houghton Mifflin.

Chapter 6

# Determinants of Innovation Processes in the Hotel Industry: Empirical Evidence from Western Austria

FABIENNE FOSS and MIKE PETERS

Innovation processes in small and/or family businesses are often informal and not institutionalized as in large international businesses. Although some recent researches focused on tourism innovations, there is still a lack in understanding of hotel businesses' processes to develop and implement innovations. Therefore this chapter elaborates on how hoteliers attempt to implement innovation processes in their companies. Based on quantitative data gathered through a survey conducted during spring 2014, the authors are able to derive the main patterns and determinants of these processes. The formalization of innovation processes is a major success factor in the eyes of the hotel managers. Implications can be drawn both for hotel management and tourism policy.

## Background

In many European countries, the tourism industry is characterized by the large proportion of small and medium-sized enterprises, with the majority of hotels being run by families (Thomas, Shaw, and Page, 2011). Such providers have to cope with competitive disadvantages, which include poor economies of scale and scope, minimal potential for diversification and innovation, as well as limited access to capital markets. A possible way to reduce these weaknesses is to change the organizational orientation of small and medium-sized business service providers towards innovative customer experiences. Innovations determine long-term business success and are a result of innovation processes that can be defined as planned activities in a firm. In these processes, companies develop new, market-ready products and services or new ways of production or distribution (Galbraith, 1999). Innovation used to be rather under-researched in the tourism industry but has become a prominent research area in the last few years. Researchers have increasingly begun to discuss innovation in tourism. Nowadays, little doubt remains about the importance of innovation for the tourism industry (Aldebert, Dang, and Longhi, 2011; Hjalager and Flagestad, 2012; Nordin, 2003). Hjalager's (2010) state of the art review comprises the most relevant research carried out so far in the field of innovation and shows that tourism innovation has been analysed in the accommodation sector (Nieves and Segarra-Ciprés, 2015; Orfila-Sintes, Crespí-Cladera, and Martínez-Ros, 2005; Orfila-Sintes and Mattsson, 2009) and in small and medium-sized tourism enterprises (Grissemann, Pikkemaat, and Weger, 2013). More research regarding innovation processes has been conducted on a destination level and it highlights the importance of cooperation within the winter sports destination for innovation (Flagestad and Christine, 2001; Pikkemaat and Weiermair, 2007).

Innovation activities in tourism are more incremental than radical in nature (Hjalager, 2002; Pikkemaat and Peters, 2006). Instead of formalized process steps or phases in small service and tourism businesses we often observe more improvised 'ad hoc' actions which lead to innovations (Hjalager, 2010; Storey and Kelly, 2001).

However, there is a need for a closer analysis of innovation processes in the hotel businesses to identify patterns or process milestones. Although, we assume that no formal innovation process exists, further empirical evidence is needed. Therefore, the research at hand attempts to investigate whether typical innovation processes are existent in hotels. In addition, this study identifies internal and external factors of successful innovation processes. The study supports an understanding of those factors that determine single innovation process steps and innovation capability in hotel businesses in order to derive implications for hotel management and tourism policy.

## Innovation and Innovation Processes

Management literature presents a number of innovation process models, which usually cover about six phases of innovation management. While the majority of these contributions discuss the generation of ideas as the first phase, Pleschak (1996) and Vahs and Burmester (2005) introduce an 'idea initialization' phase: awareness creation and problem recognition are interpreted as a critical phase of the innovation process. Other researchers describe a five-phase innovation process, starting with the generation of ideas, followed by idea evaluation or idea screening. The last phases are the idea development and commercialization phases (Brockhoff, 1999; Cooper, 1995; Reichwald and Pillar, 2009; Tidd and Bessant, 2009). Apparently, service innovation processes differ significantly from traditional product innovation processes when it comes to a detailed description of each phase. Overall, the service innovation process phase structure is quite similar and starts with the service creation (e.g., idea generation and evaluation), service engineering (development and design, introduction), and adds the service management phase in which services are implemented and evaluated (Tilebein, 2006; Walder and Pospiech, 2006). For the hotel industry Walder (2005) developed a detailed innovation process, which puts special emphasis on the training and development of personnel before the new service is going to be commercialized. The *idea initialization phase* is the awareness creation stage and is characterized by monitoring or environmental scanning initiatives.

Changes in the customer market, new technologies or a business change can lead to a new perception and recognition of changes which are needed to foster further business growth. Problem recognition stimulates the innovation processes and is the basis for further innovation management initiatives (Hartschen, Scherer, and Brügger, 2009). The *idea generation phase* is necessary as ideas are the basis for future innovations. Therefore, innovative organizations call for certain communications and reporting systems, incentives or rewards but also resources (Galbraith, 1999). In this phase creativity is of the utmost importance and an innovative organization should create the ideal framework for the generation of creativity potential. External information sources (e.g., customers) and internal sources (e.g., creativity, employees) are the foundation for the quantity and quality of generated ideas (Vahs and Burmester, 2005).

The next phase, the *idea screening and selection*, demands the estimation of financial and opportunity costs of a chosen idea. Feasibility, market attractiveness, efficiency and the fit with the overall strategy and organizational resources are major criteria used to evaluate ideas (Alam and Perry, 2002; Schori, Roch, and Faoro-Stampfli, 2006). In the *idea development phase* project management, service design and market testing are the three major management tasks. In the service industry it is often hard to develop a prototype and therefore proxies (such as similar services in other markets) are needed to further develop the new offer. However, a visualization and practical conceptualization can be done by using blueprinting and flowcharting techniques (Shostack, 1984; 1987). The *commercialization phase* is the logical final step of the innovation process. However, any innovation process should be evaluated using a control feedback loop after the initial product or service life-cycle phases (Slater and Mohr, 2006).

In the literature several variables are supposed to influence innovation output. For instance, firm size is one major variable influencing 'a firm's ability and potential to create innovations' (Pikkemaat, 2008: 189). Furthermore, the role of entrepreneurs and the psychographics of entrepreneurs have a strong impact on the degree of innovations in hospitality and tourism (Pikkemaat and Peters, 2006). A strong positive relationship between the creative firm's internal environment and innovation success was postulated by earlier research (de Brentani, 2001; Kelly and Storey, 2000; Martins and Terblanche, 2003). Employees, especially their motivation and competencies, are essential factors for the success of innovations (Ottenbacher, Shaw, and Lockwood, 2006).

Other studies support the hypothesis that active customer integration in the innovation process increases the success and number of innovations. This holds true for tourism businesses (Pikkemaat and Holzapfel, 2007; Weiermair, 2004). The same authors underline the importance of cooperation within the tourism industry because it leads to knowledge exchange processes and the generation of economies of scope, which finally positively increases the innovation output (Pikkemaat, 2008).

Finally, it can be assumed that the formalization of an innovation process supports the innovation output of a firm, as effectiveness and efficiency of innovation management will increase (de Jong, Bruins, Dolfsma, and Meijaard, 2003; de Jong and Vermeulen, 2003; Humphreys, McAdam, and Leckey, 2005). The use of instruments, such as creativity techniques or feedback analysis, also has a positive impact on the innovation output (de Jong and Vermeulen, 2003).

## Method

An online survey was conducted in June and July 2014 using the online survey software unipark of QuestBack. In the newsletter of the Austrian Hotel Association (ÖHV) a hyperlink led interested hoteliers to the online questionnaire. The link was sent to approximately 1,700 hotel managers. As only 4-star and 5-star hotels in Western Austria (Tyrol, Vorarlberg, Salzburg) were invited to participate in this study, the total number of appropriate hotels was 525. A reminder was sent after nine days and randomly selected hoteliers were contacted by phone (overall 222). Another 26 hoteliers were asked personally to fill out the online questionnaire.

The questionnaire contained 24 questions. There are 14 cover questions regarding the hotel businesses' innovation activity, innovation processes, and determinants of innovation processes. Further questions targeted demographics and business/hotel facts (for example, size measured as number of employees). Based on Pikkemaat and Peters (2006) the degree of innovation was measured asking 'Which innovations did you commercialize in the last five years?' and 'How innovative is your hotel business?' The respondents were also ask to indicate the number of innovations commercialized in the preceding five years (based on Humphreys, McAdam, and Leckey, 2005). Internal and external variables which might influence the innovativeness of a hotel business were asked using the item categories from Ottenbacher, Shaw, and Lockwood, (2006), Pikkemaat and Holzapfel (2007), Walder and Pospiech (2006), Grissemann, Pikkemaat, and Weger (2013), Alam and Perry (2002) and Martin and Horne (1995) through a five-point Likert scale for all statements listed.

## Results

Overall, of the 96 fully completed questionnaires returned, 44 respondents were female and 52 male. Respondents were relatively young: 54.2 per cent were between 20 and 40 years of age, and only 17 hoteliers were older than 50 years. The majority of businesses were located in Tyrol (64); 18 hoteliers were from Salzburg, and 14 from Vorarlberg; 10 per cent were 5-star hotels, 24 were 4-star S and 61 4-star hotels. Family-owned hotels amounted to 87.5 per cent; 54.2 per cent were small businesses with 11–49 employees; 11.5 per cent were micro businesses employing fewer than 10 employees; and 34.5 per cent were middle-sized business with 50–249 employees. More than 53 companies offered above 100 beds The majority of hotels were labelled sport and hiking hotels (29.2 per cent) or wellness hotels (27.1 per cent).

Hoteliers defined their businesses as quite innovative. The hotel managers were asked to estimate the innovativeness of their industry and their own business on a scale from 1 to 5 (1 = not innovative at all, 5 = very innovative). The industry was evaluated with a mean of 3.4, while the 'own business' innovativeness was graded with a 3.8. Referring to the number of innovations introduced to the market within the last five years, Table 6.1 shows also an optimistic self-evaluation.

Table 6.1      Number of innovations commercialized within the last five years

(*n=96*)

| No. of innovations | in % |
| --- | --- |
| No innovation at all | 0 |
| 1–5 innovations | 41 |
| 6–10 innovations | 32 |
| 11–15 innovations | 10 |
| More than 15 innovations | 17 |

The respondents were also asked '"How do you evaluate the success of the commercialization of recent innovations?' In response,". 77.1 per cent saw their innovation as '"very successful"', 24 entrepreneurs evaluated their recent innovation as '"not successful at all'," or only '"a little successful"' (25 per cent). In a next step the hoteliers were asked about the aim of their innovative activities: the majority wants to increase customer satisfaction (mean value 4.54) and benefit (4.32), others seek to improve sales (4.35) (see Table 6.2). Finding new target segment played only a minor role (3.51).

**Table 6.2    Aims of innovations**

*(n=96–93)* (1=fully disagree, 5=fully agree)

| Aim of being innovative | Mean value |
| --- | --- |
| Increase in customer satisfaction | 4.54 |
| Increase in sales | 4.35 |
| Creation of more customer benefit | 4.32 |
| Competitive advantages | 4.23 |
| Improvement of internal processes | 4.18 |
| New market shares | 3.90 |
| New target segments | 3.51 |

Of further interest were the areas where hoteliers had introduced innovations in the past ('Which innovations did you introduce in the last five years?'). Table 6.3 shows that quite heavy investments were made in architecture and design innovations (3.94, for instance, renovation of rooms, new wellness areas). The lowest scores were in the areas 'sustainability' (e.g., improved energy efficiency) (3.18) and human resource management (e.g., new working time models, reward system).

The main purpose of this survey was to assess innovation processes in hotels. It is obvious that only a few hotels implemented a formalized innovation process in their hotel. Hoteliers were asked how they evaluated certain competencies in the company which usually play a major role in the innovation processes. The hoteliers were then asked at which phase of the innovation processes did they need certain competencies. Table 6.4 shows how strong entrepreneurs evaluate the availability of their competencies to manage certain phases of the innovation process.

Table 6.3    Areas of innovation

*(n=96–91)* (1=no innovations at all, 5=many innovations)

| Area of innovation | Mean value |
|---|---|
| Architecture and design | 3.94 |
| Products and services | 3.75 |
| New IT investment | 3.67 |
| Process innovations | 3.67 |
| Marketing and distribution | 3.49 |
| Strategic innovation | 3.39 |
| Sustainability | 3.18 |
| Human resource management | 3.01 |

Table 6.4    Competencies in the innovation process phases

*(n=96–94)* (1=very weak, 5=very strong)

| Competencies | Mean value |
|---|---|
| Idea generation | 3.95 |
| Monitoring of customer demand and market opportunities | 3.94 |
| Evaluation of ideas and their potential | 3.81 |
| Selection of ideas | 3.60 |
| Implementation of ideas | 3.54 |
| Market introduction/commercialization | 3.46 |

Hoteliers were perceived to be strong in generating ideas (3.95) and in screening and monitoring market trends (3.94). They were weaker at the competencies needed in the remaining phases of the innovation process such as the implementation of ideas or the commercialization of new products or services. In a more detailed analysis, the hoteliers could evaluate a list of instruments that are useful for certain phases of the innovation process phases. Table 6.5 demonstrates that hoteliers are strong in managing customer complaints and feedback (4.03), in marketing (3.72), and in analysing markets and managing projects (both 3.33).

**Table 6.5    Self-evaluation of instruments and methods used at certain phases of the innovation process**

*(n=96–94)* (1=very weak, 5=very strong)

| Phase of innovation process | Instrument | Mean value |
|---|---|---|
| Initialization phase | Market situation analyses | 3.33 |
| Idea generation | Customer complaints and feedback management | 4.03 |
| | Employee surveys | 3.14 |
| | Competitor analyses | 3.14 |
| | Idea management and idea competition | 2.83 |
| | Market research | 2.67 |
| | Creativity techniques | 3.03 |
| Idea evaluation | Feasibility studies | 3.13 |
| | Capital budgeting techniques | 3.10 |
| | Value benefit analyses | 2.96 |
| Idea implementation | Marketing | 3.72 |
| | Project management | 3.33 |
| | Prototyping/ service design | 2.63 |
| | Product and market testing | 2.62 |

Hoteliers were asked to evaluate the influence of internal and external determinants on their innovation process (on a 5-point Likert scale, 1=very weak, 5=very strong). In their view the personality of the entrepreneur (4.33), and the entrepreneur's willingness to innovate (4.25) had an especially strong impact on the overall innovation process in a company. The firm's most influential firm-internal variable was considered to be the motivation of employees (4.10).

The most important external influential variables were changes in customer demand (4.06), new trends (3.82) and competition (3.81). Less important were subventions and subsidies (2.00) and stimuli created by government and public institutions (such as chambers of commerce) (3.04). Overall internal variables were believed to influence the innovation processes in these companies much more strongly. The 20 variables that might influence the innovation processes in business were listed, all derived from the literature. With the help of a factor analysis the authors could derive several internal and external bundles of variables or factors. For internal influences, the entrepreneur obviously distinguishes two factors: firm-specific factors, including, for instance, strategy, the entrepreneur's personality, firm size, flat hierarchies and employee-specific impact factors. Furthermore, communication within the firm structure is a firm-specific variable influencing innovation processes. Besides the firm-specific variables, internal variables load onto the second factor, the employee-specific factor, which includes employee integration and motivation, and reward systems.

Figure 6.1 illustrates that internal determinants of innovation processes can be interpreted on the one hand as a bundle of variables that creates the ideal innovative environment for employees; and on the other as a bundle of entrepreneur and enterprise structured variables.

When analysing the external factors (Figure 6.2), it can be said that entrepreneurs distinguish variables which load onto a factor that can be labelled 'market and customer needs and trends' and on a second factor to be labelled 'network and institutional structures': cooperation and public institutions fall into this category.

The next step tested which variables significantly influence the number and the success of innovations in the hotels.

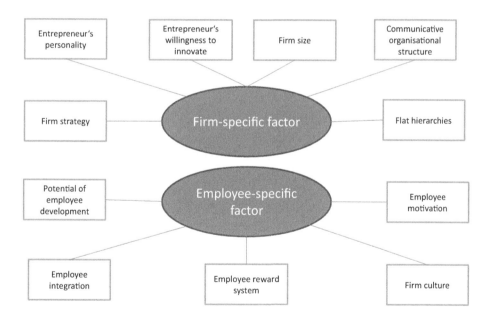

**Figure 6.1    Internal factors of innovation processes**
(all loading <0.6; variance explained: 66.37 per cent; KMO = 0.837; Bartlett Test of sphericity = 0.00)
*Source*: The authors.

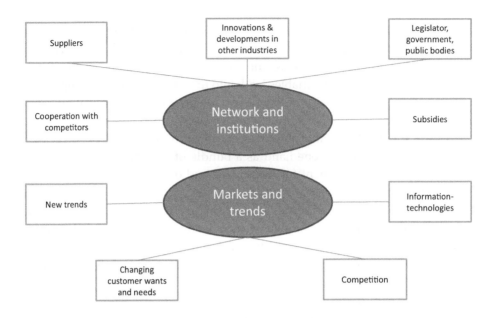

**Figure 6.2    External determinants of innovation process activities**
(All loadings >.6; variance explained: 66.37 per cent; KMO = 0.794; Bartlett test of sphericity = 0.00)
*Source*: The authors.

- *Firm size, entrepreneurship, firm internal stimuli (such as employees):* When comparing firms of various size, no significant differences can be found regarding the amount, success and degree of past firm innovations. Large companies therefore do not act more innovatively than small companies – this is based on the self-evaluation of the owner managers. However, a strong, significant relationship can be found between the entrepreneur's support and the number of innovations introduced during the preceding five years. The entrepreneur's positive attitude towards innovative activities, a cooperative leadership style, creativity and risk-orientation are variables which positively influence the innovation output of the hotels (p<.01). Innovation measures such as feedback rounds with employees and creativity techniques have positive influences on hotels' innovation management activities.
- *Customer integration and cooperation in the industry:* It cannot be postulated that stronger customer integration or a stronger degree of cooperation within the hotel industry increases the success

rate of innovations. External stimuli obviously do not influence innovation management in the way internal stimuli do.

- *Instruments of innovation management and formalization of the innovation process:* First, the formalization of an innovation process significantly influences the number of innovations introduced within the preceding five years of the firm's existence (p<.05). Second, the more instruments of innovation management are used and implemented in the company, the more successful are these innovations (p=.01).

## Conclusions

The results underline the fact that hoteliers perceive their businesses as innovative and generally state that the hotel industry in Austria is quite innovative. However, the literature in the field of innovation research in tourism tends to derive a more sceptical view and shows that tourism in general is low in terms of radical innovations. Minor or incremental improvements are certainly common and are often interpreted as innovations (Hjalager, 2002; Weiermair, 2004). The majority of innovations can be identified in the field of architecture and design and it can also be assumed that renovations of existing 'service-scapes' are labelled innovative activities. It becomes obvious that innovations are often hardware innovations, not software innovations, which is in line with earlier research (Pikkemaat and Peters, 2006). Especially low, across all firm size categories, are innovations in human resource management and personnel development.

Furthermore, the findings support earlier research, as innovations in tourism are often not the result of a formalized innovation process. Smaller businesses in particular do not follow a phase process or plan which involves more internal actors; instead, the entrepreneur dominates the innovation management (Hjalager, 2010; Peters and Buhalis, 2004; Sundbo, Orfila-Sintes, and Sørensen, 2007). This study supports these findings: approximately 75 per cent of all respondents did not implement a formal process for generating innovations. However, most entrepreneurs perceive existing innovation management competencies as strong in their businesses, especially when it comes to idea generation and evaluation. But competencies in the final phases of the innovation process are scarce, the concrete development and implementation phase in particular lacks competencies/resources. This fact is not independent of size: small businesses have more problems in providing competencies for the later phases of innovation management than larger firms (p<.05). As expected in the small-sized structured industry, the entrepreneur is crucial for innovation: personality traits such as creativity, goal orientation and the openness and attitude towards innovations strongly influence innovation success in the hotels. Beside the entrepreneur, the employees are the most important stakeholder group which nourishes innovation output in the hotels (Prantl, Grissemann, and Pikkemaat, 2009). Human resource management and innovation management are therefore strongly interrelated.

The study also underlined the fact that successful innovation depends on organization and communications structure. This is in line with Galbraith's suggestion that the innovation organization needs an optimal reward system, the organizational structure (for example, in terms of separating the organizational from the innovative entity), the communication and the existence of certain roles (for example, leaders and sponsors) (Galbraith, 1999). All these internal factors play a much more important role for the innovation output: hoteliers perceive competition and certain market trends as a pressure and call for being innovative. However external stakeholders (e.g., customers, competitors), instead of employees, play a minor but important role for the generation of innovations: they are key to initiating awareness. External stakeholders help to stimulate the awareness required to further foster an innovation process in the hotel businesses. In the later phases (starting with the idea evaluation) internal variables play the major role for the success of the innovation processes.

Figure 6.3 shows the phases of the formal innovation process and indicates the relevance of external variables to the first phase and the importance of firm internal variables to the later phases of the process. An increasing lack of innovation management competencies calls for more training and education in the field of innovation management. Hotel management can profit from more focused training and education in hotel management that allows entrepreneurs to gain competencies for the implementation phase of the innovation process. Finally, cluster initiatives to foster more exchange between researchers and hoteliers might be helpful to encourage innovation. Cluster collaboration helps hotels to gain knowledge from the external environment for the later phases of the innovation process (for example, in order to conduct feasibility studies or focus group product tests).

A major limitation of the study was the low number of questionnaires returned. Furthermore, most respondents were hotel owners or general managers; their subjective self-assessment might positively influence the results. Respondents are members of the Austrian Hotel Association (ÖHV) and 4-star and 5-star hotels in Western Austria. Owing to the low response rate, this research is of an exploratory nature and not representative and therefore has no general validity for the Austrian hotel industry.

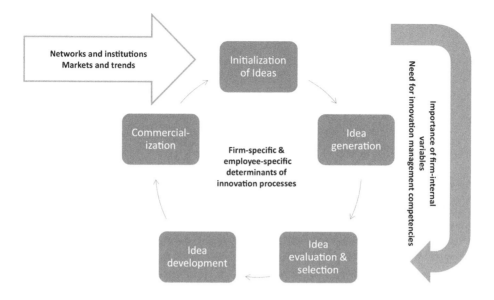

**Figure 6.3    The innovation process and its core determinants**
*Source*: The authors.

Future research should further investigate the success and failure factors of innovation processes in small and medium-sized tourism businesses. However, to guarantee a deeper and more detailed analysis it might be helpful to include employees and customers in order to shed more light upon the perception of innovation. Employees are able to identify barriers in innovation management (also on operational levels) and to describe internal innovation processes. The views of a wider complement of internal stakeholders would help to reduce whitewashing effects. Finally, it is the customer who evaluates whether a product or a service is innovative.

## References

Alam, I., and Perry, C. (2002). A customer-oriented new service development process. *Journal of Services Marketing*, 16(6), 515–534. doi: 10.1108/08876040210443391

Aldebert, B., Dang, R.J., and Longhi, C. (2011). Innovation in the tourism industry: The case of Tourism. *Tourism Management*, 32(5), 1204–1213. doi: 10.1016/j.tourman.2010.08.010

Brockhoff, K. (1999). *Forschung und Entwicklung – Planung und Kontrolle*. München: Oldenbourg Verlag.

Cooper, R.G., and Kleinschmidt, E.J. (1995). Performance typologies of new product projects. *Industrial Marketing Management*, 24, 439–456.

de Brentani, U. (2001). Innovative versus incremental new business services: Different keys for achieving success. *The Journal of Product Innovation Management*, 18(3), 169–187.

de Jong, J., Bruins, A., Dolfsma, W., and Meijaard, J. (2003). *Innovation in service firms explored: What, how and why?* EIM Business Policy Research, Strategic Study, (B200205).

de Jong, J., and Vermeulen, P. (2003). Organizing successfull new service development: A literature review. Scientific Analysis of Entrepreneurship and SMEs. *Management Decision*, 41(9), 844–858.

Flagestad, A.H., and Christine A. (2001). Strategic success in winter sports destinations: A sustainable value creation perspective. *Tourism Management*, 22(5), 445–461.

Galbraith, J.K. (1999). *Designing the Innovating Organization*. Los Angeles, USA: CEO Publication (G 99–7 (366)).

Grissemann, U., Pikkemaat, B., and Weger, C. (2013). Antecedents of innovation activities in tourism: An empirical investigation of the Alpine hospitality industry. *Tourism – An International Interdisciplinary Journal*, 61(1), 7–27.

Hartschen, M., Scherer, J., and Brügger, C. (2009). *Innovationsmanagement – die 6 Phasen von der Idee bis zur Umsetzung*. Offenbach: GABAL Verlag.

Hjalager, A.-M. (2002). Repairing innovation defectiveness in tourism. *Tourism Management*, 23(5), 465–474.

Hjalager, A.-M. (2010). A review of innovation research in tourism. *Tourism Management*, 31(1), 1–12. doi: 10.1016/j.tourman.2009.08.012

Hjalager, A.-M., and Flagestad, A. (2012). Innovations in well-being tourism in the Nordic countries. *Current Issues in Tourism*, 15(8), 725–740. doi: 10.1080/13683500.2011.629720

Humphreys, P., McAdam, R., and Leckey, J. (2005). Longitudinal evaluation of innovation implementation in SMEs. *European Journal of Innovation Management*, 8(3), 283–304. doi: 10.1108/14601060510610162

Kelly, D., and Storey, C. (2000). New service development: Initiation strategies. *International Journal of Service Industry Management*, 11(1), 45–63.

Martin, C.R.J., and Horne, D.A. (1995). Level of success inputs for service innovations in the same firm. *International Journal of Service Industry Management*, 6(4), 40–56. doi: 10.1108/09564239510096894

Martins, E.C., and Terblanche, F. (2003). Building organisational culture that stimulates creativity and innovation. *European Journal of Innovation Management*, 6(1), 64–74.

Nieves, J., and Segarra-Ciprés, M. (2015). Management innovation in the hotel industry. *Tourism Management*, 46, 51–58. doi: 10.1016/j.tourman.2014.06.002

Nordin, S. (2003). *Tourism Clustering and Innovation – Paths to Economic Growth and Development*. (U2003:14) Östersund, Sweden:. European Tourism Research Institute, MID–Sweden University.

Orfila-Sintes, F., Crespí-Cladera, R., and Martínez-Ros, E. (2005). Innovation activity in the hotel industry: Evidence from Balearic Islands. *Tourism Management*, 26(6), 851–865. doi: 10.1016/j.tourman.2004.05.005

Orfila-Sintes, F., and Mattsson, J. (2009). Innovation behavior in the hotel industry. *Omega*, 37(2), 380–394. doi: 10.1016/j.omega.2007.04.002

Ottenbacher, M., Shaw, V., and Lockwood, A. (2006). An investigation of the factors affecting innovation performance in chain and independent hotels. *Journal of Quality Assurance in Hospitality and Tourism*, 6(3–4), 113–128. doi: 10.1300/J162v06n03_07

Peters, M., and Buhalis, D. (2004). Family hotel businesses: Strategic planning and the need for education and training. *Education + Training*, 46(8/9), 406–415. doi: 10.1108/00400910410569524

Pikkemaat, B. (2008). Innovation in small and medium-sized tourism enterprises in Tyrol. *The International Journal of Entrepreneurship and Innovation*, 9(3), 187–197.

Pikkemaat, B., and Holzapfel, E. (2007). Innovationsverhalten touristischer Unternehmer: Triebkräfte und Hemmnisse, *Tourism Herausforderung Zukunft* (241–258). Berlin: LIT Verlag.

Pikkemaat, B., and Peters, M. (2006). Towards the measurement of innovation – A pilot study in the small and medium sized hotel industry. *Journal of Quality Assurance in Hospitality and Tourism*, 6(3–4), 89–112. doi: 10.1300/J162v06n03_06

Pikkemaat, B., and Weiermair, K. (2007). Innovation through cooperation in destinations: First results of an empirical study in Austria. *Anatolia*, 18(1), 67–83. doi: 10.1080/13032917.2007.9687036

Pleschak, F.S.H. (1996). *Innovationsmanagement*. Stuttgart: Schäffer-Poeschel Verlag.

Prantl, C., Grissemann, U., and Pikkemaat, B. (2009). Innovation behaviour of employees in small and medium-sized hotel enteprises. *International Journal of Tourism and Travel*, 2(2), 31–40.

Reichwald, R., and Piller F.T. (2009). *Interaktive Wertschöpfung: Open Innovation, Individualisierung und neue Formen der Arbeitsteilung*. Wiesbaden: Gabler.

Schori, K., Roch, A., and Faoro-Stampfli, M. (2006). *Innovationsmanagement für KMU*. Bern: Haupt Verlag.

Shostack, G.L. (1984). Designing services that deliver. *Harvard Business Review*, 62 (January–February), 133–139.

Shostack, G.L. (1987). Service positioning through structural change. *Journal of Marketing*, 59 (January), 34–43.

Slater, S.F., and Mohr, J.J. (2006). Successful development and commercialization of technological innovation: Insights based on strategy type. *The Journal of Product Innovation Management*, 23(1), 26–33.

Storey, C., and Kelly, D. (2001). Measuring the performance of new service development activities. *The Service Industries Journal*, 21(2), 71–90. doi: 10.1080/714005018

Sundbo, J., Orfila-Sintes, F., and Sørensen, F. (2007). The innovative behaviour of tourism firms – Comparative studies of Denmark and Spain. *Research Policy*, 36(1), 88–106. doi: 10.1016/j.respol.2006.08.004

Thomas, R., Shaw, G., and Page, S.J. (2011). Understanding small firms in tourism: A perspective on research trends and challenges. *Tourism Management*, 32(5), 963–976. doi: 10.1016/j.tourman.2011.02.003

Tidd, J., and Bessant, J.R. (2009). *Managing Innovation – Integrating Technological, Market and Organizational Change*. Chichester: John Wiley and Sons.

Tilebein, M. (2006). Ideenfindungsprozess und Unterstützungsmethoden. In K. Schmidt, R. Gleich, and, A. Richter (eds), *Innovationsmanagement in der Serviceindustrie* (111–126). Freiburg: Rudolf Haufe Verlag.

Vahs, D., and Burmester, R. (2005). *Innovationsmanagement – von der Idee zur erfolgreichen Vermarktung*. Stuttgart: Schäffer-Poeschel Verlag.

Walder, B. (2005). Entwicklung neuer Dienstleistungen und Produkte im Unternehmen. In H. Pechlaner, P. Tschurtschenthaler, M. Peters, and M. Fuchs (eds), *Erfolg durch Innovation – Perspektiven für den Tourismus – und Dienstleistungssektor* (103–118). Wiesbaden: Gabler: DUV.

Walder, B., and Pospiech, A. (2006). Innovationsprozesse im Tourismus – eine nachfrageorientierte Typologisierung. In B. Pikkemaat, M. Peters, and K. Weiermair (eds), *Innovationen im Tourismus – Wettbewerbsvorteile durch neue Ideen und Angebote* (67–84). Berlin: Erich Schmidt Verlag.

Weiermair, K. (2004). *Product Improvement or Innovation: What is the Key Success in Tourism?*. Paris: OECD.

# Chapter 7

# Correlation of Macroeconomic Development in Relation to the Development of Supply and Demand in the Hotel Trade and its Economic Efficiency

CHRISTIAN BUER

The development of new sites for hotels is not to be undertaken with the usual indicators of arrival, overnight stays and concentration of beds used as the only assessment tool. On the contrary, the analysis of economic factors in relation to supply and demand has to be studied in more detail, to create in turn an 'economic sustainability factor' that allows a secure and stable return. Unfortunately this model is not yet sufficient to determine, among investors and financiers, a rating factor that can be used to benefit small and medium-sized operators.

The investigation into developing a model based on a correlative analysis has emerged from observations of the growing professionalism within the hotel industry. This professionalization distinguishes itself in operation here as the process optimization of ongoing hotel operations (the increasing academization, for example), even though the accommodation industry reveals below-average scientific penetration (= need to catch up) (Haenschel, 2008).

## Building the Model – Preliminary Analysis

The expansion of hotel operators into opening up other hotel establishments (= spatial expansion and development of locations) is organic and opportunistic. The opportunistic approach is in turn dependent on country-specific economic structures; say, the breakdown of gross domestic product (GDP). The question arises: are hotel establishments direct creators of value – that is, the primary supply (tourism sites such as Mallorca or conference and trade fair locations, for example), and do they thereby directly influence value creation through the presence of the supply as a primary economic factor? Or do they, rather, serve as a secondary value-creator within the core economy (e.g. production, financial services, etc.)?

Depending on this question, site developments are economically driven primary factors and/or politically and strategically important safeguards, for both the operator and the business location. In this connection, strategic decision factors and the generation of soft costs such as pre-opening and planning costs are not measurable as factors in the examination and can therefore not be considered in the model.

What is relevant in the examination of economic efficiency is the return to be achieved from the property for the owner. The long-term investments, in which operators and property owners (= investors) agree on a long-term partnership, are in turn to be derived from different risk models. Investment risk is shifting increasingly towards the owners, since the hotel operators set out the management service contracts and rental or lease agreements with loss limits (= cap clause). As a result, investors are increasingly becoming, in economic terms, the 'hotel operator' and must therefore undertake risk assessment themselves. The interest of investors in hotel real estate has increased, which is in keeping with the trend that has seen hotel companies expanding despite economic instability. Investors are increasingly accepting hotels as fixed assets. In relation to the above-mentioned risks, the importance of further or supplementary performance indicators or so-called key performance indicators (KPI) could rise with increasing uncertainty (KPMG Deutschland, 2010).

The question is, therefore: are the economic indicators of the accommodation market, which have also been measured globally until now by statistics offices in the number of overnight stays, future measurement instruments for investment decision-making? The number of arrivals and overnight stays forms the basis of any feasibility study, along with knowledge of figures extrapolated from the past, which in turn is the foundation of a business plan.

The development and analysis presented here has investigated, for the first time, using Germany as the model, whether the relevant factors of the hospitality industry are sufficient for assessing future investment and operator models. The innovative approach the survey takes lies not in the technology but in the method itself! What is new and, as such, innovative is the relation of economic indicators applied to the hotel and its real estate. as well as the indicators for determining potential and possible success factors.

## The Objective, Scope and Methodology

The objective is to answer the question of whether the traditionally chosen assessment criteria for determining the expected profitability of a hotel's location are still sufficient for meeting the requirements from the perspective of investors and operators. What are the economic indicators (selection) and how do these stand in relation to the success factors in the hospitality industry? Is such a correlation observable, and can a principle be determined from this?

The study presented here is limited to an indicator analysis of the hotel market. The relevant data for surveying the specific requirements of system operators and the investment costs (= construction and manufacturing costs) are not to be gleaned interpretively by the reader, or only by the reader, from the relationship model.

The developed models are instruments that have been applied to the example of Germany as an analysis of the relationship of the indicators of the hotel market, hotel demand/performance, and economic development. This therefore serves as a reference model for the analysis options relative to the relevant regions defined.

The assessment is the question of the extent to which the indicators of economic demand can be used exclusively in practice (= nights, arrivals, origin, usage, achieved accommodation revenue) and to which supply indicators (= available capacity according to operating types and categories) are sufficient for the assessment of locations, or what other indicators can be used. In modelling theory, economic and social science apply the framework for investigating selected characteristics and the factors that influence them. The selected characteristics for investigating sites for the hotel industry are key figures, such as occupancy, the achieved net revenue per overnight stay or the statistics on overnight stays and arrivals collected by the offices of the German states and the Federal Office, as well as the occupancy of beds in relation to capacity. The industry itself collects information, on a voluntary basis, on the occupancy of rooms as well (for example STR Global, Fairmass).

The methodology applied here is the correlation, which in this survey determines the context from the development of the hotel market, of hotel performance, and of the economy in Germany based on the hypotheses advanced and with the aid of statistical methods. The correlation analysis examines whether the relationship of indices is subject to certain regularities or whether certain combinations of characteristics frequently occur and therefore correlate the examined indicators (Steland, 2010: 46). The correlation analysis as part of the descriptive research method is carried out by means of the so-called Bravais-Pearson correlation coefficients. With this method, the non-directional relationships between two quantitatively measured characteristics

(= metrically scaled values) are set against each other, whereby it is not known which figure represents the cause and which the effect. The empirical correlation coefficient (the Bravais-Pearson correlation coefficient) is a measure of the strength of the relationship (Fahrmeir, Künstler, Pigeot, and Tutz, 2010: 135).

The application of the correlation analysis has, as explained above, only an epistemological value, which is limited to the possible existence of a relationship between two of the assessed indicators. The assessed values of two variables may statistically stand within a context, which does not necessarily ensure that a causal relationship exists (= apparent correlation). Furthermore, it must also be taken into account that the span of the available statistical data material is limited to observations of eight or eighteen years at most. The descriptive state indicates that two variables have a similar process. The approach adopted here is restricted to this fact. A broader-reaching investigation using the multi-variable method could clarify this question of the cause and effect principle (Blanchard and Illing, 2007: 824 et seq.).

## THE HOTEL AS AN ELEMENT OF ACCOMMODATION SUPPLY

In academia, a distinction is made between hotels and other accommodation and tourist attractions in the accommodation market in Germany. The hospitality industry encompasses establishments such as hotels, 'Hotel Garni' (bed and breakfast), inns and pensions, as well as accommodation facilities derived from the above, such as motels and boarding houses. The Federal Statistics Office has included the latter type only for the past few years, and classes motels together with the bed-and-breakfast hotels.

The 'other accommodation and tourist attractions' category includes recreation and holiday homes, holiday lets, cabins and youth hostels, camping sites and private rooms (Haenschel, 2008: 5f).

The investigation here is confined to hotels and bed-and-breakfast establishments, which make up the core of the accommodation business. The term 'hotel' is therefore used in this chapter to describe both 'hotels' and 'Hotel Garni'.

The German state offices for statistics and the Federal Office for Statistics count every tourist accommodation establishment with more than nine guest beds The German Hotel and Restaurant Association (DEHOGA) itself recently defined a hotel as being a 'countable accommodation unit' if it has more than 20 rooms. Furthermore, the system approach for the hotel is established and transparent for investors in the 'hospitality' accommodation category as a closed investment model (= critical investment size).

## THE ECONOMIC INDICATOR INDICES IN THE HOSPITALITY INDUSTRY

The key figures of the hospitality industry, used as the first economic measured value of a hotel, are directly tied to demand. The key figures known in the hospitality industry (= Key Performance Index [KPI]) indirectly measure the profitability of companies in detail or of the location as a whole (e.g. city, region). Performance in the hotel industry, which measures the profitability of the operational activity, is simply the relationship between input and output, which in the case of real estate becomes 'capacity supplied' against 'capacity demanded'. This is the classic profitability model, as also applied in other sectors (Medlik and Ingram, 2001: 171 et seq.).

The following *hotel indicators* are used in practice (Buer, 2007: 41):

- average net room rate, i.e. net room price
- average room occupancy
- the resulting average net revenue per available room, i.e. net room revenue
- the hotel company's turnover.

The *average net room rate* (revenue per occupied room; also known as the average achieved room rate [AARR]) is, in addition to the average room occupancy (occupied rooms in relation to available rooms) (Kreuzig and Thiele, 2006: 62), the key figure, which ultimately allows a classification of quality to be made, based on the respective competition. In relation to its competitors, the willingness to book a hotel is the indicator for the service and the product. An exception is a monopoly or oligopoly situation. The indicator in the relationship of the net room rate and the average room occupancy results in the net revenue per available room unit (= Revenue per Available Room [RevPar]).

The *revenue* of the hotel operation is the total revenue from the rental of rooms and the sale of products, goods and services within the hotel. Earnings before interest, taxes, depreciation and amortization (EBITDA) is the figure that represents the operational result, i.e. the absolute return of the company. The term refers to the operating result before interest, taxes and amortization of tangible and intangible assets.

EBITDA is still used in practice in the hotel industry as gross operating profit (= GOP), according to the international standard of 'Uniform Systems of Accounts for the Lodging Industry'. Hotel establishments in direct intercompany comparison represent these three indicators in relation to the positioning of their own company. The first three indicators are used in the hospitality industry for a 'performance rating' in the competitive environment, to be able to gauge the trend of a hotel market.

## THE HOTEL REAL ESTATE RISK MODEL

The 'hotel' risk model is dependent on the *preferential strategy* of the hotel operator and hotel investor (= owner of the property).

The factors *subjective preference* and *risk aversion* are effective here. The subjective preference measures the personal benefits of the investment in relation to an individually chosen alternative. The action alternative is then, under rational criteria, optimal if the benefit value reaches its maximum. The risk factor associated with the investment reduces the expected return with a simultaneous increase of the personal benefits. There is thus a relationship between the income (expected return) and the individual risk tolerance.

The hotel operator uses the *generated cash flow (= EBITDA)* in relation to the expected return of the owner regarding the real estate gross profit and compares the cash flow with his risk propensity. This in turn depends on various factors, such as the location or type of hotel.

If the lodging is run by a single enterpriser, the *risk propensity* of the owner must closely align with that of the operator. If the real estate site is of strategic importance, the risk propensity of both the investor and the operator will be high. Sites in 1-A locations often have characteristics which induce a financial return due to the expected increase in the value of the property itself (due to location).

Investors readily distinguish between hotel investments according to the *type of hotel*, such as city or resort hotel. A significantly higher risk factor (Figure 7.1) is associated with resort hotels than city hotels, despite continued growth in demand in Germany and the orientation of hotel products towards health and conference venue services.

What is ultimately relevant to a *risk analysis* is: who is the investor that operates the hotel (basically an international hotel chain can be assumed) and how high is its *risk participation* or *risk tolerance*? As can be recognized from the risk model, the risk propensity of the operator is usually lower than that of the investor. The different risk tolerances of both parties are found in the indicator for the expected return. The operator proceeds from the EBITDA and subtracts about one-third of that amount as a 'risk bonus'. The remaining income represents the gross profit expected for the investor.

It is evident that the *transaction point* will be based on the *capital market interest rate, yield expectation* and the *risk propensity of the investor* or of the operator. The risk factor subjectively perceived by the operator is, as already

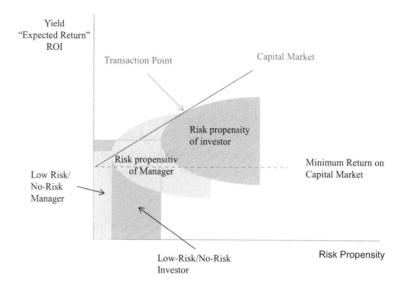

**Figure 7.1     Risk model operator/investor in the hospitality industry**
*Source*: The author.

described, higher than that of the investor, since the operator takes into account market fluctuations and incorporates this into the operating model.

## THE INDICES OF THE HOSPITALITY INDUSTRY AND THE ECONOMY

For the correlation analysis of the development of the hotel market, hotel performance and economic development, the following indicators are used:

*Hotel market*

- hotel businesses opened
- beds in hotels
- guest arrivals in hotels
  - total
  - of which guests are resident in the country
  - of which guests are resident abroad
- Overnight stays in hotels
  - total
  - of which guests are resident in the country
  - of which guests are resident abroad.

The statistical surveys of the German state offices and the Federal Office for Statistics form the database for the hotel market.

## Profitability of hotel businesses

The analysis of indicators for measuring the economic strength of the hotel industry in Germany (= performance) is carried out according to locations (= cities) and location types (= small, medium and large cities and airport locations). This assessment is carried out for various hotel categories. The following values are assessed:

- Ø Room usage (= room occupancy as a percentage), Ø room price (= achieved average room rate), Ø room revenue (= average revenue per available room):
  - in large cities
  - in medium-sized cities
  - in small towns
  - at airports
  - in hotels of the upmarket category (average room rate of more than €100, 4-star–5-star hotels)
  - in hotels of the middle category (average room rate from €50–€100, 3-star hotels)
  - in budget hotels (average room price of under €50, 1-star–2-star hotels)
- Calculating the revenues
  - total revenue
  - revenue per rented room
  - EBITDA per rented room.

The data is collected outside the official statistical surveys accompanied by IHA Germany, STR Global, and Fairmass. The survey sources originate from the publications *Hotelmarkt Deutschland* (German Hotel Market), from the Hotelverband Deutschland (IHA) e.V. (German Hotel Association), which in turn serve the database of the STR Global and Fairmass (Hotelverband Deutschland (IHA) e. V., 2009; Hotelverband Deutschland (IHA) e.V., 2010).

## ECONOMIC DEVELOPMENT OF A REGION

The economic development of a region is based on a variety of indicators, which, considered individually or in relationship to each other, result in turn in an assessment. The national accounts give a qualitative and quantitative picture of the economy of a selected region for the defined period of time (= events). The metrics of the origins, distribution, and final expenditures compilation selected for this research are: the GDP in current prices, in current prices per capita or per gainfully employed person; the gross value added (GVA) in current prices, in current prices in the hotel and catering industry or in trade, the hospitality industry and transport; the number of gainfully employed persons; the number of inhabitants; and the labour market indicators (= employment and unemployment); as well as the business tax (Database: Berlin 1991–2009; see Federal Statistics Office, 2010).

In the analysis of locations to determine a potential analysis for comparable locations, the hospitality industry used population figures and the unemployment rate. The criteria 'for comparable locations' are economic power, existing capacities in the accommodation industry, and the demand for accommodation. For this research, it was assumed that the 'business tax' indicator could be used as a measurable quantity for future location decisions.

## THE DATABASE FOR THE CORRELATION ANALYSIS

The database for the profitability of the hotel industry cannot be ascertained by the statistics offices. The database of STR Global or Fairmass is used as the basic framework. The problem is that this database must in turn be representative. The core of the database compiled by STR Global/Fairmass is made up mainly of hotels in major cities and memberships in hotel chains or partnerships. The 'private hotels' are relatively scarce entries. In Germany, around 150,000 hotel rooms have been counted in around 900 classified hotel businesses. This is around one- third of the capacity in Germany and takes in only 10 per cent of all hotels. The database for determining the profitability of the hospitality industry (= performance) covers only 10 per cent of the open hotel businesses in Germany or 30 per cent of the country's room capacity. In Munich these figures cover around 50 per cent of the hotel businesses and in Berlin 55 per cent. The validity or representativeness that can be measured for Germany is only conditionally supportable. In the differentiated observation of the categorization of hotel businesses, in Berlin and Munich around three-quarters of the existing businesses are recorded by STR Global and Fairmass. This allows a representative inference.

The evaluation of the survey by STR Global and Fairmass suggests that a growing database is being created for the major cities, which will allow conclusions to be drawn for future reviews based on the total amount. The key question will be: what correlation with the economic data will be useful?

## Correlation Analysis of Economic Development and Supply and Demand Values of Hotels using Germany as an Example

The *population* of Germany has remained constant in the last 20 years, at an average growth rate of 0.1 per cent per annum. The number of gainfully employed persons in the same period has grown by an average of 0.24 per cent. The unemployment rate has fluctuated during the period between around 7 per cent and 12 per cent and was around 7 per cent in 2013.

The *GDP* rose by an average of 2.9 per cent annually until 2008 and the GVA by 2.8 per cent. In 2009 the GDP and GVA both fell by 3.5 per cent. According to a forecast by Oxford Economics, GDP in Germany will grow over the coming years by between 1.5 to 1.7 per cent. The tax revenues in Germany have not seen any continuous growth since 1999 (decline between 2000 and 2003; growth from 2004 (+ 50 per cent), followed by a decline from 2008 to 2009 of 21 per cent). With the economy recovering, the tax on business could again in 2013 reach the levels seen in 2008 (approximately €43 billion). The economic growth had no direct positive feedback effect on the immediate revenue of local authorities in Germany. (Source: Federal Statistics Office, 2010: destatis. de, statista.de).

The rating of the accommodation demand (overnight stays) is an analysis of the correlation with the selective economic indicators. In this rating, a differentiation is made between the demand for hotels and the demand for bed-and-breakfast hotels.

The index correlation 'hotel stays' with the economic indicators for Germany gave the following results:

- The number of inhabitants and the hotel stays by guests resident in the country shows a medium correlation ($r_{HOS, resident}$=0.60).
- A high correlation exists between GDP and the hotel overnight stays in total: in current prices ($r_{HOS, GDP}$=0.98) or in current prices per capita ($r_{HOS, GDP (per cap.)}$=0.98). The same applies to the GVA in current prices in the hotel and catering industry ($r_{HOS, GVA hotel/catering industry}$=0.98). A similar close relationship exists in business tax revenues (overnight stays by guests resident in Germany, $r_{HOS res.,TR}$=0.81, overnight stays by visitors from abroad $r_{HOS non-res.,TR}$= 0.93).
- The number of people gainfully employed in Germany strongly correlates with the number of domestic overnight stays in hotels and in bed-and-breakfast hotels ($r_{HOS res., GE}$=0.96).
- The unemployment rate indicator has a direct relationship with the hotel overnight stays of domestic guests ($r_{HON res., UR}$= −0.56).

## ACCOMMODATION SUPPLY (ESTABLISHMENTS AND BEDS) IN CORRELATION WITH ECONOMIC INDICATORS

The correlation coefficient between *hotel companies* (= available capacity) and population figures, which was used in practice to determine the potential analysis, has an average value ($r_{hotels, per cap.}$=0.77). This has an inverse correlation to the economic indicator *business tax* ($r_{Hotels, BT}$= −0.89). The indicators of *GDP*, *GVA* and *gainfully employed* show only a low correlation. This allows an initial conclusion that the formation of a correlation, in the sense of determining an accommodation potential derived from the economic indicators, can generally not be attributed to the economic data. Essentially, it is important to consider that the growth of GDP or GVA in absolute numbers in relation to the growth of the hotel businesses is relatively larger and the importance of the number of hotel establishments therefore decreases. If the share of the economic power of tourism and accommodation sector is larger, so too will be the growth of the hotel businesses. It is important to check to what extent this is to be applied to all regions and hotel products (= beds or room and bed capacity).

As with the correlation of accommodation facilities, the *number of inhabitants* has a medium correlation with beds ($r_{accom., pop.}$ = 0.79). In contrast with the number of establishments, a strong relationship exists between the number of beds in 'hotels and bed-and-breakfast hotels' and the GDP (in current prices ($r_{accom., GDP}$= 0.97) and in current prices per person ($r_{accom., GDP (per cap.)}$ = 0.97)), the GVA (in current prices ($r_{accom., GVA}$=0.97)) and the number of persons in gainful employment ($r_{accom., GE}$ = 0.83). A medium correlation exists between business tax revenue and beds ($r_{accom., TR}$=0.70).

In the case of Germany, the correlation analysis based on the *accommodation demand* and *accommodation supply* in correlation with the economic indicators reveals that the number of establishments has little to no relevance. The supply of beds and the development of the economic factors of the country, as well as the number of overnight stays, do, however, have a high relevance. For the *business tax*, only a moderate relationship can be recognized.

## CORRELATION ANALYSIS OF ECONOMIC DEVELOPMENT AND HOTEL PERFORMANCE

The indicators relevant to the hotel performance are based on the surveys of STR Global or Fairmass and are differentiated by location (in large, medium and small cities and in airports) and hotel category (budget hotels, mid-range hotels and upmarket hotels).

The *room occupancy* of all categories and locations fluctuates, as affected by economic development. Airport hotels are subject to a larger fluctuation range (average is −1.38 per cent). Furthermore, the larger the city, the greater the fluctuation range. Smaller cities have a smaller fluctuation range, whereby the occupancy of upmarket hotels remains more constant than that of budget hotels. This needs to be reassessed, since the supply of 'budget establishments' has seen steady growth only since 1999 and the present time series in relation to the available database is slim.

In the correlation analysis the number of *inhabitants* has little to no relevance to occupancy. This is also confirmed by the other hotel performance indicators, so that in the further studies the number of inhabitants, in relation to the development of demand in the hotel industry, is left out. The correlation between the *labour market* (gainfully employed and the rate of unemployment) and the occupancy of rooms in hotels and bed-and-breakfast hotels in Germany gives a low correlation factor. A direct link among the gainfully employed, population figures and the *unemployment rate* for the hotel industry can therefore be ruled out as a relational factor.

The correlation between *GDP* and the room occupancy is low or medium. The correlation for occupancy in general or with major cities is therefore low. There is likewise also a low correlation with the upmarket hotels (4–5 stars). An average correlation exists for smaller cities (GDP at current prices per capita $(r_{OCC \text{ small cities, GDP (per cap)}} = 0.61)$), medium-sized cities $(r_{OCC \text{ med. cities, GDP (per cap)}} = 0.54)$, airport hotels $(r_{OCC \text{ airp. hotels, GDP (per cap)}} = 0.51)$, budget hotels (1-star–2-star) $(r_{OCC \text{ budg. hotels, GDP (per cap)}} = 0.74)$ and the medium-sized category (3 stars) $(r_{OCC \text{ med. cat. GDP (per cap)}} = 0.63)$.

The same picture can be seen for the *GVA*. An exception is the GVA in current prices in the hospitality industry in correlation to the budget hotels (1-star–2-star) $(r_{OCC \text{ Budget, GVA}} = 0.81)$.

In addition to the *development of demand* (= room occupancy) the achieved room rate measures, on one hand, the intensity of the accommodation in relation to the willingness to spend (= situation-dependent development). The fluctuation of the room prices behaves in the same scope as demand (= room occupancy). The larger the city the greater the fluctuation. In addition, the fluctuation in the upmarket category is greater than in the budget segment (Figure 7.2).

The correlation of *room price* shows little relationship to the number of inhabitants. The room price has a medium correlation to GDP, whereby the airport hotels $(r_{ADR \text{ airp., GDP}} = 0.78)$ and hotels of the medium-sized category $(r_{ADR \text{ med. cat., GDP}} = 0.78)$ have the highest relationship value. A medium-sized relationship could also be observed in upmarket hotels $(r_{ADR \text{ higher cat., GDP}} = 0.75)$. Diverging from the room occupancy rate, there is a close relationship between the GVA for airport hotels $(r_{ADR \text{ airp., GVA}} = 0.83)$ and hotels in major cities $(r_{ADR \text{ maj. cit., GVA}} = 0.58)$ as well as for hotels of the medium-sized category $(r_{ADR \text{ med.}}$

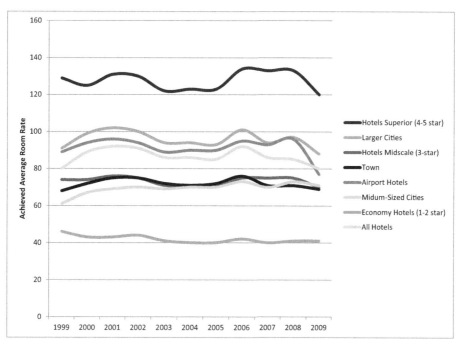

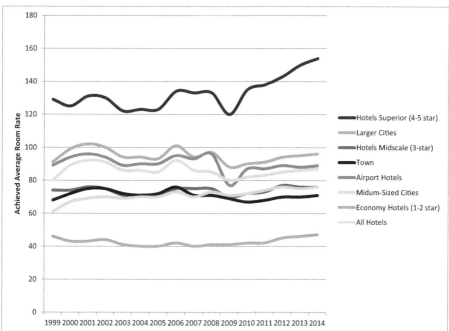

**Figure 7.2    Room price according to location and hotel category (1999–2009)**
*Source*: Hotelverband Deutschland (IHA) e.V., 2010.

$_{cat., GVA}$= 0.81). It is important to bear in mind that budget hotels are subject to lower price fluctuations (= no price and target audience-differentiated yield management/revenue management), which leads to a lower volatility in relation to GDP and therefore only a medium to low relationship exists.

The more detailed consideration of the room price and the *gainfully employed* or *unemployment rate* reveals a medium outcome for airport hotels or, in general, a weak relationship. The investigation of the relationship to the business tax reveals only a minor relationship to the room price.

The determination of the relationship of the *room yield* (= RevPar) and the economic development in Germany are moderately connected via the different relationships. Only the airport hotels ($r_{RevPAR high cat., TR}$=0.90) have a high relationship. A direct explanation for this phenomenon cannot be discerned.

The performance of the hotel business in the form of *EBITDA* against the overall economic development is an applicable indicator in Germany in this respect, since the operation-oriented response time to an altered demand behaviour is delayed and the creation and management accordingly shows a time lag.

A medium to strong relation between EBITDA and GDP/ GVA could be determined. The relationship with the EBITDA per available room and GDP ($r_{EBITDA per room, GDP}$= 0.83) is stronger than the relationship with the revenue per rented room ($_{Revenue per rented room, GDP}$ = 0.64). Furthermore, the hospitality industry revenues correlated concordantly with the number of *persons in gainful employment* ($r_{revenue, GE}$=0.64) as well as – inversely – with the *unemployment rate* ($r_{revenue, UR}$= −0.55). Business taxes and the revenues per rented room ($r_{revenue per rented room, TR}$ = 0.62) have a medium relationship and the EBITDA a strong relationship per available room ($r_{EBITDA per room, TR}$= 0.91). This strong correlation confirms the relationship between EBITDA and the tax revenues.

## SUMMARY EVALUATION OF THE CORRELATION ANALYSIS IN GERMANY

The *analysis of the demand* (= overnight stays) at a hotel has a *strong relationship to the GDP* as well as to the *GVA*. This suggests that for future forecasts in Germany, the 'overnight stays' demand-related behaviour can be deduced from the overall economic development. The revenue drivers of the economy (= export nation) and so business and conference travel (62 per cent of all hotel stays in Germany (ghh consult, 2006: 27)) play a larger role here than travel for tourism. The evaluation of the survey by STR Global and Fairmass suggests that a growing database is being created for the major cities, which will allow conclusions to be drawn for future reviews based on the total amount. The key question will be: what correlation with the economic data will be useful?

The differentiated consideration of 'domestic' and 'foreign' overnight stays plays only a subordinate role in relation to demand related to economic development. A conscious differentiation in demand-related behaviour is therefore not necessary. The room rate, to which international guests above all have a lower price sensitivity, bears no direct relationship to the indicator of an economic measured variable for the derivation of a long-term development. The lower price sensitivity of international guests has an indirect effect, since the competition of hotels is controlled and influenced by the domestic market and the price level is therefore determined by this competition.

A *positive relationship* is detected between the *number of inhabitants in Germany and the demand-related behaviour pattern (= domestic overnight stays).* The same applies to the relationship with the numbers of gainfully employed and a low unemployment rate. The German hotel market (a business travel destination) thus depends on the national purchasing power. *Focus Reisestudie* determined in 2009 that 92.1 per cent of all business trips in Germany were conducted within the country and that these in turn generated 22.4 per cent of all overnight stays in Germany (Focus (Hsrg.) 2009).

The *business tax revenue*, which is used as an indicator for the economic power of a municipality, has at least a *limited significance* for the demand-related behaviour in hotels.

The *supply of hotel beds* in *hotels and bed-and-breakfast hotels* is growing with the *number of inhabitants* in the country. This confirms that through the federal structure of the country and population growth, and through the increase in travel, the volume of demand is also increasing and thus the *hotel market* is becoming more *attractive* – that is, for more hotels to be built. The consequence of this relationship is that a positive relationship to the number of persons in employment is to be derived in the locations that have a higher number of gainfully employed, such that the number of available rooms in hotels and bed-and-breakfast hotels increases (= approx. 80 per cent of all overnight stays by domestic residents). The hotel bed capacity increases in near linear fashion with the GDP and GVA. Business tax revenues have only a conditional relationship to the supply. This lies in the nature of business taxation and location dependency. The production site is not necessarily the location where taxation is levied. Nonetheless, private hoteliers in particular are tied to their location and there hence exists a limited correlation tied to the demand for overnight stays.

The *performance of hotels*, measured among other things in room occupancy, has a *medium relationship* to the economic indicators of *GDP* and *GVA*. The performance values collected by the hospitality industry itself, by STR Global, show that smaller cities and budget hotels in particular have a positive correlation with the economic indicators, while hotels in the 'major cities' and the upmarket hotels have a relatively low correlation with the two economic indicators. This relationship can be explained by, among other things, the fact that the participants of the STR Global groups in the major cities are predominantly hotels in the upmarket category. In the specification for airport hotels, a direct relationship can be detected between economic development and room occupancy.

In the question of *economic development* and the associated room price, a *direct relationship* exists *for the airport hotels. Room price and GDP/GVA of the hotels in major cities* were also shown to be linked. By contrast, the room rates of the hotels in medium-sized and small cities are less price sensitive to the development of GDP and GVA. Regarding categorization, middle-range hotels have a medium-sized relationship of room rate to GDP/ GVA. The room price of the upmarket hotels (4-star–5-star) is less dependent on economic development.

In the relationship of *room occupancy and room price* (= yield in terms of RevPar) the *airport hotels show a positive correlation*, whereas all other indicators show a medium-sized interrelationship with economic development. The 'revenue' and EBITDA performance show a medium relationship with economic development, as does the demand in the form of overnight stays. This is due to the temporal mismatch of the economic development and to the adjustment of the operating costs, as mentioned above.

From the surveys for Germany it can be concluded that the surveys of economic development (GDP/GVA) in correlation with the number of overnight stays (= demand correlation coefficient) and the accommodation supply (=supply correlation coefficient) are a proven forecasting tool.

For the surveys of hotels of various categories and forms of use (= airport hotels, holiday hotels, etc.) as well as the location-specific factors (= size of the city) there are different respective factors that can be used individually for the forecasts.

The *business tax* as an indicator of the potential demand-related behaviour in hotels is relevant only if economically (GDP/GVA) there is a positive relationship with the volume of business tax. This is not, as a rule, to be deduced unconditionally, and so the commercial tax revenue at one location can be applied only to a limited extent. The business tax revenue can be used as an indicator to derive the expected overall profitability in the form of the EBITDA for the hotel. The higher the tax revenue at the location, the greater the willingness could be to push the room price higher and thus achieve a higher corporate profit (EBITDA).

*Smaller and medium-sized locations* have greater price stability, can assume a more continuous occupancy rate and are directly influenced by the employment rate or the economic factors. Small and medium-sized locations or regions which show population growth and growing economic indicators (GDP/GVA) are suitable for hotels of the medium and lower category (= budget hotels).

For the *prognosis for the determination of location factors* and potential economic success factors it can be summarized that supply and demand-related factors are the number of gainfully employed, the GDP and the GVA. The business tax, however, serves as an indicator for the possible readiness for (= tendency towards) a better profitability ratio (= EBITDA). The performance data used by the hospitality industry (KPIs) – net logistics revenue and room occupancy – have a medium relevance to the economic indicators of a location. They serve as an indicator of current market developments and reflect the economic demand in the hotels, which is relevant mainly in larger cities (= greater price and demand fluctuations). In medium and smaller cities, both the price and demand volatility are low and serve as an indicator for a long-term allocation and pricing policy.

## Derivation of the Relationships for Investors

The investment behaviour in the hotel business, as already stated, depends on the figure for investment per room or the income per room. The investments are divided at core into the real estate and development costs, construction and manufacturing costs, equipment and furnishing costs, as well as consulting and architect fees. For the investors in hotel real estate the separation of 'construction and technical equipment' from 'equipment and furnishing costs' must increasingly be taken into account. If approximately €1,250– €1,500 (depending on the technology used) is spent per room in the building, including technical equipment, the ranges for the equipment and furnishings will vary depending on the area or the selected category. For a simple 1-star to 2-star hotel, an average of approximately €3,500–€5,500 is spent per room for the equipment and furnishings. In this category, the public spaces (such as restoration, lobby, spa facilities, conferences) are minimized. In the upmarket to luxury category, which basically has no upper ceiling, an average of €25,000– €35,000 is spent per room.

Ultimately, the previous *indicators* of the *hospitality industry can be applied* if the following is observed.

Derived from the market analysis, the basic interest paid on the capital invested is determined by the possibility of generating a return. Sites that are of strategic importance for operators, among others, or that achieve a higher demand (= returns to scale), usually attain a higher yield (EBITDA), which in turn can be used to cover debt servicing. On the so-called B and C locations, this will achieve stable capital servicing corresponding to a stable demand, a manageable operational size, and a stable room price at concurrent low volatility. This means that, in relation to the investment, the savings potential lies in the construction sector. The initial investment in 'construction and technical equipment' is guided by the service area. The interior and decor are ultimately determined by the operator. In developing and building a hotel in the stable markets of smaller cities (= lower fluctuation), savings must be achieved in construction in order to secure return on capital.

The *return on capital* is defined in the industry as rental per room per month. In locations such as Berlin, this return is around €1,000 for an upmarket hotel. A comparable product (small enterprise) at a B and C location can be expected to return around 20–35 per cent less than this. As a result, the spaces in the building must be correspondingly smaller. Furthermore, the entry-level price will be lower and the equipment and facility standards accordingly modified. A significant reduction of the spaces dedicated as public areas is to be expected, as hotels with lower numbers of rooms also need no large conference rooms.

*Capital servicing* of €1,000 per room per month allows, at a seven per cent interest rate, an investment per room of approximately €175,000. With a corresponding lower capital servicing, the investment per room falls to approximately €110,000–€140,000. These savings can be achieved through the price of the land and the space. In Germany, irrespective of location, the construction costs will shift within a certain range. The second savings potential lies in the facilities and furnishings, with the result that the investment will be in the context of economic expectations.

## Conclusion

This analysis has concluded that potential for more hotels in the polypolic hotel market is to be sought at locations where a stable economic development prevails and there is a low range of fluctuations. Nonetheless, the hotel market in Germany continues to focus its development primarily on the major cities, a fact that can be derived, for instance, from the risk diversification and risk behaviour of operators. Regional or even local hotel developments use as a basis the distinctive individual interests of on-site investors.

Nevertheless, the identified indicators and their correlations serve to establish a future foundation for evaluating economically stable regions and markets as preferred real estate investments.

# References

Blanchard, O., and Illing, G. (2007). *Makroökonomie* (4. aktualisierte und überarbeitete Ausg.). München: Pearson Studium.

Buer, C. (2007). Kennziffern und Besonderheiten von Hotelimmobilien. In F. (Hrsg.), *Hotel Real Estate Management – Grundlagen, Spezialbereiche, Fallbeispiele.* Berlin: Erich Schmidt Verlag.

Fahrmeir, L., Künstler, R., Pigeot, I., and Tutz, G. (2010). *Statistik – Der Weg zur Datenanalyse* (7. Ausg.). Heidelberg, Dordrecht, London, New York: Springer Verlag.

Federal Statistics Office, destatis.de, 2010: Destatis. Statistisches Bundesamt (Federal Statistics Office), Retrieved from: https://www.destatis.de/

Statista. Das Statistik-Portal, 2010, http://de.statista.com/

Focus (Hrsg.) (2009). *Focus Reisemarktstudie – Der Markt für Urlaub und Geschäftsreisen – Daten, Fakten, Trends.* München: Focus.

ghh consult (2006). *Der Hotelmarkt in Deutschland 2005.* Wiesbaden.

Haenschel, K. (2008). *Hotelmanagement.* München, Wien: Oldenbourg Verlag.

Hotelverband Deutschland (IHA) e. V. (2009). *Hotelmarkt Deutschland 2009.* Berlin.

Hotelverband Deutschland (IHA) e.V. (2010). *Hotelmarkt Deutschland 2010.* Berlin.

KPMG Deutschland (2010). *Hotelimmobilien in Deutschland – Analyse zum Einfluss der Wirtschaftsentwicklung auf die Hotel-Performance.* München.

Kreuzig, K.-H., and Thiele, R. (2006). *Betriebsvergleich Hotellerie and Gastronomie Deutschland 2006.* Düsseldorf: BBG Consulting.

Medlik, S., and Ingram, H. (2001). *The Business of Hotels.* 4th Revised Edition. Oxford: Butterworth-Heinemann.

Steland, A. (2010). *Basiswissen Statistik – Kompaktkurs für Anwender aus Wirtschaft, Informatik und Technik* (2. Ausg.). Heidelberg, Dordrecht, London, New York: Springer Verlag.

# PART III
# Innovation in Destinations

# Chapter 8

# The Impact of Innovativeness on Mountain Destination Development

KIR KUŠČER and TANJA MIHALIČ

This chapter examines two different aspects of tourism development in the context of mountain tourism destinations. First, there is an increasing awareness that the development of destinations is shaped by the ability to innovate. Second, destinations differ in their technological, socio-cultural, natural, political and legal environments, and these different characteristics influence their competitiveness and development. The purpose of this chapter is to develop a theoretical model and to better understand the relationships between tourism development, innovativeness and destination environments. In this context, the mountain destination innovativeness model has been constructed and empirically tested in Alpine mountain tourism destinations. The results confirm that environmental attributes directly influence development of the destinations and also shape the capacity for being innovative, which in turn also has a substantial impact on destination development. More specifically, innovativeness is a mediator: it can mitigate the effects of adverse changes or emphasize the effects of favourable changes in environments, which contributes to proper tourism development. These findings can help destination managers refine their current and future responses in regard to mountain destination development and adapt to changes in tourism environments by shaping their innovativeness policy.

## Introduction

Researchers in the field of tourism call for further understanding of the relative importance of different dimensions of destination development and competitiveness (Bornhorst, Ritchie, and Sheehan, 2010; Dwyer and Kim, 2003). It is crucial for destinations to monitor the changes in different environments, such as economic, environmental, social, technological.

(Dwyer et al., 2008; Ritchie and Crouch, 2003). In order to avoid a strategic drift in tourism development (Dwyer and Edwards, 2009), a destination needs to constantly adapt to external changes, e.g., to the changes in environments mentioned above. This has also been emphasized by other authors (Dwyer and Kim, 2003; Pechlaner, 1999) who argue that a destination's development should be future-oriented, thus forward-looking, e.g. innovative. In the above context, we focus our research on the triangle formed by tourism destination development, a destination's environments and a destination's innovativeness.

Another characteristic of our research is derived from the fact that destination attributes vary across locations (Dwyer, Knežević Cvelbar, Edwards, and Mihalič, 2012) and that different elements are relevant for different kinds of destinations (Dwyer and Kim, 2003). In order to study the relationships between the aforementioned destination dimensions, we selected a homogeneous group of mountain tourism destinations. The existing literature offers a measurement tool that focuses on the development–environments–innovativeness triangle in the context of mountain tourism destinations (Kuščer, 2012; 2013; Kuščer and Mihalič, 2011). This research tool provides lists of relevant mountain tourism destination indicators for each of the aforementioned dimensions based on the answers of the panel of tourism experts from the field of mountain tourism. Their findings have been incorporated into our structural equation model, the mountain destination innovativeness model (MDIM); the purpose of this study is to determine the relationships between mountain destination development, innovativeness and environments. The goals are to measure the impact of mountain tourism environments on innovativeness and to uncover how innovativeness influences destination development by mitigating the possible negative impacts of environmental changes, or emphasizing the possible positive ones on destination development.

## Mountain Destinations

There is a vast amount of tourism literature that focuses on mountain tourism destinations (Bourdeau, 2009; Brida, Osti, and Barquet, 2010; Charters and Saxon, 2007; Curto, 2006; Debarbieux and Price, 2008; Gunya, 2007; Lasanta, Laguna, and Vicente-Serrano, 2007; Nepal and Chipeniuk, 2005). A mountain destination is usually defined as a geographical, economic and social entity that incorporates companies, organizations, activities, areas and infrastructure developed to satisfy the specific needs of mountain tourists (adapted from Flagestad and Hope, 2001). The specific characteristics of mountain destinations have been defined by the Nordic Centre for Spatial Development (2004) and are shown in Table 8.1.

Table 8.1    Mountain destination altitude and slope criteria

| Class (elevation in m) | Additional criteria |
|---|---|
| > 2500 | |
| 1500–2499 | > 2° slope within 3 km radius |
| 1000–1499 | >5° slope within 3 km radius and/or local elevation range local elevation range >300 m within 7 km radius |
| 300–999 | local elevation range >300 m within 7 km radius |
| 0–299 | standard deviation > 50 m for cardinal points |

*Source*: Nordic Centre for Spatial Development, 2004.

However, in order to constantly adapt to external changes and to maintain destination development, the interest in this chapter is in the relationships between mountain destination development, their environments and innovativeness in order to recommend actions for qualitative and quantitative destination maintenance and development (Figure 8.1).

Previous relevant research (Kuščer, 2012; 2013; Kuščer and Mihalič, 2011), was based on the opinions and expertise of an international sample of approximately 200 tourism researchers, destination managers and other stakeholders in mountain destinations. They evaluated lists of potential indicators of tourism development, innovativeness and environments, which have been gathered from the existing tourism literature and research. Firstly, all proposed indicators in each category were evaluated in regard to their relevance for measuring the corresponding dimension and then grouped into factors. These dimensions and factors are presented in the following sections.

## MOUNTAIN DESTINATION DEVELOPMENT

Destinations strive to protect, maintain and improve their destination development and to remain competitive on the tourism market. Mountain destination developments need to be properly managed and adapted to the fragility of mountain destinations.

There is a need for more general agreement on how to measure destination development (Dwyer and Kim, 2003). Destination development is very frequently studied from its economic perspective or focused on quantitative growth, such as growth in visitor numbers, overnight stays or tourism expenditure. However, the qualitative component of tourism development

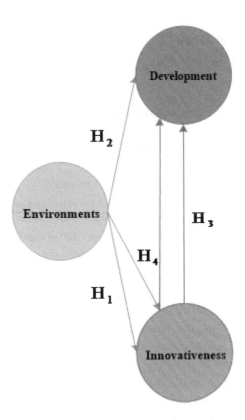

**Figure 8.1     Dimensions of the mountain destination innovativeness model and the corresponding hypotheses**

*Source*: The authors.

is also important. In this context, non-financial destination performance in regard to its natural, social or cultural environments also becomes relevant. Such a broader understanding of destination development is covered by the established sustainable tourism development concept. Mainstream tourism literature on sustainable development follows the three-pillars model as promoted by the UNWTO (2004). These are the traditional economic, environmental and socio-cultural pillars. In addition to this, some other dimensions of sustainable development that are gaining the attention of tourism researchers and international organizations are also noteworthy. More specifically, some advise taking customer satisfaction into consideration, as it is a market-oriented measure of a destination's success and competitiveness (Dmitrović et al., 2009; Mihalič, 2013; UNWTO, 2004). However, the former indicator should be used with caution, since it is influenced by uncontrollable factors, such as weather and snow conditions (Perdue, 2002).

According to the previously mentioned research on measuring mountain tourism destination performance, mountain destination development is measured by indicators that relate to the protection of the natural environment, tourist traffic and expenditure, visitor satisfaction, and socio-economic prosperity (Table 8.2).

**Table 8.2    Factors and elements for measuring mountain destination development**

| Preservation of natural environment | Reference |
| --- | --- |
| Water consumption in tourism sector | Cruz, 2011 |
| Amount of soil erosion | Zhang et al., 2010 |
| Usage of clean energy (wind, sun, geothermal, photovoltaics, etc.) in tourism sector | Karamanis, 2011 |
| Energy consumption in tourism sector | Cruz, 2011 |
| Frequency of environmental accidents related to tourism | Choi and Sirakaya, 2006 |
| Share of recycled waste in tourism sector | Yaw, 2005 |
| $CO_2$ emissions in tourism sector | Lin, 2010 |
| Share of recycled water in tourism sector | Gössling et al., 2012 |
| Air quality | Choi and Sirakaya, 2006 |
| Water pollution from sewage | Gössling et al., 2012 |
| **Tourist traffic and expenditure** | **Reference** |
| Growth rate in average length of stay | Barros and Machado, 2010 |
| Growth of market share in terms of nights spent | Dwyer and Kim, 2003 |
| Growth of market share in terms of tourist arrivals | Dwyer and Kim, 2003 |
| Average length of stay | Barros and Machado, 2010 |
| Visits to parks, recreation areas | McCool et al., 2001 |
| Hotel occupancy rate | O'Neill and Mattila, 2006 |
| Growth rate in daily visitor expenditure | Sun and Stynes, 2006 |
| **Visitor satisfaction** | **Reference** |
| Share of returning visitors | Chi and Qu, 2008 |
| Share of very satisfied visitors | Chi and Qu, 2008 |
| Perceived value for money of tourist services | Tam, 2004 |
| Perceived quality of tourist services | Konu et al., 2011 |
| Visitor satisfaction with environmental issues | G. Miller, 2001 |
| Availability of tourism infrastructure services | Konu et al., 2011 |

**Table 8.2**    *Concluded*

| Socio-economic prosperity | Reference |
| --- | --- |
| Average wage in tourism sector compared to other sectors of the economy | Lundberg, 2008 |
| Contribution of tourism sector to economic growth | Arslanturk et al., 2011 |
| Seasonality of employment in tourism sector | Charters and Saxon, 2007 |
| Lodging revenues | McCool et al., 2001 |
| Employment growth in tourism | Choi and Sirakaya, 2006 |

*Source*: Kuščer, 2012.

## MOUNTAIN DESTINATION INNOVATIVENESS

Innovative tourism destination is forward-looking, advanced in its strategies and operations, and is implementing new solutions. Wang and Ahmed (2004) define an innovative destination as an organization that is capable of 'introducing new products to the market, or opening up new markets, through combining strategic orientation with innovative behaviour and process'. Similarly, Huang, Li and Chen (2009) relate innovativeness to a firm's inclination to develop new products and services. New innovative approaches and solutions can increase the destination's ability to meet and adjust to the global changes faster than the competitors and thus gain a competitive advantage. That enables destinations to become 'future makers', rather than 'future takers' (Dwyer et al., 2012).

Innovations are needed to provide the flexibility to face the challenges imposed by the environment (Bourdeau, 2009; Macchiavelli, 2009). Consumers demand innovation in tourism products and this includes new trends, such as those in the economic, natural and socio-cultural environments in mountain destinations (Franch, Martini, Buffa, and Parisi, 2008). Therefore, being innovative in all aspects of development, marketing, cooperation and education, as well as prolonging the season, are the future priorities of sustainable mountain destination development (Müller and Weber, 2008). Climate change can provide an incentive for innovation, so mountain destinations have to rethink what they offer, as well as the changing importance of the summer and winter seasons (Shih, Nicholls, and Holecek, 2009). However, climate change can also represent a serious threat for winter mountain tourism (Falk, 2013). The adoption of sustainable innovations at ski resorts is influenced by the perceived simplicity of such innovations, and opinion leadership (Smerecnik and Andersen, 2011).

Tourism research suggests many indicators to measure destination innovativeness, such as local support for change, capacity to change, use of alternative energy resources, use of opportunities created by climate change, or adapting to it, use of dynamic web resources, etc. Previous research states that the mountain destination innovativeness construct relates to innovativeness in the socio-cultural and natural environments and the proactiveness of tourism destinations (Table 8.3). More specifically, proactiveness as a significant factor can be measured by the formation of a destination's innovation strategy, the creation of innovative vision, adaptations to changing demand, etc.

**Table 8.3    Factors and elements of mountain destination innovativeness**

| Socio-cultural sustainability and stakeholder participation | Reference |
| --- | --- |
| The local population's support for change | Fallon and Kriwoken, 2003 |
| The local population's capacity for change | Fallon and Kriwoken, 2003 |
| Participation of all stakeholders in tourism planning | Soliva et al., 2008 |
| Collaboration of all stakeholders in decision-making processes | Gunya, 2007 |
| Interests of the local community taken into account | Debarbieux and Price, 2008 |
| Organizational structure that supports involvement of all stakeholders | Lebe and Milfelner, 2006 |
| Availability of knowledge resources and education | Dredge, 2006 |
| Respect for the socio-cultural authenticity of host communities (conservation of cultural heritage and traditional values) | Meleghy et al., 1985 |
| Local products offered in combination with experience of local craftsmanship | Brandth and Haugen, 2011 |
| **Environmental sustainability** | **Reference** |
| Energy policies that support use of alternative sources of energy | Heagle et al., 2011 |
| Environmental policies that promote sustainable development | Castellani and Sala, 2010 |
| Optimal use made of environmental resources (environmental sustainability) | Kuniyal, 2002 |
| Transport policies that favour alternative transport modes and public transport | Reilly et al., 2010 |
| Maintenance of ecological processes and help with conservation of natural resources and biodiversity | Kruk et al., 2007 |
| Exploitation of opportunities created by changing climate conditions | Franch et al., 2008 |
| Implementation of new practices in environmental management | Mihalič, 2000 |
| Adaptation to changing climate conditions | UNWTO and UNEP, 2008 |

**Table 8.3    *Concluded***

| Proactiveness | Reference |
|---|---|
| Dynamic content on the web portal | B'Far, 2005 |
| Creating distinctive image of the destination | Govers et al., 2007 |
| Logistics adapted to changing demand (last-minute reservations, new reservations systems, etc.) | Marom and Seidmann, 2011 |
| Web portal providing rich user experience | Woodside et al., 2011 |
| Tourism products adapted to changing demand (last-minute reservations, increased price sensitivity, etc.) | Vanhove, 2011 |
| Formation of destination's innovation strategy | Dwyer et al., 2009 |
| Creation of innovative vision | Dávid, 2011 |
| Ease of access to information through a highly developed communications system | Stamboulis and Skayannis, 2003 |

*Source*: Kuščer, 2013.

## MOUNTAIN DESTINATION ENVIRONMENTS

Different kinds of destination environments, such as natural, cultural, social or technological environments, are crucial for destination development (Dwyer and Kim, 2003; Kaynak and Marandu, 2011; Ritchie and Crouch, 2003). Some researchers also indicate political and legal environments as needing more research (Clarimont and Vlès, 2009). No matter which environment type is discussed, the fact remains that tourism environments generally either support or hinder tourism destination development (Mihalič, 2006). In the case of mountain destinations, it is argued that their fragile environments are extremely sensitive to tourism influences (Flagestad and Hope, 2001). Mountain destination development should take into account the characteristics and protection of these natural and socio-cultural environments, which are the core of sustainable tourism practices, based on recognition of their importance for economic development (Holden, 2000). In contrast, the effects of mountain destination environments on destination development can also be negative (Lama and Sattar, 2004; Lasanta, Laguna, and Vicente-Serrano, 2007; Nepal and Chipeniuk, 2005). Examples are numerous and vary from bad weather or green winters to underdeveloped web promotion and marketing that may have a negative impact on tourism visitation and development. The aforementioned panel of mountain tourism destination experts recognized the technological, socio-cultural, natural, political and legal environments as being important (Table 8.4).

Table 8.4      Factors and elements of mountain destination environments

| Technological environment | Reference |
| --- | --- |
| Mobile phone signal coverage | Kurihara and Okamoto, 2010 |
| Presence of Internet connection facilities and internet coverage | Buhalis and Law, 2008 |
| Acceptance of credit cards and presence of ATMs | Kurihara and Okamoto, 2010 |
| Efficient health/medical facilities | Briassoulis, 2002 |
| Efficient electricity infrastructure | Chaoqun, 2011 |
| Efficient water supply infrastructure | Gössling et al., 2012 |
| **Socio-cultural environment** | **Reference** |
| Presence of multilingual written instructions/guides (traffic signs, maps, restaurant menus) | Kurihara and Okamoto, 2010 |
| Ease of oral communication (in English or other languages) | Leslie and Russell, 2006 |
| Local managerial and staff skills | Pyo, 2005 |
| Hospitality of local population | Bornhorst et al., 2010 |
| Support for tourism development by local population | Yoon et al., 2001d |
| **Natural environment** | **Reference** |
| Carrying capacity | Schianetz et al., 2007 |
| Variety and diversity of terrains for different sports | Papadimitriou and Gibson, 2008 |
| Favourable climate conditions | Ritchie and Crouch, 2003 |
| Visual appeal | Whitlock et al., 1991 |
| **Political and legal environment** | **Reference** |
| Support of government at the regional level | McCool et al., 2001 |
| Support of government at the municipality level | McCool et al., 2001 |
| Efficiency of decision making | Pellinen, 2003 |
| Efficiency of regulatory framework | Robson and Robson, 1996 |

*Source*: Kuščer, 2011.

## Relations in the Mountain Destination Innovativeness Model

Some previous tourism destination research discusses relationships among the main categories of our MDIM. Volo (2005) stated that additional research is needed on destination level interactions with innovativeness. Weiermair (2003) and Paget, Dimanche and Mounet (2010) acknowledged the impact of innovativeness on mountain destination development. Crouch and Ritchie (1999) claimed that the effective usage of tourism environments can impact on destination competitiveness and development. Based on the above knowledge, the following hypotheses have been created (Figure 8.1):

*H1:* Mountain destination environments positively influence mountain destination innovativeness.

*H2:* Mountain destination environments positively influence mountain destination development.

*H3:* Mountain destination innovativeness positively influences mountain destination development.

*H4:* Mountain destination innovativeness partially mediates the relationship between mountain destination environments and mountain destination development.

## Method and Data

The data have been gathered by collecting the opinions of mountain destination managers from Alpine mountain destinations in Austria, France, Germany, Italy, Slovenia and Switzerland. In order to avoid problems with the language barrier, the survey was available in English, French, German, Italian and Slovenian. According to Crouch (2011), managers from destination management organizations (national tourism administrations, state or provincial tourism offices, regional tourism organizations, convention and visitor bureaux and similar types of bodies) possess appropriate knowledge for such research. The country of origin of the respondents and the number of completed surveys received are presented in Table 8.5.

**Table 8.5    Country of origin of the survey respondents**

| Country* | CH | SI | AT | IT | DE | FR | Sum |
|---|---|---|---|---|---|---|---|
| Number of cases | 31 | 30 | 27 | 18 | 11 | 10 | 127 |
| Share (%) | 24.4 | 23.6 | 21.3 | 14.2 | 8.7 | 7.9 | 100.0 |

*AT = Austria; CH = Switzerland; DE = Germany; FR = France; IT = Italy; SI = Slovenia (ISO (International Organization for Standardization 2-letter codes).

The problem of attaining proper and comparable numerical data in regard to innovativeness, environments and development in all destinations has been avoided by using a seven-point Likert scale (1 = Very unimportant, 2 = Unimportant, 3 = Slightly unimportant 4 = Neither unimportant nor important, 5 = Slightly important, 6 = Important, 7 = Very important), which is a common practice in tourism literature (Barquet, Osti, and Brida, 2010; Borchgrevink and Knutson, 1997; Peters, 1993). Respondents have been asked to grade the state of elements of the MDIM in their own destination in comparison to other mountain destinations. Using competitors to benchmark the performance measure is a widely used practice (Crouch, 2011; Enright and Newton, 2005).

First, validity and reliability analyses were performed, since it must be proven that the factors identified in previous research are a good fit for the data gathered from this sample. This was performed with a confirmatory factor analysis (CFA), which was also used to evaluate the measurement model. Analyses show that the convergent and discriminant validity is supported. For evaluating the measurement model and also for inputting the factors to LISREL, summated scales for each factor were created by averaging the elements comprising each factor. This technique is being applied increasingly frequently (Chen and Tsai, 2007; Chi and Qu, 2008) and is mainly advocated for two reasons (Hair, Black, Babin, and Anderson, 2010): it provides a means of overcoming, to some extent, the measurement error inherent in all measured variables, and has the ability to represent the multiple aspects of a concept in a single measure.

The LISREL model that analyses covariance structures has been used for the construction and testing of the MDIM. The LISREL model has been widely used to determine structural relationships; it has been used to measure performance (Vaughan, 1999; Vaughan and Tague-Sutcliffe, 1997) and innovativeness (Eickelpasch, Lejpras, and Stephan, 2007; Huang, Li and Chen, 2009). Research areas in which the LISREL model has been used indicate that it is an appropriate tool for measuring the relationships between the constructs of the MDIM.

## Analyses

Once the measurement model had been tested for validity and reliability, path coefficients were established. First, the data were examined using PRELIS to determine potential violations of assumptions underlying a structural equation model. Then, structural equation modelling with the maximum likelihood (ML) estimation method was applied for testing the model. In our case, the ML method has withstood the test of robustness and was chosen as the preferred method of estimation in the LISREL program, using a covariance matrix as an input.

Taking into account all of the goodness-of-fit measures, provided in Table 8.6, including their strengths and weaknesses, we can conclude that, though not achieving the most desirable levels of fit, the hypothesized model (as shown in Figure 8.2) does represent a quite acceptable fit to the empirical data.

Table 8.6     Goodness-of-fit measures for the research-based mountain destination innovativeness model

| Goodness-of-fit measures | Criteria | Value |
| --- | --- | --- |
| $\chi^2$ | p>0.05 | 89.450 (p=0.000) |
| $\chi^2$/df | <3.00 | 2.180 |
| RMSEA | <0.05 | 0.098 |
| GFI | >0.90 | 0.884 |
| AGFI | >0.90 | 0.813 |
| SRMR | <0.08 | 0.067 |
| CFI | >0.95 | 0.963 |
| IFI | >0.95 | 0.963 |
| NNFI | >0.95 | 0.950 |

Relationships between the latent constructs and their factors are also researched. Firstly, all factor loadings are significant (at $p<0.01$ or better), indicated by the $t$-values well in excess of 2.58 in absolute terms, thus validating the proposed relationships among latent constructs and their factors. Secondly, the SMCs for y-factors range from 0.257 to 0.682 and for x-factors from 0.221 to 0.650, indicating fairly high reliability of the measurement model. Lastly, the composite reliability (CR) for each latent construct surpasses the threshold value of 0.6 (Table 8.7) (Diamantopoulos and Siguaw, 2000), and we can therefore conclude that all factors provide reliable measurements of the related constructs.

Relationships between the endogenous and exogenous latent constructs are shown in Figure 8.2. The LISREL results show that all the paths proposed in the model are statistically significant (at $p<0.05$ or better), indicated by $t$-values well in excess of 1.96 in absolute terms, and of the appropriate direction (positive) (Diamantopoulos and Siguaw, 2000). Results in Figure 8.2 show that mountain destination environments positively influence

Table 8.7      LISREL results for measurement model

| Constructs and factors | Loading | Completely standardized loading | t-value | SMC | CR |
|---|---|---|---|---|---|
| Exogenous: mountain destination environments | | | | | 0.752 |
| Technological environment | 1.000 | 0.612 | – | 0.735 | |
| Socio-cultural environment | 1.080 | 0.716 | 6.223 | 0.512 | |
| Natural environment | 0.595 | 0.470 | 4.486 | 0.221 | |
| Political and legal environment | 1.308 | 0.806 | 6.678 | 0.650 | |
| Endogenous: mountain destination innovativeness | | | | | 0.832 |
| Socio-cultural sustainability and stakeholder participation | 1.000 | 0.798 | – | 0.637 | |
| Environmental sustainability | 1.040 | 0.742 | 8.500 | 0.551 | |
| Proactiveness | 1.347 | 0.826 | 9.509 | 0.682 | |
| Endogenous: mountain destination development | | | | | 0.787 |
| Preservation of natural environment | 1.000 | 0.507 | – | 0.257 | |
| Tourist traffic and expenditure | 1.953 | 0.769 | 5.411 | 0.591 | |
| Visitor satisfaction | 1.719 | 0.702 | 5.189 | 0.492 | |
| Socio-economic prosperity | 2.262 | 0.777 | 5.435 | 0.604 | |

mountain destination innovativeness and mountain destination development. Moreover, mountain destination innovativeness positively influences mountain destination development. Furthermore, since the introduction of the innovativeness construct lowers the path loading between the environments and development constructs from the initial 0.886 ($t$=4.495), it can also be concluded that mountain destination innovativeness partially mediates the relationship between mountain destination environments and mountain destination development. All three conditions for a construct to act as a mediator have been fulfilled: the paths are significant, and the introduction of

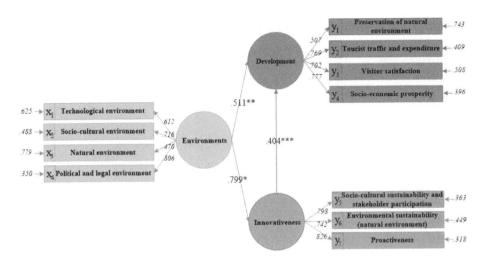

**Figure 8.2    The estimated mountain destination innovativeness model**

*Notes*: *Completely standardized coefficient; *t*-value = 5.798; **Completely standardized coefficient; *t*-value = 2.619; ***Completely standardized coefficient; *t*-value = 2.274
*Source*: The authors.

a mediator lowers the path loading between the independent construct and the dependent construct, while the direct path loading is still significant; hence the mediator has a partial effect (Baron and Kenny, 1986). As it is logical to assume that not all changes and trends in destination environments a priori benefit destination development, this mediating role of innovativeness becomes even more important, since it can amplify the positive changes and trends in the environments and mitigate the negative ones.

All hypotheses are therefore confirmed, indicating causal relationships among mountain destination environments, mountain destination innovativeness, and mountain destination development.

## Study Limitations and Recommendations for Further Research

The model has been developed based on the list of indicators, which have been perceived as important by a panel of around 200 mountain tourism destination experts. However, the structural equation model has been tested only on Alpine mountain destinations in Europe. In order to confirm the potential for wider application of the model, similar studies should be replicated elsewhere, for instance, in mountain destinations in North American or other Alpine destinations. The model therefore carries the potential of generalizability for mountain destinations.

It may be the case that environments and innovativeness have a lagged effect on mountain destination development. However, incorporating a time delay effect into the LISREL model would make the model overly complicated (Vaughan, 1999). Nevertheless, future research has potential for improvement in this area, and incorporating the time delay might provide even more accurate results.

This research was based on the opinions given by destination managers at mountain destinations. It would be worth expanding the research to examine the opinions from other stakeholders in mountain destinations. With such an approach, there is a possibility of benchmarking the results from different stakeholder groups. Future research could even focus on testing the perceptions of mountain destination development, innovativeness and environments from the tourists' perspective. However, there are considerable barriers to such an approach, such as the knowledge of tourists with regard to the destination elements. Nevertheless, with careful and consistent transformation of the elements into the consumers' perspective, these barriers can be substantially reduced.

## Conclusion

This chapter builds on previous research regarding the key indicators of tourism development, innovativeness and environments for mountain tourism destinations. Previous research findings have been expanded by using already developed indicators in order to study how to maintain and assure mountain destination development in the context of environmental changes and trends. The value of the research for mountain destination managers and other stakeholders in mountain destinations has been confirmed by demonstrating that more favourable environments and innovativeness together contribute to improved and sustainable mountain destination development. Moreover, more tourism-supporting environments also positively influence mountain destination innovativeness. However, the confirmed indirect impact of innovativeness on destination development that helps to mitigate the adverse environmental changes and to enhance positive environmental changes to the benefit of destination development represents a relevant input for destination managers. They can avoid strategic drift and assure continuous quantitative and qualitative destination growth if they follow changes and trends in the destination's development and constantly react and apply new (innovative) managerial solutions. The research suggests this because it has proved that the influence of environments on mountain destination development is partially mediated by innovativeness. Innovation at mountain destinations is a crucial factor for success, since more can be achieved with the same predispositions. More specifically, destination managers can innovate by optimizing the use of environmental resources, employ new information and communications technologies, and create an organizational structure that enables collaboration by all stakeholders. In this context, the list of innovativeness factors and the corresponding elements represent a useful tool for mountain destination managers.

The relationship between innovativeness and environments is complex, yet vital for destination management. First, changes in environments can have a negative impact on the development of destinations, which destinations with high innovativeness potential can mitigate. Innovativeness can therefore be used to reduce the negative impact of, for instance, a deteriorating natural environment, with the introduction of environmentally friendly technologies. Furthermore, this mediating ability of innovativeness can also emphasize the positive impact of environmental changes on destination development: the effect is therefore two-sided.

This research has also produced a tool that enables management at destinations to evaluate the state of their environments and provides the means of identifying and improving problematic areas in order to increase mountain destination development. Such approaches can better uncover strengths, weaknesses, opportunities and threats, and also aid in business and strategic planning. Evaluation and the improvement of development, innovativeness and environments can enable destinations to better cope with the rapidly changing environment and support sustainable destination development.

## Acknowledgments

This chapter has been written in the course of the doctoral dissertation research entitled 'Modeling mountain tourism destination development with focus on innovativeness'. We wish to thank Sašo Sever and Matic Jeločnik for their help with the chapter.

## References

Arslanturk, Y., Balcilar, M., and Ozdemir, Z.A. (2011). Time-varying linkages between tourism receipts and economic growth in a small open economy. *Economic Modelling*, 28(1–2), 664–671. doi: 10.1016/j.econmod.2010.06.003

B'Far, R. (2005). *Mobile Computing Principles: Designing and Developing Mobile Applications with UML and XML.* Cambridge: Cambridge University Press.

Baron, R.M., and Kenny, D.A. (1986). The moderator–mediator variable distinction in social psychological research: Conceptual, strategic, and statistical considerations. *Journal of Personality and Social Psychology*, 51(6), 1173–1182. doi: 10.1037/0022–3514.51.6.1173

Barquet, A., Osti, L., and Brida, J.G. (2010). Residents' attitudes and perceptions of tourism impacts and their policy implications. Working Paper Series, 1–14. Available at: http://ssrn.com/abstract=1559991 [accessed 15August 2011].

Barros, C.P., and Machado, L.P. (2010). The length of stay in tourism. *Annals of Tourism Research*, 37(3), 692–706. doi: 10.1016/j.annals.2009.12.005

Borchgrevink, C.P., and Knutson, B.J. (1997). Norway seen from abroad: Perceptions of Norway and Norwegian tourism – an image study. *Journal of Hospitality and Leisure Marketing*, 4(4), 25–46. doi: 10.1300/J150v04 n04_02

Bornhorst, T., Ritchie, J.R.B., and Sheehan, L. (2010). Determinants of tourism success for DMOs and destinations: An empirical examination of stakeholders' perspectives. *Tourism Management*, 31(5), 572–589. doi: 10.1016/j. tourman.2009.06.008

Bourdeau, P. (2009). Mountain tourism in a climate of change. In R. Jandl, A. Borsdorf, H. Van Miegroet, R. Lackner, and R. Psenner (eds), *Global Change and Sustainable Development in Mountain Regions* (39–52). Innsbruck: Innsbruck University Press.

Brandth, B., and Haugen, M.S. (2011). Farm diversification into tourism – Implications for social identity? *Journal of Rural Studies*, 27(1), 35–44. doi: 10.1016/j.jrurstud.2010.09.002

Briassoulis, H. (2002). Sustainable tourism and the question of the commons. *Annals of Tourism Research*, 29(4), 1065–1085. doi: 10.1016/ S0160–7383(02)00021-X

Brida, J.G., Osti, L., and Barquet, A. (2010). Segmenting resident perceptions towards tourism – a cluster analysis with a multinomial logit model of a mountain community. *International Journal of Tourism Research*, 12(5), 591–602. doi: 10.1002/jtr.778

Buhalis, D., and Law, R. (2008). Progress in information technology and tourism management: 20 years on and 10 years after the Internet – the state of eTourism research. *Tourism Management*, 29, 609–623. doi: 10.1016/j. tourman.2008.01.005

Castellani, V., and Sala, S. (2010). Sustainable performance index for tourism policy development. *Tourism Management*, 31(6), 871–880. doi: 10.1016/j. tourman.2009.10.001

Chaoqun, C. (2011). Researches on application of the renewable energy technologies in the development of low-carbon rural tourism. *Energy Procedia*, 5, 1722–1726. doi: 10.1016/j.egypro.2011.03.293

Charters, T., and Saxon, E. (2007). *Tourism and Mountains: A Practical Guide to Good Practice*. Paris: UNEP.

Chen, C.-F., and Tsai, D. (2007). How destination image and evaluative factors affect behavioral intentions? *Tourism Management*, 28(4), 1115–1122. doi: 10.1016/j.tourman.2006.07.007

Chi, C. G.-Q., and Qu, H. (2008). Examining the structural relationships of destination image, tourist satisfaction and destination loyalty: An integrated approach. *Tourism Management*, 29(4), 624–636. doi: 10.1016/j.tourman.2007.06.007

Choi, H.C., and Sirakaya, E. (2006). Sustainability indicators for managing community tourism. *Tourism Management*, 27(6), 1274–1289. doi: 10.1016/j.tourman.2005.05.018

Clarimont, S., and Vlès, V. (2009). Pyrenean tourism confronted with sustainable development: Partial and hesitant integration. *Revue de Géographie Alpine/ Journal of Alpine Research*, 97(3). Available at: http://rga.revues.org/978 [accessed 8 May 2010].

Crouch, G.I. (2011). Destination competitiveness: An analysis of determinant attributes. *Journal of Travel Research*, 50(1), 27–45. doi: 10.1177/0047287510362776

Crouch, G.I., and Ritchie, J.R.B. (1999). Tourism, competitiveness and societal prosperity. *Journal of Business Research*, 44(3), 137–152. doi: 10.1016/ S0148–2963(97)00196–3

Cruz, R. (2011). Preserving the natural environment. Available at: http://www. pikespeakqualityoflife.org/uploads/8/8/7/4/8874289/2011_qli_natural_ environment.pdf [accessed 15 February 2012].

Curto, J. (2006). *Resident Perceptions of Tourism in Rapidly Growing Mountain Tourism Destinations*. Waterloo, Canada: University of Waterloo.

Dávid, L. (2011). Tourism ecology: Towards the responsible, sustainable tourism future. *Worldwide Hospitality and Tourism Themes*, 3(3), 210–216. doi: 10.1108/17554211111142176

Debarbieux, B., and Price, M.F. (2008). Representing mountains: From local and national to global common good. *Geopolitics*, 13(1), 148–168. doi: 10.1080/14650040701783375

Diamantopoulos, A., and Siguaw, J. (2000). *Introducing Lisrel*. London: Sage Publications.

Dmitrović, T., Cvelbar, L.K., Kolar, T., Brencic, M.M., Ograjenšek, I., and Žabkar, V. (2009). Conceptualizing tourist satisfaction at the destination level. *International Journal of Culture, Tourism and Hospitality Research*, 3(2), 116–126. doi: 10.1108/17506180910962122

Dredge, D. (2006). Policy networks and the local organisation of tourism. *Tourism Management*, 27(2), 269–280. doi: 10.1016/j.tourman.2004.10.003

Dwyer, L., and Edwards, D. (2009). Tourism product and service innovation to avoid 'strategic drift'. *International Journal of Tourism Research*, 11(4), 321–335. doi: 10.1002/jtr.690

Dwyer, L., Edwards, D., Mistilis, N., Roman, C., and Scott, N. (2009). Destination and enterprise management for a tourism future. *Tourism Management*, 30(1), 63–74. doi: 10.1016/j.tourman.2008.04.002

Dwyer, L., Edwards, D., Mistilis, N., Roman, C., Scott, N., and Cooper, C. (2008). *Megatrends Underpinning Tourism to 2020: Analysis of Key Drivers for Change*. Gold Coast, Australia: Sustainable Tourism Cooperative Research Centre (STCRC).

Dwyer, L., and Kim, C. (2003). Destination competitiveness: Determinants and indicators. *Current Issues in Tourism*, 6(5), 369–414. doi: 10.1080/13683500308667962

Dwyer, L., Knežević Cvelbar, L., Edwards, D., and Mihalič, T. (2012). Fashioning a destination tourism future: The case of Slovenia. *Tourism Management*, 33(2), 305–316. doi: 10.1016/j.tourman.2011.03.010

Eickelpasch, A., Lejpras, A., and Stephan, A. (2007). Hard and soft location factors, innovativeness and firm performance. *Electronic Working Paper Series*, 109. Available at: http://www.infra.kth.se/cesis/documents/WP109.pdf [accessed 15 August 2010].

Enright, M.J., and Newton, J. (2005). Determinants of tourism destination competitiveness in Asia Pacific: Comprehensiveness and universality. *Journal of Travel Research*, 43(4), 339–350. doi: 10.1177/0047287505274647

Falk, M. (2013). Impact of long-term weather on domestic and foreign winter tourism demand. *International Journal of Tourism Research*, 15(1), 1–17. doi: 10.1002/jtr.865

Fallon, L.D., and Kriwoken, L.K. (2003). Community involvement in tourism infrastructure – The case of the Strahan Visitor Centre, Tasmania. *Tourism Management*, 24(3), 289–308. doi: 10.1016/S0261–5177(02)00072–9

Flagestad, A., and Hope, C.A. (2001). Strategic success in winter sports destinations: A sustainable value creation perspective. *Tourism Management*, 22(5), 445–461. doi: 10.1016/S0261–5177(01)00010–3

Franch, M., Martini, U., Buffa, F., and Parisi, G. (2008). 4L tourism (landscape, leisure, learning and limit): Responding to new motivations and expectations of tourists to improve the competitiveness of Alpine destinations in a sustainable way. *Tourism Review*, 63(1), 4–14. doi: 10.1108/16605370810861008

Gössling, S., Peeters, P., Hall, C.M., Ceron, J.-P., Dubois, G., Lehmann, L.V., and Scott, D. (2012). Tourism and water use: Supply, demand, and security.

An international review. *Tourism Management*, 33(1), 1–15. doi: 10.1016/j.tourman.2011.03.015

Govers, R., Go, F. M., and Kumar, K. (2007). Virtual destination image a new measurement approach. *Annals of Tourism Research*, 34(4), 977–997. doi: 10.1016/j.annals.2007.06.001

Gunya, A. (2007). *Cross-border cooperation at local level in the Alps, the Caucasus and the mountains of Central Asia*. Input for the Sixth Ministerial Conference 'Environment for Europe', Belgrade 2007. Available at: http://www.mtnforum.org/sites/default/files/pub/949.pdf [accessed 14 November 2011].

Hair, J.F., Black, W., Babin, B.J., and Anderson, R.E. (2010). *Multivariate Data Analysis*. 7th Edition. Upper Saddle River, NJ: Prentice Hall.

Heagle, A.L.B., Naterer, G.F., and Pope, K. (2011). Small wind turbine energy policies for residential and small business usage in Ontario, Canada. *Energy Policy*, 39(4), 1988–1999. doi: 10.1016/j.enpol.2011.01.028

Holden, A. (2000). Winter tourism and the environment in conflict: The case of Cairngorm, Scotland. *International Journal of Tourism Research*, 2(4), 247–260. doi: 10.1002/1522–1970(200007/08)2:4<247::aid-jtr214>3.0.co;2-x

Huang, Y.-H., Li, E.Y., and Chen, J.S. (2009). Information synergy as the catalyst between information technology capability and innovativeness: Empirical evidence from the financial service sector. *Information Research*, 14(1), paper 394. Available at: http://informationr.net/ir/14–1/paper394.html [accessed 22 March 2010].

Karamanis, D. (2011). Management of moderate wind energy coastal resources. *Energy Conversion and Management*, 52(7), 2623–2628. doi: 10.1016/j.enconman.2011.01.002

Kaynak, E., and Marandu, E.E. (2011). Variations in tourism market potential in an emerging economy: Theoretical perspectives and analytical insights. *Journal of Quality Assurance in Hospitality and Tourism*, 12(1), 1–27. doi: 10.1080/1528008x.2011.541814

Konu, H., Laukkanen, T., and Komppula, R. (2011). Using ski destination choice criteria to segment Finnish ski resort customers. *Tourism Management*, 32(5), 1096–1105. doi: 10.1016/j.tourman.2010.09.010

Kruk, E., Hummel, J., and Banskota, K. (eds) (2007). *Facilitating Sustainable Mountain Tourism*. Kathmandu, Nepal: International Centre for Integrated Mountain Development (ICIMOD).

Kuniyal, J.C. (2002). Mountain expeditions: Minimising the impact. *Environmental Impact Assessment Review*, 22(6), 561–81. doi: 10.1016/S0195–9255(02)00031–8

Kurihara, T., and Okamoto, N. (2010). Foreign visitor's evaluation on tourism environment. *Journal of the Eastern Asia Society for Transportation Studies*, 8(0), 912–925.

Kuščer, K. (2011). *Determining Factors of Mountain Destination Innovativeness. Proceedings of TTRA 2011 European: Creativity and Innovation in Tourism,* Archamps, France, 11–13 April 2011.

Kuščer, K. (2012). *Determining Indicators of Mountain Destination Development. Proceedings of TTRA Europe 2012: Performance Measurement and Management in Tourism,* Bilbao, Spain, 18–20 April 2012.

Kuščer, K. (2013). Determining factors of mountain destination innovativeness. *Journal of Vacation Marketing,* 19(1), 41–54. doi: 10.1177/1356766712461404

Kuščer, K., and Mihalič, T. (2011). *Determining Factors of Tourism Environments in Mountain Destinations. Proceedings of the World Research Summit for Tourism and Hospitality, Hong Kong, China, 10–13 December 2011.*

Lama, W.B., and Sattar, N. (2004). Mountain tourism and the conservation of biological and cultural diversity. In M. F. Price, L. Jansky and A.A. Iatsenia (eds), *Key Iissues for Mountain Areas* (111–148). Tokyo: United Nations University Press.

Lasanta, T., Laguna, M., and Vicente-Serrano, S.M. (2007). Do tourism-based ski resorts contribute to the homogeneous development of the Mediterranean mountains? A case study in the Central Spanish Pyrenees. *Tourism Management,* 28(5), 1326–1339. doi: 10.1016/j.tourman.2007.01.003

Lebe, S.S., and Milfelner, B. (2006). Innovative organisation approach to sustainable tourism development in rural areas. *Kybernetes: The International Journal of Systems and Cybernetics,* 35(7–8), 1136–1146. doi: 10.1108/03684920610675139

Leslie, D., and Russell, H. (2006). The importance of foreign language skills in the tourism sector: A comparative study of student perceptions in the UK and continental Europe. *Tourism Management,* 27(6), 1397–1407. doi: 10.1016/j.tourman.2005.12.016

Lin, T.-P. (2010). Carbon dioxide emissions from transport in Taiwan's national parks. *Tourism Management,* 31(2), 285–290. doi: 10.1016/j.tourman.2009.03.009

Lundberg, M.C. (2008). A word-of-mouth approach to informal information sharing among part-time and short-term employed front-line workers in tourism. *Journal of Vacation Marketing,* 14(1), 23–39. doi: 10.1177/1356766707084217

Macchiavelli, A. (2009). Alpine tourism: Development contradictions and conditions for innovation. *Revue de géographie alpine,* 97(1). Available at: http://rga.revues.org/index843.html [accessed 13 September 2010].

Marom, O., and Seidmann, A. (2011). Using 'last-minute' sales for vertical differentiation on the Internet. *Decision Support Systems,* 51(4), 894–903. doi: 10.1016/j.dss.2011.02.008

McCool, S.F., Moisey, R.N., and Nickerson, N.P. (2001). What should tourism sustain? The disconnect with industry perceptions of useful indicators. *Journal of Travel Research*, 40(2), 124–131. doi: 10.1177/004728750104000202

Meleghy, T., Preglau, M., and Tafertshofer, A. (1985). Tourism development and value change. *Annals of Tourism Research*, 12(2), 181–199. doi: 10.1016/0160–7383(85)90056–8

Mihalič, T. (2000). Environmental management of a tourist destination: A factor of tourism competitiveness. *Tourism Management*, 21(1), 65–78. doi: 10.1016/S0261–5177(99)00096–5

Mihalič, T. (2006). *Tourism and its Environments: Ecological, Economic and Political Sustainability Issues*. Ljubljana: Faculty of Economics, University of Ljubljana.

Mihalič, T. (2013). Performance of environmental resources of a tourist destination: Concept and application. *Journal of Travel Research*, 20(19), 1–17. doi: 10.1177/0047287513478505

Miller, G. (2001). The development of indicators for sustainable tourism: Results of a Delphi survey of tourism researchers. *Tourism Management*, 22(4), 351–362. doi: 10.1016/S0261–5177(00)00067–4

Müller, H., and Weber, F. (2008). Climate change and tourism – scenario analysis for the Bernese Oberland in 2030. *Tourism Review*, 63(3), 57–71. doi: 10.1108/16605370810901580

Nepal, S.K., and Chipeniuk, R. (2005). Mountain tourism: Toward a conceptual framework. *Tourism Geographies*, 7(3), 313–333. doi: 10.1080/14616680500 164849

Nordic Centre for Spatial Development (2004). *Mountain Areas in Europe: Analysis of Mountain Areas in EU Member States, Acceding and other European Countries*. Available at: http://ec.europa.eu/regional_policy/sources/docgener/studies/pdf/montagne/mount1.pdf [accessed 18 June 2012].

O'Neill, J.W., and Mattila, A.S. (2006). Strategic hotel development and positioning: The effects of revenue drivers on profitability. *Cornell Hotel and Restaurant Administration Quarterly*, 47(2), 146–154. doi: 10.1177/0010880405281519

Paget, E., Dimanche, F., and Mounet, J.-P. (2010). A tourism innovation case: An actor-network approach. *Annals of Tourism Research*, 37(3), 828–847. doi: 10.1016/j.annals.2010.02.004

Papadimitriou, D., and Gibson, H. (2008). Benefits sought and realized by active mountain sport tourists in Epirus, Greece: Pre- and post-trip analysis. *Journal of Sport and Tourism*, 13(1), 37–60. doi: 10.1080/14775080801972056

Pechlaner, H. (1999). The competitiveness of Alpine destinations between market pressure and problems of adaptation. *Turizam*, 47(4), 332–343.

Pellinen, J. (2003). Making price decisions in tourism enterprises. *International Journal of Hospitality Management*, 22(2), 217–235. doi: 10.1016/S0278–4319(03)00019–7

Perdue, R.R. (2002). Perishability, yield management, and cross-product elasticity: A case study of deep discount season passes in the Colorado ski industry. *Journal of Travel Research*, 41(1), 15–22. doi: 10.1177/0047287502041001003

Peters, M. (1993). Succession in tourism family business: The motivation of succeeding family members. *Tourism Review*, 60(4), 12–18. doi: 10.1108/eb058461

Pyo, S. (2005). Knowledge map for tourist destinations – Needs and implications. *Tourism Management*, 26(4), 583–594. doi: 10.1016/j.tourman.2004.03.001

Reilly, J., Williams, P., and Haider, W. (2010). Moving towards more eco-efficient tourist transportation to a resort destination: The case of Whistler, British Columbia. *Research in Transportation Economics*, 26(1), 66–73. doi: 10.1016/j.retrec.2009.10.009

Ritchie, J.R.B., and Crouch, G.I. (2003). *The Competitive Destination: A Sustainable Tourism Perspective*. Wallingford: CABI Publishing.

Robson, J., and Robson, I. (1996). From shareholders to stakeholders: Critical issues for tourism marketers. *Tourism Management*, 17(7), 533–540. doi: 10.1016/S0261–5177(96)00070–2

Schianetz, K., Kavanagh, L., and Lockington, D. (2007). The learning tourism destination: The potential of a learning organisation approach for improving the sustainability of tourism destinations. *Tourism Management*, 28(6), 1485–1496. doi: 10.1016/j.tourman.2007.01.012

Shih, C., Nicholls, S., and Holecek, D.F. (2009). Impact of weather on downhill ski lift ticket sales. *Journal of Travel Research*, 47(3), 359–372. doi: 10.1177/0047287508321207

Smerecnik, K.R., and Andersen, P.A. (2011). The diffusion of environmental sustainability innovations in North American hotels and ski resorts. *Journal of Sustainable Tourism*, 19(2), 171–196. doi: 10.1080/09669582.2010.517316

Stamboulis, Y., and Skayannis, P. (2003). Innovation strategies and technology for experience-based tourism. *Tourism Management*, 24(1), 35–43. doi: 10.1016/S0261–5177(02)00047-X

Sun, Y.-Y., and Stynes, D.J. (2006). A note on estimating visitor spending on a per-day/ night basis. *Tourism Management*, 27(4), 721–725. doi: 10.1016/j.tourman.2005.04.008

Tam, J.L.M. (2004). Customer satisfaction, service quality and perceived value: An integrative model. *Journal of Marketing Management*, 20(7–8), 897–917. doi: 10.1362/0267257041838719

UNWTO (2004). *Indicators of Sustainable Development for Tourism Destinations: A Guidebook*. Madrid: World Tourism Organisation.

UNWTO and UNEP (2008). *Climate Change and Tourism – Responding to Global Challenges*. Madrid: United Nations World Tourism Organization and the United Nations Environment Programme.

Vanhove, N. (2011). *The Economics of Tourism Destinations*. 2nd Edition. London: Elsevier.

Vaughan, L.Q. (1999). The contribution of information to business success: A LISREL model analysis of manufacturers in Shanghai. *Information Processing and Management*, 35(2), 193–208. doi: 10.1016/S0306–4573(98)00048-X

Vaughan, L.Q., and Tague-Sutcliffe, J. (1997). Measuring the impact of information on development: A LISREL-based study of small businesses in Shanghai. *Journal of American Society for Information Science*, 48(10), 917–931. doi: 10.1002/(sici)1097–4571(199710)48:10<917::aid-asi6>3.0.co;2–4

Volo, S. (2005). Tourism destination innovativeness. In P. Keller and T. Bieger (eds), *Innovation in Tourism – Creating Customer Value* (Vol. 47: 199–211). St. Gallen: AIEST.

Wang, C.L., and Ahmed, P.K. (2004). The development and validation of the organizational innovativeness construct using confirmatory factor analysis. *European Journal of Innovation Management*, 7(4), 303–313. doi: 10.1108/14601060410565056

Weiermair, K. (2003). *Product Improvement or Innovation: What is the Key to Success in Tourism?* Paper presented at the OECD Conference on Innovation and Growth in Tourism, Lugano, Switzerland.

Whitlock, W., Van Romer, K., and Becker, R.H. (1991). *Nature Based Tourism: An Annotated Bibliography*. Clemson, SC: Strom Thurmond Institute, Regional Development Group.

Woodside, A.G., Vicente, R.M., and Duque, M. (2011). Tourism's destination dominance and marketing website usefulness. *International Journal of Contemporary Hospitality Management*, 23(4), 552–564. doi: 10.1108/09596111111130038

Yaw Jr. F. (2005). Cleaner technologies for sustainable tourism: Caribbean case studies. *Journal of Cleaner Production*, 13(2), 117–134. doi: 10.1016/j.jclepro.2003.12.019

Yoon, Y., Gursoy, D., and Chen, J.S. (2001). Validating a tourism development theory with structural equation modeling. *Tourism Management*, 22(4), 363–372. doi: 10.1016/S0261–5177(00)00062–5

Zhang, X., Wu, B., Ling, F., Zeng, Y., Yan, N., and Yuan, C. (2010). Identification of priority areas for controlling soil erosion. *CATENA*, 83(1): 76–86. doi: 10.1016/j.catena.2010.06.012

## Chapter 9

# Drivers of Innovation in Tourism – From Imitation to Adaptation? *An Interview with Josef Margreiter, Managing Director of the Tyrolean Tourism Board*

ELISA INNERHOFER and HARALD PECHLANER

This chapter discusses driving forces of innovation in tourism and describes which special forms of innovation occur in the tourism sector and how innovation processes are addressed in tourism businesses. After a short introduction, the chapter continues with a brief theoretical discussion of forces that drive innovation in tourism. In this context, the market-based view and its counterpart, the resource-based view, with a special focus on the dynamic capability approach, is presented. The main body of the chapter consists of an interview conducted by the authors.

The interview shows that internal as well as external, and tangible as well as intangible factors are driving forces of innovation. Besides the customers and their feedbacks, human resources are crucial prerequisites for the development of successful innovation. It can be observed that tourism acquires knowledge and competences from other industries and that imitation is a special mode of innovation in tourism. Furthermore, it emphasizes that the ability to adapt imitated ideas is a key resource for achieving sustainable success and above-average performance through innovation.

## Background

Even if the tourism industry in the 1970s and 1980s was not perceived as being very innovative (Peters and Weiermair, 2002; Peters and Pikkemaat,

2005; Pikkemaat and Peters, 2005), structural changes in the tourism industry do occur – tourism businesses regularly alter their product portfolio and new products and services appear on the market. The Walt Disney Company, for example, introduced media-synergized theme parks, attracting not only locals but also a global interest (Weth, 2007). Thomas Cook, a pioneer of tourism, developed a concept that included travel and entertainment for a new target group and implemented an organizational system that allowed him to provide tourism services at appropriate prices (Brendon, 1991; Hjalager, 2010). The innovative aspect of Thomas Cook's contribution to the development of tourism and travelling was that he gave customers the option to choose services on a modular basis, to buy a variety of travel services from one source and to claim travel discounts. With these offerings, he paved the way for mass tourism (Mundt, 2014). This raises the question of which forces drive innovation in tourism.

Several global social and economic dynamics and trends influence employment, consumer behaviour, demographic behaviour, the living conditions of societies and, last but not least, the development of the economy. One major factor of change and development in almost all industries and service sectors is technological progress – the use of new technologies, especially new uses of information and communications technologies (Volo, 2004; Christensen, 1997, 2011). New technologies and digitalization affect several aspects of business, society, entertainment, etc. and are crucial to how products and services are produced, designed and distributed. In tourism new forms of business have appeared. New uses of information and communications technologies in the tourism industry pose the challenge of adapting daily business to changed framework requirements, for example, in the hotel industry (Aldebert, Dang, and Longhi, 2011). As well as new technological skills, businesses are having to develop new management and interactive skills relating to their relationships with employees and customers (Weiermair, 2006).

A second main factor of changing markets are changing values and their impact on customer requirements. New products and services are introduced into the market that would not have brought returns several years ago. With new accommodation concepts and product offerings like serviced apartments, tourism businesses try to satisfy the changing needs of customers (Eger, 2008). For quite some time, tour operators have been committed to the principle of sustainable tourism and they launch online platforms, where they guarantee customers environmentally sound and socially acceptable products and offers (Forum Anders Reisen, 2015). Radical changes in customer needs and requirements followed by changing demands put pressure on tourism businesses and boost their drive for innovation.

## Driving Forces in the Context of Strategic Management Approaches

Besides new technologies and changing values, other forces drive innovation. According to Arzeni (2006), competition is the main driving force of innovation in tourism. Innovation literature in general also highlights the importance of competitive interaction for search activities, innovation and learning (Aime, Johnson, Rigde, and Hill, 2010; White, 1981). This theoretical perception underlines the core argument of the market-based view of strategic management (Hill and Jones, 2012). The market-based approach deals with the general principle that a firm's strategic orientation is geared towards competitors and customers. Customers' needs and requirements, as well as competitors' products and offers, are indications and points of reference for product development and innovation (Greenley, 1995; Rasche and Wolfrum, 1994). According to this interpretation, successful market-based innovation would best be achieved by customer integration in innovation processes and by observing competitors.

Open innovation and the integration of external sources have become increasingly important (Gyurácz-Németh, Friedrich and Clarke, 2013; Grissemann, Pikkemaat and Weger, 2013; Döpfer, 2013) – as, for example, for the automotive industry (Rese, Saenn, and Homfeldt, 2015), or for the development of new technologies (Enkel, Perez-Freije, and Gassmann, 2005). Critics of the market-based view point out that a one-sided and strong strategic orientation towards markets leads to the development of products and services, which are easy to imitate and thus may not assure sustainable competitive advantages (Saá-Pérez and García-Falcón, 2002). As an alternative to the market-based view, the resource-based view of strategic management argues that firms should look inside the company and take the firm's tangible and intangible resources as sources of competitive advantages (Talaja, 2012). This approach assumes that organizations may achieve superior organizational performance by using the company-specific bundle of resources as a starting point for the development of products and services (Wernerfeldt, 1984; Rasche and Wolfrum, 1994). The resource-based view asserts that strategic and competitive advantages derive from the existence of heterogeneous, intra-organizational, company-specific resources (Wernerfeldt, 1984; Freiling, 2001).

Studies of the driving forces of innovation in tourism highlight the importance of customer integration in the form of customer feedback loops (Innerhofer, 2012; Grissemann, Pikkemaat and Weger, 2013) and (creative) imitation from competitors (Pompl and Buer, 2006; Frehse, 2005; Mukoyama, 2003) for search activities and innovation. Imitation can help small and medium-sized companies in reaching competitiveness (Hoelzl, Pechlaner, and Laesser,

2005). In order to ensure sustainable success through innovation, knowledge and competences from other industries should be acquired. The transfer of knowledge is an important managerial competence. It refers to the integration of benchmarks and competences from other industries into the company's own network of competences. By applying this strategy, managers critically analyse and review their own competence base. This allows them to learn from other industries and makes innovation an ongoing learning process (Pechlaner, 2010). Cohen and Levinthal (1990) talk about the 'ability of a firm to recognize the value of new, external information, assimilate it and apply it to commercial ends' and call this ability an 'absorptive capacity', which is crucial for a firm's innovative capabilities. Thus, successful innovations emerge when ideas are not simply imitated but combined with the firm's resources and core competences. This combination requires flexibility and dynamic capabilities, which allow companies to be adaptable to changing environments (Meffert, 1999; Burmann, 2001). In the tradition of the resource-based view, dynamic capabilities are those by which managers integrate, build, and reconfigure internal and external competences to address dynamic markets (Teece, Pisano, and Shuen, 1997; Easterby-Smith, Lyles, and Peteraf, 2009). The dynamics of organizational competences and capabilities are an important prerequisite for the evolvement of competences and for innovation development. Eisenhardt and Martin (2000) describe dynamic capabilities as processes embedded in companies that create value by manipulating resources into new value-creating strategies (innovations). These capabilities are similar across successful organizations and thus have greater homogeneity across organizations and firms than the resource base has according to the resource-based view. Due to this substitutability across companies, dynamic capabilities are not the source for competitive advantages, but the value for above-average performance lies in the resource and competence configuration that they create (Eisenhardt and Martin, 2000).

The insights into dynamic capabilities combined with the imitation discussion lead to the conclusion that the ability to adapt and improve can be seen as dynamic capability. The ability to adapt allows the reconfiguration of the organization's resource base in order to meet changing market conditions and to achieve competitive advantages (Zahra and George, 2002). Thus, the ability to adapt is the collection of abilities to recognize the value of external knowledge, incorporated in the imitated idea, and to combine this information with the resource base, finalized in the commercial outcome. According to this interpretation, the ability to adapt can be identified as an absorptive capacity (Cohen and Levinthal, 1990).

Based on the above analysis, innovation processes in tourism can be described as 'adoption–adaptation–improvement' processes (Innerhofer, 2012; Mukoyama, 2003). This assumes that an imitation undergoes a further development within the company in order to succeed as an innovation. In this process organizational learning occurs. Based on the knowledge companies obtain from others, they often develop new products (Mukoyama, 2003).

In summary, tourism businesses need knowledge about competitors, customers and markets as the learning environment in which they operate, and their own organizational, entrepreneurial and human resources and competences to realize innovations and to create and sustain competitive advantages.

## Interview

The following is a summary of an interview with the director of the regional tourism organization of the Austrian federal state of Tyrol, Josef Margreiter, carried out by the authors. Tyrol has a long tradition and history of tourism. The region has long been a destination for tourists in search of culture, leisure, recreation and experiences. Since the beginning of the 20th century ski resorts have constituted one of the main driving forces behind tourism. Nowadays, Tyrol is known as a popular destination for winter sports – most innovations in winter tourism in Austria were implemented for the first time in the western federal states of Tyrol, Salzburg and Vorarlberg (Job and Mayer, 2005). Its capital, Innsbruck, twice hosted the Olympic Winter Games (in 1964 and 1976), which constituted important landmarks for the development of tourism in the region. Offerings in the hospitality and lodgings sector cover tourist accommodation on farms and in bed and breakfast hotels, as well as health resorts and luxury wellness and spa hotels (Forcher, 2014). As a popular winter destination Tyrol accounts for 44.9 million overnight stays and 10.2 million arrivals (2013/2014) (Tirol Werbung GmbH, 2015). It was one of the first tourist destinations to build a destination brand and it is still a pioneering Alpine region in new product development and innovation in tourism (Forcher, 2014; Standortagentur Tirol and Institut für innovativen Tourismus, 2012; HTW Chur Hochschule für Technik und Wirtschaft, 2012). Josef Margreiter explains his perception of driving forces of innovation in tourism and gives an overview of innovation and innovativeness in tourism in Tyrol.[1]

### What is innovation in tourism? What is driving innovation and how are innovations in tourism created? How do they appear?

Over the last few decades, one of the most important driving forces of innovation in Alpine tourism has been courageous and active entrepreneurship,

---

1   The interview, conducted in German, was translated and edited by the authors.

which has helped the agricultural regions to prosperity and wealth. Innovative entrepreneurs developed new product and business ideas and many imitators appeared. This led to highly intensive competition in tourism, which in turn pushed tourism businesses and companies to innovate in order to develop unique selling points and to gain competitive advantages. However, most tourism businesses do not carry out a detailed analysis and they operate without any strategic planning.

### Would you say that innovations in tourism are most of the time ad hoc innovations without strategically managed innovation processes?

Exactly, usually tourism businesses act on an ad hoc basis. Most of the hotel businesses in Tyrol and the entire Alpine region are small and medium-sized enterprises. The entrepreneur collects ideas, concentrates on inspiration and brings the two together. In the end, an entrepreneur relies on 'gut feeling', instead of continually analysing and casting doubt on new projects. I believe that this is the reason why Alpine entrepreneurs have been so successful. They are willing to take some risk. That is the strong sense of entrepreneurship.

### Which role are other industries and sectors playing in the development of innovation in tourism?

Industry outsiders and impacts from outside the tourism sector are very important drivers of innovation in tourism. Architects, for example, often have a completely different lifestyle and corporate culture from tourism companies and entrepreneurs. Let me give another example: In Lermoos, a village in Tyrol, we have a very successful children's hotel called Alpenrose Kinder Hotel. The owners were teachers when they inherited the little bed and breakfast establishment from their parents. They developed a very professional family hotel focusing on the needs and requirements of children and parents. Besides the fact that they used their knowledge acquired in their profession as teachers, the couple's strong sense of entrepreneurship played an important role.

Therefore, many innovative ideas come from outside the tourism sector, but tourism businesses are very successful in integrating them and adapting the ideas to their own businesses. More and more tourism providers look outside their own, sectors, especially to areas of industry. For example, one destination, Sölden, is interested in attracting visitors from the automotive world and the cruise industry and in the development of the theme and adventure parks. They think outside the box. In Seefeld, another destination in Tyrol, they implemented an interdisciplinary summit meeting called 'Tourism meets Industry', where industrial companies and tourism businesses come together, network and discuss themes which are of mutual interest. Crossover observations occur.

Furthermore, tourism businesses, in general, have a high sensitivity for social trends, more than companies from other sectors, because they have direct contact with their customers and get regular feedback on guests' satisfaction with the services. In response to the low fat diet trend, hotel kitchens implemented new menus very rapidly. Tourism businesses observe their competitors and take over those things at which the others are successful.

## Could this method be described as 'creative imitation'?

I would call it 'adaptation'. They observe competitors and monitor trends, and then they adapt existing ideas to their own businesses. Besides that, it is the competition between hotel businesses within a destination which drives creativity and contributes to innovation. In a competitive landscape in which companies observe each other's strategies, the superior performance of one actor forces a search for responses by its competitors. Especially in destinations with a high density of hotels, they push each other. As soon as one hotel has introduced a new service or offer, the neighbouring hotel has to react. If there is just one innovative and successful actor in a destination, he has no incentive to go further and he tends to rest on his success.

We talked about innovative entrepreneurship as a key component of Alpine tourism. The innovative entrepreneurs are courageous and willing to bear a certain risk, they are open-minded, think outside the box, collect innovative ideas and adapt them to their own businesses. These are often ad hoc activities without clearly planned and strategically managed processes of innovation. Thinking about governance instruments – what can be done at a destination level? What should be managed or governed from outside to increase innovativeness in tourism?

There is already some governance from outside. However, I believe that we should focus more on education, information and awareness training. Tourism actors often are not aware of the fact that, for example, art and architecture are quality drivers and fuel for innovation that can be used in the development of tourism products. Or they do not know how to sustainably capitalize on rural culture to add value to tourism. How should they know all the technical solutions and digital media they could use in their daily businesses? Education is an essential factor and it should be more diverse and varied. It should be approached from a holistic point of view. Excellent, modern hotel architecture is not enough, the building has to be integrated harmoniously into the landscape and into the regional context and it has to have a certain functionality plus a unique identity to fulfil its intended purpose.

Nowadays, there is some governance through training and education measures. The many different training trips and travel offered for tourism actors did not exist until 20 years ago. Excursions became very important for companies. If entrepreneurs know what is going on outside their little world, they can create their own profiles. Besides regular study tours, visits to conferences and events are increasing as well and consultancies are becoming more and more popular.

## The South Tyrolean Tourism Board (Agentur Südtirol Marketing – SMG) organizes excursions for hoteliers and employees of tourism organizations to emphasize the importance of innovative development. Has the Tourism Board implemented an initiative to foster innovation?

Yes, we have an initiative for our staff members. We have an ideas workshop. Every employee can present ideas which are evaluated in a neutral way through a professional process. The employee experiences recognition, which in turn leads to improved performance. Employee participation to foster innovation is part of our corporate culture. In addition, it is an important aspect of employer branding, which is crucial in tourism. The tourism industry is a service industry where people work with people. Tourism businesses need good and appropriately qualified and committed employees, who like to work with humans. Hence, the tourism industry has to present itself on the labour market as a competitive employer offering attractive places to work. This is a big challenge, because working hours are not very attractive, especially in the hospitality sector. People have to work when all the others have time off. This has to be compensated for with extra benefits. What I want to say is that staff are a crucial success factor in tourism and can be a driver of innovation. It is our task and responsibility to present our industry as an attractive one to work in.

## The employee is one side of the service offer; on the other side is the customer. As production and consumption of a service occurs simultaneously, they need each other to provide services. If employees can be drivers of innovation, what about guests? Does co-creation of innovation occur?

What we increasingly notice is that employees participating in our programme (ideas workshop) often perceive guests not just as consumers but also as 'prosumers'. This is especially important for hotel businesses. The exchange with guests and in particular with repeat visitors takes place almost daily or at least regularly. This feedback loop in combination with the monitoring of behaviour changes and social developments and trends is one of the key prerequisites for the development of successful innovation.

### Trend researchers identified digitalization and changing values as two key megatrends influencing the development of tourism. Do you agree? How does the tourism industry in Tyrol tackle these developments, or how does tourism deal with them? Would you consider the destination an early adopter or a creative adopter?

The tourism industry is not an early adopter, in my opinion it is somewhere in the middle, like lots of consumer goods industries. One of the key drivers is definitely the digitalization and, compared to other destinations, Tyrol is here a pioneering region. Hotels and tourism businesses were much faster in going online than those in other destinations. We created the Tirol Information System – TIS – in 1990 and pioneered the new Internet after 1995 with Tiscover, which is a now privatized online platform that offers bookable accommodation in the Alpine region and back office solutions for tourism organizations (Tiscover, 2015). Meanwhile social media has become another very important communications tool. The best advertising for destinations and hotels has always been word-of-mouth promotion and social media is something like the digital and online version of word-of-mouth communication. People assess, evaluate, communicate and share their pictures, videos and experiences in hotels and at destinations. Information technology and technological systems were implemented very fast in the daily routines of Tyrolean tourism and hospitality industries. They perceived and recognized corporate communication as a key success factor.

The second trend you mentioned, the changing values, have a direct and very strong impact on innovation and developments in tourism. They determine the needs and requirements and thus the demands of guests. The combination of digitalization and changing values leads to new business models and a new 'sharing economy', such as couch surfing. More and more people consider it a valuable alternative to stay with locals instead of booking a hotel and they appreciate the hospitality offered by those people.

Therefore I would emphasize that the most important driving force of innovation in tourism, particularly in hotel and leisure tourism, are guests. They represent changing values, express needs and requirements, put pressure on providers to look for alternatives and drive the development in one specific direction.

## Which target or guest group can provide the most significant innovation inputs or new impulses?

Guests visiting mountain regions and destinations like Tyrol often come from cities and urban areas, where social developments and trends appear earlier than in rural areas. The observation of these types of guests can help to better understand societies. These trendsetters are usually between 25 and 45 years old and often work in sectors influenced by the creative industry, technology and design, fashion, art, and entertainment.

## On the supply side in the IT industry, for example, Apple tells its competitors and its clients what they need. Other IT companies notice the trend and produce similar products.

Yes, but the crucial point regarding innovation in tourism is that tourism providers in most cases do not entirely imitate, they adapt. The digitalization megatrend produces increasing transparency for the customer. This transparency is another driver of innovation in tourism. There is more transparency regarding quality and the price than ever before. Customers can find evaluations and pictures of hotels and destinations on the Internet and gather information, pictures and videos posted by other users. From the guest's perspective, this information seems to be more credible than that distributed by the provider. Comparisons can be carried out easily and quickly. The same applies to prices. This focuses attention on the price/performance ratio and increases the competition between hotels and destinations. Providers are forced to secure high customer satisfaction and to create unique selling points to justify a certain price level. Transparency puts pressure on hotels, restaurants and other service businesses to develop new services, which cannot be compared with services offered by competitors. This brings me to the point: owing to transparency in favour of the customer, it is not enough to imitate competitors; rather, ideas or products have to be adapted creatively. Hotel businesses can pick up ideas from competitors, but they have to bring them in line with their own resources, competences and identities. They must adapt them to the expectations of their guests. The further implementation of an innovation through the utilization of one's own or otherwise exclusive resources and competences makes it excessively difficult for competitors to imitate the innovation.

This is why I would say that successful innovations in tourism are successful adaptations rather than successful imitations of ideas developed by competitors or by entrepreneurs from other sectors.

## Conclusion

This interview shows that external market-related factors, as well as internal company-related forces, have a direct impact on the innovativeness of tourism businesses and destinations. Furthermore, imitation and innovative sourcing may be a successful way for small and medium-sized tourism businesses to be innovative. In general, the innovation management literature highlights the importance of a comprehensive strategic concept for managing innovation processes (from the generation of ideas to market launch) (Trout and Wied, 2014). While most innovations in Alpine tourism businesses are ad hoc and introduced without developing an adequate strategic response, managerial and entrepreneurial qualities are important prerequisites. Thus, innovation is often the result of successful innovative activities of a single entrepreneur who was courageous enough to open a special hotel or to offer a new service. However, two of the most crucial elements in the innovation process are customers and qualified employees, who have to interact in order to produce and consume the service in question.

Compared to other industries, like the manufacturing sectors, for example, innovation in tourism takes on completely different features. Innovation in tourism rarely has a radical dimension, but comes about mostly through incremental changes (Gyurácz-Németh, Friedrich and Clarke, 2013). To create innovative tourism offers, it is important for those formulating such offers to look outside their own sectors. Imitation is a valuable alternative to being innovative, but in order to achieve better performances on a long-term basis, adaptation has to follow. The ability to adapt can be identified as a dynamic capability. Next to flexibility, the ability to adapt is essential for tourism businesses to adjust to changing conditions and to alter the resource base for processes of change. The ability to modify and adapt new products and services through the use of company-specific resources and competences, rather than simply imitate new products and services used by other industries and competitors is a key resource for successful innovation and sustainable competitive advantage.

With regard to digital technologies, social media platforms become progressively more significant as communications tools and this constitutes a trend with enormous potential for tourism. Those organizations and businesses which have the resources and competences as well as the ability to alter the resource base and to react quickly to changing conditions may achieve competitive advantages.

## References

Aime, F., Johnson, S., Ridge, J.W., and Hill, A.D. (2010). The routine may be stable but the advantage is not: Competitive implications of key employee mobility. *Strategic Management Journal*, 31, 75–87.

Aldebert, B., Dang, R.J., and Longhi, C. (2011). Innovation in the tourism industry: The case of Tourism@. *Tourism Management*, 32, 1204–1213.

Arzeni, S. (2006). Foreword. In OECD – Organisation for Economic Co-operation and Development (ed.), *Innovation and Growth in Tourism* (3), Paris: OECD.

Brendon, P. (1991). *Thomas Cook: 150 Years of Popular Tourism*. London: Secker & Warburg.

Burmann, Ch. (2001). Strategische Flexibilität und Strategiewechsel in turbulenten Märkten. Neue theoretische Ansätze zur Unternehmensflexibilität. *Die Betriebswirtschaft*, 61(2), 169–188.

Christensen, C.M. (1997). *The Innovator's Dilemma: When New Technologies Cause Great Firms to Fail*. Cambridge, Massachusetts: Harvard Business School.

Christensen, C.M. (2011). *The Innovator's Dilemma: The Revolutionary Book That Will Change the Way You Do Business*. New York: Harper Business.

Cohen, W.M., and Levinthal, D.A. (1990). Absorptive capacity: A new perspective on learning and innovation. *Administrative Science Quarterly*, 35, 128–152.

Döpfer, B. (2013). *Co-Innovation Competence. A Strategic Approach to Entrepreneurship in Regional Innovation Structures*. Wiesbaden: Gabler.

Easterby-Smith, M., Lyles, M.A., and Peteraf, M.A. (2009). Dynamic capabilities: Current debates and future directions. *British Journal of Management*, 20, 1–8.

Eisenhardt, K.M. and Martin, J.A. (2000). Dynamic Capabilities: What are They? *Strategic Management Journal*, 21, 1105–1121.

Enkel, E., Perez-Freije, J., and Gassmann, O. (2005). Minimizing market risks through customer integration in new product development: Learning from bad practice. *Creativity and Innovation Management*, 14(4), 425–437.

Forcher, M. (2014). *Zu Gast im Herzen der Alpen: Eine Bildgeschichte des Tourismus in Tirol*. Innsbruck: Haymon Verlag.

Frehse, J. (2005). Innovative product development in hotel operations. *Journal of Quality Assurance in Hospitality and Tourism*, 6(3/4), 129–146.

Freiling, J. (2001). *Ressourcenorientierte Reorganizationn: Problemanalyse und Change Management auf der Basis des Resource-based View*. Wiesbaden: Gabler.

Greenley, G. (1995). Forms of market orientation in UK companies. *Journal of Management Studies*, 32(1), 47–66.

Grissemann, U.S., Pikkemaat, B., and Weger, C. (2013). Antecedents of innovation activities in tourism: An empirical investigation of the Alpine hospitality industry. *Tourism*, 61(6), 7–27.

Gyurácz-Németh, P., Friedrich, N., and Clarke, A. (2013). *Innovation in Special Hotels as a Key to Success. Active Citizenship by Knowledge Management and Innovation. Proceedings of the Management, Knowledge and Learning, International Conference* 2013, 643–653.

Hill, C.W.L., and Jones, G.R. (2012). *Strategic Management. An Integrated Approach.* Mason, Ohio: South Western CENGAGE Learning.

Hjalager, A.-M. (2010). A review of innovation research in tourism. *Tourism Management*, 31, 1–12.

Hoelzl, B, Pechlaner, H., and Laesser, C. (2005). Imitation processes of SMEs – A special form of innovation? In P. Keller; and T. Bieger (eds), *Innovation in Tourism – Creating Customer Value* (311–332). St. Gallen: E-Druck AG St. Gallen.

Innerhofer, E. (2012). *Strategische Innovationen in der Hotellerie. Eine ressourcenorientierte Fallstudienanalyse touristischer Dienstleistungsunternehmen.* Wiesbaden: Springer Gabler Verlag.

Job, H., and Mayer, M. (2005). Spatial and temporal diffusion patterns of innovation in tourism – the example of ropeways and ski lifts in the Austrian Alps. In P. Keller and T. Bieger (eds), *Innovation in Tourism – Creating Customer Value* (262–276). St. Gallen: E-Druck St. Gallen.

Meffert, H. (1999). Größere Flexibilität als Unternehmenskonzept. *Marktorientierte Unternehmensführung im Wandel*, 467–488.

Mundt, J.W. (2014). *Thomas Cook. Pionier des Tourismus.* Konstanz: UVK Verlagsgesellschaft.

Mukoyama, T. (2003). Innovation, imitation, and growth with cumulative technology. *Journal of Monetary Economics*, 50(2), 361–380.

Pechlaner, H. (2010). Innovation gelingt durch Lernen von anderen. In H. Pechlaner, C. Engl, and H. Hofer (eds), *Lernen von anderen Branchen. Imparare da altri settori* (9–10), Bozen: Athesia.

Peters, M., and Pikkemaat, B. (2005). Innovation in Tourism. *Journal of Quality Assurance in Hospitality and Tourism*, 6(3/4), 1–6.

Peters, M., and Weiermair, K. (2002). Innovationen und Innovationsverhalten im Tourismus. In T. Bieger and C. Laesser (eds), *Jahrbuch 2001/2002 Schweizer Tourismuswirtschaft* (157–178). St. Gallen: IDT-HSG.

Pikkemaat, B., and Peters, M. (2005). Towards the measurement of innovation – a pilot study in the small and medium sized hotel industry. *Journal of Quality Assurance in Hospitality and Tourism*, 6(3/4). 89–112.

Pompl, W., and Buer, Ch. (2006). Notwendigkeit, Probleme und Besonderheiten von Innovationen bei touristische Dienstleistungen. In B. Pikkemaat, M. Peters, and K. Weiermair (eds), *Innovationen im Tourismus. Wettbewerbsvorteile durch neue Ideen und Angebote* (21–35). Berlin: Erich Schmidt Verlag.

Rasche, C., and Wolfrum, B. (1994). Ressourcenorientierte Unternehmensführung. *Die Betriebswirtschaft*, 54, 501–517.

Rese, A., Sänn, A., and Homfeldt, F. (2015). Customer integration and voice-of-customer methods in the German automotive industry. *International Journal of Automotive Technology and Management*, 15(1), 1–19.

Saá-Pérez, P., and García-Falcón, J.M. (2002). A resource-based view of human resource management and organizational capabilities development. *The International Journal of Human Resource Management*, 13(1), 123–140.

Standortagentur Tirol, and Institut für innovativen Tourismus (2012). *Von der Idee zur Innovation. Ein praktischer Wegweiser für touristische Unternehmen*, Innsbruck.

Talaja, A. (2012). Testing VRIN framework: resource value and rareness as sources of competitive advantage and above average performance. *Management: Journal of Contemporary Management Issues*, 17(2), 51–64.

Teece, D.J., Pisano, G., and Shuen, A. (1997). Dynamic capabilities and strategic management. *Strategic Management Journal*, 18(7), 509–533.

Trout, J., and Wied, L. (2014). Positionierung von Innovationen. In P. Granig, E. Hartlieb, and H. Lecher (eds), *Innovationsstrategien – Von Produkten und Dienstleistungen zu Geschäftsmodellinnovationen* (43–52). Wiesbaden: Springer Gabler.

Volo, S. (2004). Foundations for an innovation indicator for tourism: An application to SME. In P. Keller and T. Bieger (eds), *The Future of Small and Medium Sized Enterprises in Tourism* (361–376). St. Gallen: E-Druck AG St. Gallen.

Weiermair, K. (2006). Product Improvement or Innovation: What is the Key to Success in Tourism?. In OECD (ed.), *Innovation and Growth in Tourism* (Chapter 4: 53–69), Paris: OECD.

Wernerfeldt, B. (1984). A resource-based view of the firm. *Strategic Management Journal*, 5, 171–180.

Weth, A. (2007). *Innovations and Creativity – How Disney Keeps Ideas Coming.* München: GRIN Verlag.

White, H.C. (1981). Where do markets come from? *American Journal of Sociology*, 87, 517–547.

Zahra, S., and George, G. (2002). Absorptive capacity: A review, reconceptualization, and extension. *Academy of Management Review*, 27, 185–203.

## SOURCES

Eger, B. (2008). Internationaler Living-Lifestyle: 'Serviciertes Wohnen' – ein neuer Trend setzt sich durch. *Deal-Magazin*, 05. Available at: http://www.deal-magazin.com/index.php?cont=detailandseite=740    [accessed    13 February 2015].

Forum Anders Reisen (2015). Available at: www.forumandersreisen.de [accessed 13 February 2015].

HTW Chur Hochschule für Technik und Wirtschaft (2012). Lernen von den Besten. Innovation im alpinen Tourismus: Eine Reise durch Tourismusregionen in Graubünden, Vorarlberg, Tirol und Südtirol, Chur. Available at: http://www.htwchur.ch/fileadmin/user_upload/institute/SIFE/3_Forschungsthemen/Start-up/Lernen_von_den_Besten_Final_Web.pdf [accessed 27 January 2015].

Tirol Werbung GmbH (2015). Unternehmen – Geschichte. Available at: http://www.tirolwerbung.at/xxl/de/geschichte/index.html [accessed 27 January 2015].

Tiscover (2015). *Tiscover. My Bed in the Alps*. Available at:. http://www.tiscover.com/ [accessed 15 February 2015].

# Chapter 10

# Experience Design: Competencies for Innovation

## SARAH GARDINER and NOEL SCOTT

The development of innovative and exciting experiences is central to the competitiveness of a tourist destination. There is a small emerging literature on the design of such experiences, but few if any case studies and discussion of successful examples of innovative experience design. This chapter discusses results of a project that involved working with five small businesses on the Gold Coast, Australia, to adapt their experiential offering to the developing China market. The project involved a series of qualitative and quantitative data collection stages, along with phases of interaction with the managers. This chapter provides case studies of the process and outcomes of this experience design project and reflections on the competencies required for its success.

Innovation is the lifeblood of business and small businesses are a significant source of innovative products and services. Indeed, the majority of small businesses in the tourism industry are small or micro businesses. However small businesses often lack the resources and competency to develop innovative new products. Their time is often taken up with day-to-day management issues and they may not have the knowledge and ability to conduct the required market research. However, if the energy and passion (Gardiner and Scott, 2014) of small business managers can be captured, then tourism destinations can adapt to changing markets and opportunities.

## Australia's Gold Coast

The City of Gold Coast is the main non-capital city leisure tourism destination in Australia. It is a classic beach, sun and sand destination that received $4.7 billion in tourist expenditure in 2012/2013. Around 19 per cent of the 4.2 million overnight visitors to the Gold Coast each year are from overseas (Tourism and Events Queensland, 2015) and there is an increasing number of Asian visitors. Traditionally the primary tourism origin market for the Gold Coast was New Zealand, which contributes approximately 187,000 visitors and 1.7

million visitor nights per year. However, recently China has emerged as a major tourism origin market for the Gold Coast with 186,000 visitors and over 1 million visitor nights per year (Tourism and Events Queensland, 2015). For many of the smaller tourism businesses on the Gold Coast, such as 'learn to surf' operators, this may create a challenge as it means that they need to be able to adapt their products to a new market – Chinese visitors.

The beach is one of the main attractions on the Gold Coast. Gold Coast surf beaches stretch for some 36 kilometres. Along this coastal strip is a series of coastal villages that have grown together over the past century into a continuous built-up area. The Gold Coast is home to a series of surfing-related events, the largest event being the World Surf League professional surf competition, Quiksilver Pro Gold Coast. The Gold Coast also regularly hosts surf life-saving and amateur surfing competitions. The relaxed atmosphere and safe beaches are patrolled by Australia's largest professional lifeguard service in Australia; lifeguards patrol 26 beaches along the Gold Coast all year round (City of Gold Coast, 2015), making them popular with locals and visitors from other parts of Australia. Most Australians and New Zealanders are able to swim, are aware of beach safety and able to deal with breaking waves. For these tourists, visiting the beach and swimming in the ocean are popular leisure activities.

Chinese visitors share a strong interest in visiting beaches in Australia. In a survey of Chinese visitors to Australia, a visit to the beach was reported as the most important activity (Yu and Weiler, 2001); however, these visitors may not be aware of beach safety (Ballantyne, Carr, and Hughes, 2005). It also appears likely that older visitors from China are more interested in sightseeing and famous attractions (Wang and Qu, 2004), while younger visitors are more interested in active tourism activities such as participatory marine tourism activities (sailing and surfing), as well as hiking (Agrusa, Kim, and Wang, 2011).

On the Gold Coast, there is anecdotal evidence that Chinese visitors are interested in visiting the beach. Although no formal study has been conducted, it is common to see tour groups visiting the main tourist beach at Surfers Paradise on the Gold Coast, yet these visitors do not engage in swimming. The beaches of the Gold Coast are surf beaches and as discussed below, this environment can be intimidating for people with poor swimming skills.

There is a small emerging literature on the design of innovative and exciting tourism experiences (Mansfeldt, Vestager, and Iversen, 2008; Tussyadiah, 2014; Wang, Park, and Fesenmaier, 2012), but few if any case studies and discussions of successful examples of innovative experience design. This chapter discusses the innovation process used to develop new beach experiences for Chinese visitors on the Gold Coast, Australia (see also Scott, Gardiner, and Carlini, 2014).

## Designing New Tourist Experiences

Overall the research discussed in this chapter originated in discussions with existing tourism operators concerning developing innovative water-based experiences for Asian visitors.

In the past, tourists may have been thought of as buying a mass-produced, predetermined product, such as a hotel room or a tourism package. As a result, there was limited diversity in the visitor experience and, as a result, visitors felt like they were getting a homogeneous experience that was unvaried and created a feeling of sameness, one that lacked personalization. Today's travellers are seeking to create their own travel stories through experiences, where they play their role as both the producers and consumers of experiences (Binkhorst and Den Dekker, 2009), shaping a unique experience that has a personal meaning to them (Diller, Shedroff, and Rhea, 2006). Experiences by their nature are not tangible but instead co-opt and involve the visitor by cognitive processes and psychological engagement. The degree of involvement and the resultant emotional outcome of an experience is closely related to how it can help the customer fulfil a particular need or want and meet an important goal. Because of this it is necessary to clearly understand the reasons a customer has for engaging in an experience.

Design of experience-centric services therefore must have a customer-centric focus (Tussyadiah, 2014) and commonly involve multiple sources of customer research (Martinson, Schwartz, and Vaughan, 2002). Designing for experiences calls for the conceptualization of the experience through naturalistic enquiry, by gathering information and observing user behaviour in natural experience settings and real use situations (i.e., tourists at tourism destinations), while taking into consideration the relevant sociocultural contexts (Tussyadiah, 2014: 552).

This research involved three different research methods: a series of focus groups with Chinese students studying at universities on the Gold Coast and in Brisbane; visits by these students to undertake the experiential activity; and a quantitative survey of both Australian and Chinese students regarding these experiences. This chapter only discusses the results of the first two qualitative research studies.

A second issue concerning the experiences examined in this research is that they are offered by small business operators on the Gold Coast. Such businesses do not often have the *research competencies* to conduct the research necessary to provide the necessary visitor insights and arguably do not have the need to develop these skills as they may engage in experience enhancement only irregularly. Experience design projects are also typically ill-defined where there is a conjecture–analysis cycle (Tussyadiah, 2014). This means that presuppositions are important as the origins of solution concepts, and designers and other participants need to refine their understanding of problems and solutions in parallel. The competencies to undertake such a design process are complex and require considerable expertise and experience. In this way the researchers provided the research competencies instead of the business owners.

Small business may also not have the resources (time and money) to undertake the necessary experience development. In this particular case, the funding for the research came from an Australian government grant which was jointly sourced and partly funded by the local government – City of Gold Coast, the destination marketing organization – Gold Coast Tourism and the authors, who are based at Griffith University on the Gold Coast. However, in this project the business owners were involved in all aspects of the actual study. The business owners were recruited for this study through a process in which expressions of interest were canvassed from adventure tourism operators on the Gold Coast who were members of the Gold Coast Tourism. Interested operators were interviewed and the successful operators were chosen for the interest in working collaboratively, as well as their likely ability to implement the results of the research. Therefore, another competency necessary for experience design of the type discussed here is *ability to collaborate* and the willingness and ability to engage in the design process. The complete process took 18 months, which is a significant investment for small business operators. As a result of this recruitment process five tourism operators were selected, although this chapter only discusses results relevant to one business – the Get Wet Surf School.

After recruitment, the particular business operations and objective of each business owner were documented. The Get Wet Surf School provides lessons on how to surf to visitors to the Gold Coast, whereby those undertaking a one-day course are guaranteed to be able to stand on the board by the end of the lesson. This business recognized the growth in Asian visitors to the Gold Coast and sought to gain their share of this market, but had been unsuccessful in the past, so their aim in participating in this project was to develop an experience to suit this market. Kerri Jekyll, Director and owner of Get Wet Surf School, noted that in recent years there has been a shift in the typical customers wanting to learn to surf. In the past, the key market was backpackers travelling around Australia, whereas now the international student market has come to her attention. Statistics on international students told her that there were about 500,000 students studying each year in Australia. These students were mostly from China, India and South East Asia. She recognized the potential to grow her business if she could capture this emerging Asian-focused international student youth tourism market. This change in focus from European backpackers to international students has meant challenges for her, with innovation needed to modify products to suit the new market. She decided to focus on the China market, since Chinese students represented approximately one-third of all international students studying in Australia and the numbers of Chinese visitors to Australia was forecast to grow over the next decade.

The next step involved conducting eight focus groups to uncover travel behaviour and attitudes of younger Chinese students. The key findings were indexed into categories including; destinations, travel behaviour – influences, experiences – relating experiences to things they know, adventure – contrasting views on adventure, water-based activities, surfing, water-based touring, wildlife, and technology and accommodation options.

During these focus groups the students were offered the opportunity to undertake one of the experiences they had discussed through on-site visits. The choices included a jet boat tour, learn to surf lesson, kayaking tour and wildlife sanctuary visit. Participants were interviewed immediately following the experience. This approach was an important research component, as some students had never participated in these activities and their perceptions and attitudes were altered significantly as a result of their experience. Key outcomes included the importance of images to share their experience with family and friends back home through social media, quality assurance and safety reinforced through accreditation and memberships of governing bodies (such as Gold Coast Tourism and Surfing Australia), the importance of a caring instructor who was sensitive to the cultural and personal needs of the participants and the delight experienced in successfully standing on the board. Although the company offers a guaranteed 'stand up', many participants did not expect they would be able to do it and therefore felt surprise and gratification at this unexpected outcome. Finally, an online survey of domestic and international students in Australia was then conducted with the purpose of testing the findings of the previous qualitative research. The survey also provided feedback to the partner businesses about the attractiveness of their product and suggested changes to innovate to match the international student market expectations.

## Findings

### FOCUS GROUPS

To begin to explore ways to make these experiences more appealing to the students, eight focus groups were conducted with international students studying English language and undergraduate degree programmes at Griffith University and The University of Queensland in South East Queensland, Australia. Seven of the focus groups were conducted with Chinese students and a mixed nationality focus group was also conducted. Most English language student participants had been in Australia less than six months and most university student participants had been in Australia one to five years. There was a slight gender bias in the sessions, with more females than males participating.

Focus groups enable participants to provide detailed accounts of their views and beliefs about the tourism experiences, thus providing in-depth insights into their travel behaviour. The group interviews also provide an opportunity for focus group members to interact with each other, as well as with the interviewers, creating an environment where they can discuss their travel experiences and perceptions with their peers.

Each session had four to eight participants and two interviewers and was of approximately 45 minutes duration. Each session began by asking the students open-ended questions about the tourism and leisure activities that they had undertaken since arriving in Australia, to get a general understanding of their travel behaviour. The students were then presented with images of various tourism experiences, including learn to surf, kayaking and snorkelling. They were then asked to talk about the experience that most and least interested them. Probing questions aimed to elicit insights into their reasoning for their views and beliefs about the experiences. As part of this probing, perceived barriers and limitations to engaging in the experience were also discussed.

The results indicated that most of the information about the beach and water came during their university orientation and students believed what was told them during orientation. Tertiary colleges have a duty of care to their students, however the information presented tends to instil fear within the students, for example, swimming between the flags, rips in the water and stingers. Steps to change the messaging during orientation with a more positive spin would prove beneficial. By educating the students on where to swim and what not to do, instead of advising them not to participate because it is dangerous, would be far more beneficial.

It is worth noting that the beach was a very strong attractor for the students coming to the Gold Coast and selecting it as a study destination. They really like the beach, but most of the time they just tended to look and visit the beach, they did not actually enter the water.

The research suggested that the group was interested in learning about the surf beach and how to swim and surf in the waves, but it was perceived as too difficult. The idea of entering the water was viewed as challenging and the thought of standing up on a board and surfing on a wave was viewed as exciting and would be a significant goal achievement. To send a surfing image back home was seen as something to provide social kudos because many of their friends and family had not engaged in this experience before. It is quite interesting that often the thought process in undertaking an activity relates to perception of the activity rather than the reality of it; many participants had been nervous and hesitant to participate in the experience beforehand, but they were delighted that they had overcome their fear and expressed having enjoyed the activity afterwards.

The research into water-based adventures uncovered an interesting point. Predominately among the students from China, but somewhat across some of the other countries as well, there was an unfamiliarity with and fear of the water. Many were fearful because they could not swim and there was a considerable fear of the surf because many had never experienced it before. Many of the countries where they lived had still water. They might have ventured into flat water, but adding a surf dynamic creates quite a difficulty. This was interesting because the beach was the main attractant for them to choose the Gold Coast to study over a number of other destinations. Yet all they wanted to do at the beach was stand there and look across the sand at the water and leave, and that made them happy.

One comment regarding how the student might assess the safety of the ocean highlighted the importance of third party endorsement: 'Maybe search online and have some feedback on Facebook or someone else sharing their experience online saying it's safe.'

Interestingly, this was not just with water, there was a fear of anything to do with staying at a hostel. If a third party were to tell them that they would be safe, they would accept it. Membership of governing bodies and accreditation, especially government accreditation, provided visual cues to the safety of the experience.

Sun exposure was also a concern. The majority of students were worried about getting sunburnt because they did not want to get brown, and they wanted to stay whiter. Promoting sun protection, such as the use of sunscreen and hats and offering long-sleeved rash vests, helped to elevate this concern and resulted in fewer participants being sunburnt. If someone is sunburnt on tour, despite having had an enjoyable experience, they will be quite negative about the tour experience and may tell others about it through word-of-mouth and social media. Hence, operators must be mindful of this.

## TESTING EXPERIENCE THROUGH ON-SITE VISITS

During the focus groups the students were shown images of the activities and were given the opportunity to sign up and participate in the experience at no charge to them. Despite this incentive, it proved difficult to encourage the students to participate in a number of activities, including the learn-to-surf lesson, because of their concerns about their ability to undertake the activity, and about its safety.

A group of international students were taken on a Get Wet Surf School lesson and later questioned. Students thought that the 'lesson was better than expected' as they 'didn't expect to stand up' and this experience evoked feelings of excitement, satisfaction and pride. While standing up on the surfboard was an important aspect of the experience, also important was the ability to share images with friends via social media. Most students have a Weibo social media account, which they use to share images with family and friends back home and in Australia, as well as a Facebook social media account to share images with their friends from other nationalities in Australia. This was particularly important for Chinese students, as their parents expected that their only child would experience Australia as a tourist and as a student.

The majority of students had never surfed before and likened it to snowboarding. The perception was that the activity was difficult and they did not expect to be able to stand on the surfboard. Key learnings from this experience highlighted the need for digital photographs of the participants surfing to enable them to share these images with friends and family. There was also a requirement for the provision of long-sleeve rash vests to protect against the sun. Prior to the research, the Get Wet Surf School only had short-sleeve rash vests; however investment in long-sleeve rash vest based on this research has since resulted in increased satisfaction and patronage among Asian visitors. Students were looking for group discounts and only wanted to pay $25 for the experience. They also wanted information before the trip on sun protection, as many Asian participants were very concerned about sunburn resulting in the darkening of their skin. Darker skin was associated with farmers and agricultural workers, who were perceived as lower class than Asian international students. These students were from cities and middle- to upper-class families, who preferred fairer skin to represent their social status.

There was a lot of excitement and people were proud and satisfied because they confronted their fears of the activity. They really did not expect to be able to stand up on a surfboard, so when they did stand, it was a moment of great joy. The professionalism and enthusiasm of the instructor also rated highly.

## Outcome of the Design Process

The results indicated that the Get Wet Surf School had unique challenges with the change to an Asian dominated market due to their clients' concern about the safety of entering the water, especially the waves in the surf and fear of drowning. While the proximity of the ocean was a key factor for students choosing to study at the Gold Coast, it was discovered during focus groups that they were content to look at the ocean rather than enter it, because many Asian students have never learnt to swim or have experience the surf. With the new Asian market being more fearful and less adventurous than the previous backpackers, Get Wet Surf School needed to reconsider their current strategy.

Based on these findings, the Surf School changed its emphasis from thrill and adventure to customer safety, with the focus on the surf skills and the accreditation of their instructors. They also have designed a new experience, 'Surf and Sizzle', which focuses less on surfing and more on socializing through offering barbequed sausages at the end of the lesson to encourage interaction among the guests and with the instructors. Sun sensitivity is also a characteristic of this market, so that long sleeve rash vests were introduced to avoid sun exposure. Another feature of the international student market is value for money. Understanding this aspect means that Get Wet Surf School was able to offer group discounts, free transfers and bundling with other activities and accommodation to increase the perceived value. Finally, the Get Wet Surf School has also introduced surfing lessons in a wave pool available at a theme park nearby so that participants could learn to surf in an environment they were more familiar with (i.e., a pool) and which has more predictable conditions, that is, no rips or marine stingers and consistent wave size.

## Conclusion

This chapter has described a case study of the development of an innovative new learn-to-surf experience using a structured design process. The key aspects of this process are a focus on the deep customer understanding using multiple methods of research and continuous engagement with the business owner. As a result, a number of changes were successfully implemented by the business owner and further enhancements are planned. Early results are positive, as Get Wet Surf School has had over 500 students from Griffith University and The University of Queensland express interest in participating in a learn-to-surf lesson at orientation week.

Reflecting on the research process, two significant competencies appear necessary for the effective experience design in tourism: an ability to conduct research and an ability to collaborate. These competencies are unlikely to be possessed by many small business operators. The ability to conduct deep market research may be related to the market orientation found in successful businesses (Polo Peña, Frías Jamilena, and Rodríguez Molina, 2013; Sin, Tse, Heung, and Yim, 2005; Wu, 2004) as many small business owners are close to their customers. However, in this case the target market was new and not visiting the surf school and thus a customer-oriented approach would not work. Instead the research was conducted by external researchers from the local university.

The consequence of this externalization of the research on new customers was that the business owner required an ability to collaborate with the researchers, as well as an interest in developing their business. This ability involves relationship-building and trust. Relationships are also two-way and require the researchers to be able to build trust and collaboration with the business owner. Therefore we find that the ability to develop innovative new experiences to match the needs of new markets requires a university researcher having particular qualitative and quantitative research competencies to work with a small business operator having collaboration competencies. This means that such innovation requires two parties with the right competencies located at the same destination.

This co-location of researcher and business owner with the appropriate competencies may be a relatively rare occurrence, which may explain why there is less innovation in the tourism sector (Hjalager and Flagestad, 2011; Mei, Arcodia, and Ruhanen, 2012).

## Acknowledgements

This project, undertaken by researchers from Griffith University and the University of Queensland, was funded by the Australia Government TQUAL grant, City of Gold Coast and Gold Coast Tourism.

## References

Agrusa, J., Kim, S.S., and Wang, K.-C. (2011). Mainland Chinese tourists to Hawaii: Their characteristics and preferences. *Journal of Travel and Tourism Marketing*, 28(3), 261–278. doi: 10.1080/10548408.2011.562853

Ballantyne, R., Carr, N., and Hughes, K. (2005). Between the flags: An assessment of domestic and international university students' knowledge of beach safety in Australia. *Tourism Management*, 26(4), 617–622. doi: 10.1016/j.tourman.2004.02.016

Binkhorst, E., and Den Dekker, T. (2009). Agenda for co-creation tourism experience research. *Journal of Hospitality Marketing and Management*, 18(2–3), 311–327.

City of Gold Coast. (2015). *Gold Coast Lifeguards*. Available at: http://www. goldcoast.qld.gov.au/thegoldcoast/gold-coast-lifeguards-152.html [accessed 13 March 2015].

Diller, S., Shedroff, N., and Rhea, D. (2006). *Making Meaning: How Successful Businesses Deliver Meaningful Customer Experiences*. Berkeley, CA: New Riders.

Gardiner, S., and Scott, N. (2014). Successful tourism clusters: Passion in paradise. *Annals of Tourism Research*, 46, 171–173.

Hjalager, A.-M., and Flagestad, A. (2011). Innovations in well-being tourism in the Nordic countries. *Current Issues in Tourism*, 15(8), 725–740. doi: 10.1080/13683500.2011.629720

Mansfeldt, O.K., Vestager, E.M., and Iversen, M.B. (2008). Experience design in city tourism. *Experience Economy and Tourism/Creative Industries*. Oslo: Nordic Innovation Centre.

Martinson, A.M., Schwartz, N., and Vaughan, M.W. (2002). Women's experiences of leisure implications for design. *New Media and Society*, 4(1), 29–49.

Mei, X.Y., Arcodia, C., and Ruhanen, L. (2012). Towards tourism innovation: A critical review of public polices at the national level. *Tourism Management Perspectives*, 4, 92–105.

Polo Peña, A.I., Frías Jamilena, D.M., and Rodríguez Molina, M.Á. (2013). Market orientation as a strategy for the rural tourism sector: Its effect on tourist behavior and the performance of enterprises. *Journal of Travel Research*, 52(2), 225–239. doi: 10.1177/0047287512459108

Scott, N., Gardiner, S., and Carlini, J. (2014). *Experience Gold Coast: Innovative Products for Asian Visitors*. Griffith Institute for Tourism Research Report Series Report No 3. Gold Coast, Australia: Griffith Institute for Tourism.

Sin, L.Y.M., Tse, A.C.B., Heung, V.C.S., and Yim, F.H.K. (2005). An analysis of the relationship between market orientation and business performance in the hotel industry. *International Journal of Hospitality Management*, 24(4), 555–577. doi: 10.1016/j.ijhm.2004.11.002

Tourism and Events Queensland (2015). *Gold Coast Regional Snapshot*. Brisbane: Tourism and Events Queensland.

Tussyadiah, I.P. (2014). Toward a theoretical foundation for experience design in tourism. *Journal of Travel Research*, 53(5), 543–564. doi: 10.1177/0047287513513172

Wang, D., Park, S., and Fesenmaier, D.R. (2012). The role of smartphones in mediating the touristic experience. *Journal of Travel Research*, 51(4), 371–387. doi: 10.1177/0047287511426341

Wang, S., and Qu, H. (2004). A comparison study of Chinese domestic tourism: China vs the USA. *International Journal of Contemporary Hospitality Management*, 16(2), 108–115.

Wu, J.J. (2004). Influence of market orientation and strategy on travel industry performance: An empirical study of e-commerce in Taiwan. *Tourism Management*, 25(3), 357–365.

Yu, X., and Weiler, B. (2001). Mainland Chinese pleasure travelers to Australia: A leisure behavior analysis. *Tourism Culture and Communication*, 3(2), 81–91.

# How to Create Destination Capabilities in the Field of New Product Development

RUGGERO SAINAGHI and MANUELA DE CARLO

This chapter aims to identify the key elements underlying a destination capability, and to examine *how* these components interact to foster destination development. The chapter uses the model presented by Haugland et al. (2011), which is structured around three major concepts: (1) destination capabilities, (2) coordination at the destination level, (3) inter-destination bridge ties.

To answer the research questions we carried out a preliminary study based on an inductive single-case study, represented by Skipassfree (Livigno, Italy). Skipassfree case study is analysed along three stages: its 'genesis', its development, and last but not least its implementation through the use of a contractual form.

## Destination Development

The issue of development is decisive for any tourism destination and the firms operating in it (Crouch and Ritchie, 1999). Numerous researchers have underlined the role areas play in increasing competitiveness of both destinations and local firms (Molina-Azorín, Pereira-Moliner, and Claver-Cortés, 2010).

In attempting to explore this connection, various issues giving content to destination management have emerged. The numerous approaches and themes are closely linked to the complexity of the destination, often described as a tourism district (Dredge, 1999; Sainaghi, 2006), a social network (Baggio, Scott, and Cooper, 2010), or a complex system (Baggio and Sainaghi, 2011; Sainaghi and Baggio, 2014), while the firms operating within it take on the features of co-producers of goods and services (Murphy, Pritchard, and Smith, 2000). Destination is a competitive subject (Go and Govers, 2000), which needs a clear strategic definition that allows it to position itself and its products. This task is generally undertaken by the Destination Management Organizations (DMOs)

(Pike, 2004; Sheehan, Ritchie, and Hudson, 2007). In this context, dealing with the development issue demands finding suitable forms of coordination, able to integrate the contributions of the single firms and to manage the different levels on which development itself takes place.

Some authors put forward the usefulness of analysing the development issue within the stream of capabilities, underlining the central role played by the latter in enacting concrete growth processes (Rodríguez-Díaz and Espino-Rodríguez, 2008). One crucial question remains, however: how to generate a destination capability. To contribute to filling this gap, this chapter analyses the development of a product (Skipassfree) achieved by the Livigno resort, Italy.

## Destination Capabilities

This chapter aims to identify the key elements underlying a destination capability (DC), and to examine *how* these components interact to foster destination development. The chapter uses the model of Haugland et al. (2011), which is structured around three major concepts: i) destination capabilities, ii) coordination at the destination level, iii) inter-destination bridge ties. Capabilities have been defined by Teece, Pisano, and Shuen as 'a set of differentiated skills, complementary assets, and routines that provide the basis for a firm's competitive capacities and sustainable advantage in a particular business' (1997: 28). A destination capability is thus called upon to integrate and reassume the resources distributed between the various local actors with the aim of creating or strengthening the destination's competitive advantage (Mei, Arcodia, and Ruhanen, 2012). Haugland et al. (2011) identify two main destination capabilities: one relating to the use of distributed resources and competences for the creation or renewal of new products (new product development capability) and a second one, which is related to the capability to develop a destination image and branding. The identification of the importance of these two capabilities open up a crucial question: how is a collective capability created at destination level?

The second variable of the model (coordination at destination level) springs from the fragmented structure of the tourism supply, which demands integration mechanisms that differ according to the type of destination, its maturity and its strategic objectives (d'Angella, De Carlo, and Sainaghi, 2010). According to Haugland et al. (2011), four types of coordination forms may be identified, along a continuum ranging from the absence of structured forms to administered, contractual forms and hierarchy. The four forms do not exclude each other, but are different tools which may exist side by side. As far as the goals of the present study are concerned, the issue of coordination is functional to dealing with the research question: how to develop a destination capability. We must thus highlight the role which coordination plays in favouring or hindering the process of creating a destination capability.

Lastly, the inter-destination bridge ties focus attention on the relationships existing between various destinations. Above all, it is useful to link the importance of this dimension to the social capital issue (Bourdieu, 1986) and to the importance of the ties, whether they are weak (Burt, 1992) or strong (Coleman, 1988, 1990). According to the extent a destination has developed relationships with other areas, the latter will be part of its social capital and may offer useful resources and competences to generate destination capabilities (Ansari, Munir, and Gregg, 2012). The contribution offered by the inter-destination bridge ties may be traced along two dimensions: imitation and innovation (Haugland et al., 2011).

## Methodology

To answer the research questions underlying this chapter – how a destination capability is created and how this contributes to the destination's development – we carried out a preliminary study based on an inductive single-case study (Eisenhardt, 1989). In particular the empirical analysis focuses on the Skipassfree scheme launched by Livigno, an Italian Alpine destination. The case is an appropriate field of study, since the destination: i) has shown a significant development in terms of overnight stays as a result of a new product development initiative; ii) has completed all the phases of the new product development process, up to commercialization; iii) compared with other cases with similar features, it offers authors a privileged access to data and observations over a significant period of time (30 years). Data collection relies on interviews, documentation and archival records.

*In-depth interviews* were carried out with key players involved in the Skipassfree project. The executives belonged to the DMO (Azienda di Promozione Turistica, or APT Livigno), the ski company association (Associazione Ski Pass Livigno), the local Municipality (Comune di Livigno) and the hoteliers' association (Associazione Albergatori Livigno). Some in-depth analyses were then carried out relating to the incoming agencies, the hospitality sector (apartments and hotels), and the ski lift operators. All the interviews were recorded and transcribed verbatim to generate approximately 150 pages of text.

## The Livigno Context

Livigno is an Alpine destination accounting for approximately 1 million annual overnight stays, mainly concentrated in the winter season. The small town (approximately 6,000 inhabitants) is located at 1,816 metres; the altitude ensures abundant snowfall and a potentially long winter season from the end of November to the beginning of May. Livigno is a duty-free area.

The winter supply hinges on cable car firms, hospitality firms and the shopping sector. The cable car operators work under concession and have to respect a tender with the Livigno Municipality. The only valid travel passes are those issued by the Ski Pass Livigno Association, which groups together the 13 companies operating within the destination. Two of these are owned by the same company, achieving over 50 per cent of overall turnover; together with a third, they account for almost 90 per cent of business. The passes issued by the Association permit skiing on all ski slopes and the use of all lifts. The single companies pay an association quota amounting to 4.5 per cent of turnover, generating a budget for the Ski Pass Association of approximately €1 million per year.

While the cable car business shows a high concentration, the hospitality sector is fragmented. The destination numbers 106 hotel structures for a total of 5,046 beds The hotels are supplemented by numerous apartments rented by the week, owned by the residents, which enable the destination to host up to 13,000 tourists. Lastly, the duty-free system has favoured the development of over 250 shops, specializing mainly in the sale of perfumes, tobacco, and sports equipment. Approximately 70 per cent of annual flows are concentrated in the winter season, but this reveals a clear problem of seasonality: at the start and at the end of the season, despite optimal skiing conditions, the tourism flows show a lower volume of presences compared with the central months.

In order to increase tourist flows at the start and at the end of the season, the operators acted mainly on prices, offering discounts, while at local level a bundle of services was set up, called Natur.card (developed during the 1990s), coinciding with the organization of sports events. However, these attempts were not able to modify seasonality, but encouraged a 'price war', leading the destination to offer particularly low prices in December and April (in the post-Easter period).

## The Process of New Product Development

During winter 2007/2008, jointly with the Ski Pass and Hotelier Association, the DMO proposed a package including the ski pass and accommodation (hotel or apartment). The product was called Skipassfree since the accommodation price included the cost of the pass offered free of charge to end clients. Lodgings firms paid 50 per cent of the costs and ski companies 50 per cent. The promotion is valid only during seasonal tails; at the beginning of season, Skipassfree is sold for approximately four weeks, from the opening of the winter season until Christmas, while at the end of winter the package is offered after Easter until the end of the winter season in April. According to the different dates of Easter, the end of season can be a very long period (such as 37 days in 2011–2012) or only few days (for example, 16 days in 2009–2010 and 2010–2011,).

In particular, focusing attention on hotels, for which a greater historic series is available, we may note that the initiative produces a clear discontinuity regarding past data (last 30 years). This chapter explores the role played by Skipassfree to achieve this result. To deal with this issue, the Skipassfree case study is reread along three stages: its 'genesis', its development, and last but not least its implementation through the use of a contractual form.


## SKIPASSFREE – GENESIS

The Skipassfree idea arose during the 2006–2007 season, stimulated by the positive experience gained by a competitive destination (Trentino, Italy), which had introduced a similar product, called 'Free Ski'. A Livigno entrepreneur, who manages a small ski lift and operates in the incoming sector through the weekly renting of apartments, discussed the opportunity of repeating the idea in Livigno with several tour operators,

> *Occupation in the reception sector was very low, as were the prices applied. Attempts enacted with the winter.card product and events had had no effect. We had to try out an innovative idea. The proposal to give free passes, although it was a shock, could be an interesting approach. (Interview no. 1)*

An impassioned exchange of ideas began, exclusively on an informal level. The entrepreneur discussed the scheme with a friend, an APT Livigno councillor, and other fellow operators of ski lifts. This dialogue made it possible to formulate several hypotheses, which later became the distinctive features of Skipassfree.

> *During the winter the idea was informally discussed by various operators. The talks helped to better clarify the problem, but also to see its complexity. (Interview no. 2)*

It was felt that the new product had to involve the entire reception sector and not exclusively the apartments managed by the local incoming agencies. This approach made it clear, however, that a *super partes* [impartial] 'director' was needed for the initiative; the APT's involvement was put forward. The Skipass Association did not possess the relational competences to involve and manage a product interfacing with a fragmented sector like the reception sector. Questions were raised about who would bear the costs for the pass offered to customers free of charge, and the hypothesis arose of sharing its costs between the accommodation sector (hotels and apartments) and the ski lifts. It was suggested that the free Ski Pass might be offered only to customers staying for longer periods, avoiding the creation of a 'short break' sector, also because of Livigno's distance from catchment areas. It seemed necessary to have a suitable promotional budget to support the initiative and to involve an agency, which is able to develop a suitable marketing plan.

## SKIPASSFREE – DEVELOPMENT

The second phase began with the first roundtable discussion. It is important to clarify that no hierarchic or institutional tie existed between the actors. The roundtable discussion was an opportunity in which the DMO and the two associations (hoteliers and ski pass operators) freely decided to take part. Moreover, the decisions taken did not automatically bind the respective organizations, but had to be approved by the formal structures of each firm. All the actors had a profound knowledge of the location as well as of its strengths and weaknesses; some members were entrepreneurs in the reception, incoming and commercial divisions. All those invited to participate had very close relationships with other operators in Livigno, which made it possible to share different experiences and risks.

The first meeting took place on 14 May 2007, the last on 9 July the same year. The development stage opened and closed in 57 days, The actors wished to make the new product operative in the coming 2007–2008 season, which made it necessary to proceed very rapidly and in a concrete manner. Tables 11.1 and 11.2 show the salient decisions made during the six meetings, maintaining chronological order, but linking the work carried out to some relevant features related to the creation of Skipassfree (Table 11.1) and communications and marketing processes (Table 11.2).

**Table 11.1  Salient decisions carried out in the development area of the new product**

| | 1st meeting (14/05/07) | 2nd meeting (18/05/07) | 3rd meeting (14/06/07) | 4th meeting (02/07/07) | 5th meeting (06/07/07) | 6th meeting (09/07/07) |
|---|---|---|---|---|---|---|
| Seasonality | Performance analysis of the last season | First definition of Skipassfree promotional periods | Seasonal tails and last two weeks of January | | | Only seasonal tails |
| Sharing mechanism | 50% ski company, 50% lodging firms | Cost evaluation for hotels and apartments of free of charge ski pass | 50% ski company, 50% lodging firms | | | |
| Firms involved | Ski companies and lodging firms | Lodging sector: hotels and aparments | Inclusion of aparments managed by incoming agencies | Aparments: one free of charge ski pass for two people | Aparments: one free of charge ski pass for two people | Aparments: one free of charge ski pass for each person |

**Table 11.2  Salient decisions carried out in communications and marketing processes**

| | 1st meeting (14/05/07) | 2nd meeting (18/05/07) | 3rd meeting (14/06/07) | 4th meeting (02/07/07) | 5th meeting (06/07/07) | 6th meeting (09/07/07) |
|---|---|---|---|---|---|---|
| Seasonality | Performance analysis of the last season | First definition of Skipassfree promotional periods | Seasonal tails and last two weeks of January | | | Only seasonal tails |
| Sharing mechanism | 50% ski company, 50% lodging firms | Cost evaluation for hotels and apartments of free of charge ski pass | 50% ski company, 50% lodging firms | | | |
| Firms involved | Ski companies and lodging firms | Lodging sector: hotels and aparments | Inclusion of aparments managed by incoming agencies | Aparments: one free of charge ski pass for two people | Aparments: one free of charge ski pass for two people | Aparments: one free of charge ski pass for each person |

## The product

The minutes and interviews suggest several issues which are crucial for the development of the Skipassfree: (1) the choice of promotional periods; (2) the sharing mechanism of the free pass offered to customers; (3) the firms involved.

The choice of seasonality focused on periods marked by smaller flows, i.e. at the start and at the end of the season. During the work, it was suggested that the promotions should be extended to the last two weeks in January, when the resort shows smaller flows (but not a drastic drop) after the Christmas holidays. However, finally it was decided to focus attention on the tails.

The sharing mechanism remained anchored to the subdivision of the free ski pass between the reception industry (hotels and apartments) and the ski lifts. As is recalled above, a significant majority share of the reception supply is composed of apartments rented by the week. Thus, one of the first choices was to extend Skipassfree to apartments (second meeting), whether managed by private individuals or incoming agencies (third meeting). A reduction in free passes was, however, hypothesized, and a free pass was offered for every two guests (fourth and fifth meetings). It was finally decided to use the same measure planned for hotels: a free pass for each guest.

> The apartment managers immediately showed opposition to Skipassfree since the cost of free passes appeared too high. The value of the free pass is the same as that paid by hotel owners; the sale price of an apartment is however decidedly lower. The APT however succeeded in demonstrating that the fees paid to the tour operators were actually higher. (Interview no. 3)

The work carried out on the communications and marketing front was expressed in four main issues: (1) the initiative's payoff and brand, (2) target definition, (3) choice of sales channels, (4) tariff policy.

As far as the new product was concerned, the payoff suggested the central role which the free pass should play (second meeting), while the brand remained linked to the name 'Livigno Free Ski' right up to the last meeting, when 'Skipassfree' was chosen, also thanks to the work which the APT had developed with a communications agency. The target choice had been fairly clear: the new product was geared above all to permanent visitors and hence, given Livigno's distance from large cities, it should address primarily distant areas, and foreigners in particular, with a longer average stay. Skipassfree should also be offered to families with children and attention was paid to single guests, as well as to those buying through agencies and tour operators. A progressive opening in channels was in fact seen: while at the beginning the accent was put on the commercial channel managed by the APT (front office and Internet), the importance of a multichannel strategy was progressively seen, confirming a total freedom on sales tools during the last meeting.

One last, particularly important issue concerned the price policy. The reception structures communicated their winter fees six to eight months ahead, publishing them through the DMO's promotional channels (price lists, Deskline, Internet sites). The result was that when the roundtable discussion structured the Skipassfree offer, the entire reception industry had already communicated prices for winter 2007–2008.

> *Skipassfree called for the reception firms to bear a high cost, above all for apartments. When the offer was formulated, the firms had in fact already communicated their prices, without knowing that they would have to take on 50 per cent of the pass costs. (Interview no. 5)*

## SKIPASSFREE – CONTRACT FORMULA

The third stage moved Skipassfree towards start-up and contained two decisive activities: (1) the definition of a contract format to offer local firms, in particular to the reception sector, given their fragmentary nature; (2) the structuring of the communications plan and marketing.

Without going into details of single aspects, it is interesting to note several trends. The contract provided a cost structure which was almost exclusively variable for the reception firms: a modest fee (€200), was charged to participate in the initiative while the main part of the costs were covered by 50 per cent of the pass offered free of charge, which took on the features of a variable cost.

All the communications relating to the contract took on the form of letters signed jointly by the three organizations involved in the development table. The letters were also divided according to issues: from the project presentation (first letter), to the contract format (second), from the use of logos (third), to relations with tour operators (sixth), from the technical forms of information circulation to receive the free passes (seventh and eighth).

> *The role played by the Hoteliers' Association was important to involve the reception structures, both hotels (over 100 firms), and apartments (several hundred operators). Without solid support, Skipassfree would not have achieved the results it later generated. The close relationship developed with the APT definitely increased the project's credibility, favouring broad participation. (Interview no. 7)*

On the communications front, the APT developed a capillary marketing plan, involving commitment especially on international markets with particular focus on the continental and East European areas. The tools utilized involved advertisements in specialized reviews, the presentation of the Skipassfree product in fairs and workshops in which the DMO had already taken part, index-linking of several keywords on Google (including 'free' and 'Livigno'), the organization of educational programmes for various international tour operators, the purchase of advertising spaces on the Eurosport television channel, enabling the association of the Skipassfree promotion with World Cup ski competitions, the use of radio, but only domestic radio. The overall cost of the operation was €200,000, financed by the Ski Pass Association.

## Conclusion

In this section, we would like to retrace the process to outline some points on how destination capabilities related to the development of new products are generated.

The case study shows the importance of relations with other destinations: innovation may in fact be inspired by successful initiatives already developed by other areas. It is interesting to note that none of the actors interviewed had a detailed knowledge of the Free Ski product developed in Trentino; however, this experience had set off informal thinking among the actors, leading to a first, inevitably sketchy formulation of the new product. This made it possible to realize the complexity of the process and thus prompted the formulation of a more structured organizational form.

The second phase (development) made it possible to examine and outline the operating contents, working both on the specific issues concerning the new product, and on the communications strategy and marketing. This led to the usefulness of involving the actors with a sufficiently broad vision to deal with this 'focused' work. It is in fact important to understand the problems and harmonize decisions with the destination's features. For example, the question of a fragmented reception sector, with its numerous apartments, also demanded the inclusion of this offer, involving the incoming agencies. This decision, in turn, made it necessary to rethink the sales channels, the forms of information circulation, and to potentially enable all the structures to join the Skipassfree project. This definition work gradually called for the structuring of the relationship between the firms involved, suggesting the transition to a contractual form.

In the last phase, the new product entered the implementation stage through the creation of a contractual format. Hence the utility of translating the work previously carried out informally into actual norms makes it possible to give content to the product, its image and brand. The need to codify the relationship was dictated, in the case in question, by the fragmentation of the reception sector. The norms therefore represent an 'operationalization' of the decisions taken in the previous phase. In order to structure communications with the firms, it was important to involve the local DMO (APT Livigno) because of its high reputation.

This chapter confirms the central role played by destination capabilities and the usefulness of setting up intrusive studies to compare the features which the capability's creative process took on in the Livigno case with other experiences, marked by different types of tourism, a different collocation in the life cycle and different governance structures.

A second development area pertains to the analysis of the dynamic destination capabilities, i.e. to their evolution in time. Two research questions appear particularly important: once a particular destination capability has been developed, is it possible to enhance it and apply it to other types of processes? How can a destination capability be preserved and further developed to prevent its imitation and diffusion?)

## References

Ansari, S., Munir, K., and Gregg, T. (2012). Impact at the 'Bottom of the Pyramid': The role of social capital in capability development and community empowerment. *Journal of Management Studies*, 49(4), 813–842.

Baggio, R., and Sainaghi, R. (2011). Complex and chaotic tourism systems: Towards a quantitative approach. *International Journal of Contemporary Hospitality Management*, 23(6), 840–861.

Baggio, R., Scott, N., and Cooper, C. (2010). Network science – a review focused on tourism. *Annals of Tourism Research*, 37(3), 802–827.

Bourdieu, P. (1986). The forms of capital. In J.G. Richardson, *Handbook Theory and Practice for the Sociology of Education* (241–258). New York: Greenwood.

Burt, R.S. (1992). *Structural Holes: The Social Structure of Competition*. Cambridge, MA: Harvard University Press.

Coleman, J.S. (1988). Social capital in the creation of human capital. *American Journal of Sociology*, 94(S1), 95–120.

Coleman, J.S. (1990). *Foundations of Social Theory*. Cambridge, MA: Harvard University Press.

Crouch, G.I., and Ritchie, J.R. (1999). Tourism, competitiveness, and societal prosperity. *Journal of Business Research*, 44(3), 137–152.

d'Angella, F., De Carlo, M., and Sainaghi, R. (2010). Archetypes of destination governance: A comparison of international destinations. *Tourism Review*, 65(4), 61–73.

Dredge, D. (1999). Destination place planning and design. *Annals of Tourism Research*, 26(4), 772–791.

Eisenhardt, K.M. (1989). Building theories from case study research. *Academy of Management Review*, 14(4), 532–550.

Go, F.M., and Govers, R. (2000). Integrated quality management for tourist destinations: A European perspective on achieving competitiveness. *Tourism Management*, 21(1), 79–88.

Haugland, S.A., Ness, H., Grønseth, B.O., and Aarstad, J. (2011). Development of tourism destinations. An integrated multilevel perspective. *Annals of Tourism Research*, 38(1), 268–290.

Mei, X.Y., Arcodia, C., and Ruhanen, L. (2012). Towards tourism innovation: A critical review of public polices at the national level. *Tourism Management Perspectives*, 4, 92–105.

Molina-Azorín, J.F., Pereira-Moliner, J., and Claver-Cortés, E. (2010). The importance of the firm and destination effects to explain firm performance. *Tourism Management*, 31(1), 22–28.

Murphy, P., Pritchard, M., and Smith, B. (2000). The destination product and its impact on traveler perceptions. *Tourism Management*, 21(1), 43–52.

Pike, S. (2004). *Destination Marketing Organizations*. New York: Elsevier.

Rodríguez-Díaz, M., and Espino-Rodríguez, T.F. (2008). A model of strategic evaluation of a tourism destination based on internal and relational capabilities. *Journal of Travel Research*, 46(4), 368–380.

Sainaghi, R. (2006). From contents to processes: Versus a dynamic destination management model (DDMM). *Tourism Management*, 27(5), 1053–1063.

Sainaghi, R., and Baggio, R. (2014). Structural social capital and hotel performance: Is there a link? *International Journal of Hospitality Management*, 37, 99–110.

Sheehan, L.R., Ritchie, J.R., and Hudson, S. (2007). The destination promotion triad: understanding the asymmetric stakeholder interdependencies between the city, the hotels and the DMO. *Journal of Travel Research*, 46(1), 64–74.

Teece, D.J., Pisano, G., and Shuen, A. (1997). Dynamic capabilities and strategic management. *Strategic Management Journal*, 18(7), 509–533.

# Chapter 12

# Competence-based Innovation in New Zealand Wine Tourism: Partial Strategies for Partial Industrialization

TIM BAIRD and C. MICHAEL HALL

This chapter discusses innovation in New Zealand wine tourism. Using the results of surveys and interviews of wine tourism businesses and wineries, the chapter highlights the relationships between different areas of innovation and different business strategies. Some of these relationships are deliberate and some are potentially 'accidental'. However, their nature is strongly connected to firm focus and, in particular, the partially industrialized nature of many tourism businesses. A number of areas of competence for innovative practices are examined, with the research highlighting that the respondents are primarily internally focused and that there are clearly significant issues in leveraging external competences. Many winegrowers appear risk averse, with New Zealand wineries appearing to adopt innovations only if there is a proven track record of their success. Nevertheless, tourism appears as one mechanism by which new competence innovation may be addressed, rather than existing competence enhancing sources.

## Introduction

Innovation is increasingly seen as an important element of wine tourism, particularly as environmental concerns and climate change become major issues for wineries (Brannon and Wiklund, 2014; Doloreux, Chamberlain, and Ben-Amor, 2013; Doloreux and Lord-Tarte, 2013; Ferreira and Muller, 2013; Lenzi, 2013; Ohmart, 2008). Wine tourism is defined as 'visit[s] to vineyards, wineries, wine festivals and wine shows for which grape wine tasting and/or experiencing the attributes of a grape wine region are the prime motivating factors for visitors' (Hall, 1996: 1). Mitchell and Hall (2006) underline the fact that wine tourism is an important catalyst for providing potential opportunities for wine producers to add value to their existing market offerings. However, in the New Zealand context, wine producers are also operating in a volatile marketplace prone to significant economic fluctuations (Deloitte, 2010), including with respect to volatility of currency and supply. As a direct result of this, a degree of caution with respect to the adoption of new business and environmental practices currently exists within the New Zealand wine industry (Baird and Hall, 2013; Deloitte, 2010). This cautious approach potentially suggests that the competences of local firms with respect to innovation are internally driven and that they appear reluctant to utilize external competences for knowledge transfer (Argote and Ingram, 2000; Goh, 2000; Mowery and Oxley, 1996).

The competence concept in innovation embraces not only all forms of available capabilities, knowledge, know-how and skills that exist internally within a firm but also other assets that contribute to a firm's competitive potential (Goh, 2000). In the case of tourism businesses, and wine tourism in particular, the focus on other assets is extremely significant, as innovation is also going to be connected to tourists as a source of knowledge, other firms that exist within the various wine and tourism clusters and networks within which the firm is embedded. Leverage is also provided with respect to place branding and connectivity (Figure 12.1). Place is also significant because over the long-run innovation capacity relies not just on the competences that exist within the firm but also the improvement of the competences that exist within the broader place setting (Hall and Williams, 2008). However, perhaps somewhat ironically, the competences that exist within place may rely on inflows of extra-local or global knowledge that are complementary to existing competences in a region in order to improve innovation capacity (Asheim, Boschma, and Cooke, 2011). Firms' internal and external competences that contribute to innovation may be further understood in terms of competence-enhancing innovation (i.e. innovation that builds upon and reinforces existing knowledge and capacities) and new competence innovation (innovation that is based on competences new to the firm and requires it to reach beyond existing skills and knowledge) (Nambisan, 2013).

This chapter presents the results of a study of innovation among New Zealand winegrowers based on whether the businesses surveyed chose to offer cellar door sales to wine tourists. Following a review of some of the key issues associated with innovation in the context of wine tourism, this chapter then explores innovation within the New Zealand wine industry in order to provide some background and context. The third and final part of this chapter reviews the results of a survey of New Zealand wineries with respect to their engagement with wine tourism and innovation and seeks to identify the extent

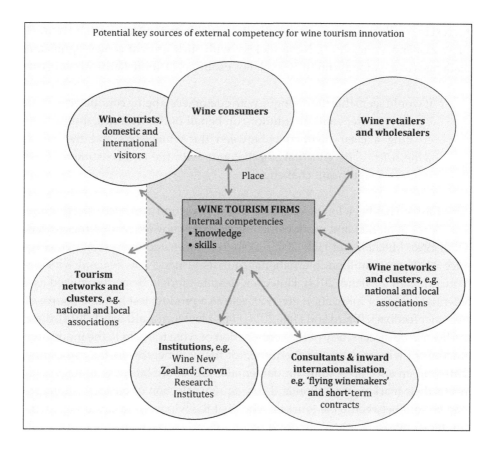

**Figure 12.1    Internal and external competences of wine tourism firms**
*Source*: The authors.

to which internal and external competences are utilized by winegrowers that are engaged in wine tourism.

## Innovation Within the New Zealand Wine Industry

The New Zealand wine industry has witnessed a growth in wine production that has also seen an explosion in the number of registered vineyards and wineries in New Zealand since 1997, although growth may now be starting to level out. The 2014 *Australian and New Zealand Wine Directory* lists 508 wineries (Winetitles, 2014) compared with 511 listed in 2009 (Winetitles, 2009), 419 in 2003 (Christensen, Hall, and Mitchell, 2004) and 270 listed wineries in 1997 (Hall and Johnson, 1998). This same period has also seen a rise in the amount of interest in locally produced wine products available on the New Zealand market (New Zealand Wine, 2014). Nevertheless, with such growth comes significant challenges at a national and firm level. For example, Deloitte (2010: 21) suggest:

> It would seem that the dialogue with customers is being conducted by the exporters and distributors on behalf of the wineries, thus creating a clear distinction between the wine*makers* and the wine *sellers*. The winemaker's dialogue with the end consumer remains a significant challenge.

Wine tourism has been long recognized as an opportunity for such dialogue and as a source of market and product intelligence and knowledge for winegrowers (Hall, 1996; Mitchell and Hall, 2003; 2004). It is estimated that in the five years since 2010 over 1 million international tourists visited New Zealand wineries (Tourism New Zealand, 2014). However, despite tourism being recognized as a potential source of innovation given its role as a product test bed and source of customer feedback (Baird and Hall, 2014; Hall, Heyworth, and Baird, 2014), there has been little direct study of the contribution of wine tourism to the innovative practices of winegrowers. Furthermore, for many winegrowers the association with tourism also raises some fundamental issues about business strategy, as it means their market orientation and consequent selection of business strategies may be split between wine tourists, who visit the winery, and consumers, who purchase and drink wine. Although there is clearly an overlap, the groups will have distinct demands on firms with respect to products required, as well as the allocation of capital (Hall and Mitchell, 2005; 2008). Indeed, many studies of tourism innovation arguably fail to recognize the significance of what Leiper et al. (2008) describe as the partial industrialization of tourism systems (Hall and Page, 2010). This means that only a proportion of a firm's customer base and income is derived from tourism and, therefore, any analysis of innovation or other aspects of firm strategy and management requires close examination so as to distinguish the role of tourism in business decision-making as well as the relative mix between tourism and non-tourism influences. In the case of wine tourism, for example, many firms may have a substantial proportion of their income derived directly or indirectly from cellar-door sales, but may have only a weak connection to tourism industry networks, or may not even see themselves as being in the business of tourism at all (Baird and Hall, 2014; Weidenfeld and Hall, 2014). Furthermore, and reflecting the wider context of partial industrialization, tourism and innovation policies in New Zealand appear to have little formal interrelationship. Hall (2009: 15) suggests that 'it is possible that one of the reasons for the lack of recognition of tourism in innovation policy is that it is perceived as an industry that is not particularly innovative'.

## Innovation, Wine, and Tourism

Four main categories of innovation are identified, consisting of product and process innovations and organizational and marketing innovations (OECD, 2005). In the context of sustainable winemaking, which has become integral to winegrowing in New Zealand (Hall and Baird, 2014a), this also potentially applies to wine tourists who are attracted to wineries because of the process and production methods used on site, and the end consumer who purchases a particular brand of wine because it is manufactured using sustainable methods (Baird and Hall, 2013; Gössling and Hall, 2013a; Hall and Gössling, 2013; Hall and Mitchell, 2008). However, the very nature of the OECD (2005) definition of innovation suggests a potential dilemma for New Zealand wine tourism. On one hand, for example, you have the approach taken by the Sustainable Winegrowing New Zealand (SWNZ) scheme, whereby sustainable processes, methods and products must meet a predetermined criteria (SWNZ, 2010), while on the other there are many wineries which predate the introduction of SWNZ in 1995 (SWNZ, 2010), and arguably have already created their own innovations with respect to sustainability without external intervention (Baird and Hall, 2013).

Studies of the relationship between wine tourism and innovation draw on a number of strands of innovation research. Examining how innovation serves to improve wine production techniques (Aylward, 2002; Gilinsky et al., 2008) has also led to research into the effect of innovation on wine exports (Aylward, 2004a; 2004b; Olavarría et al., 2009) and the levels of knowledge sharing which exist between wine producers (Aylward, 2005; Chiffoleau, 2005). This embraces knowledge-sharing in the development of wine trails (Preston-Whyte, 2000) and in the contribution to regional development (Hall, 2012; Hall, Johnson, and Mitchell, 2000; Hall, Mitchell, and Sharples, 2003). Studies have also been conducted that review how successful tourism developments have benefited from the implementation of organizational, production or process changes (Gössling and Hall, 2013b; Hjalager, 2009). However, this research has not readily focused on the competences of firms or of the wider wine region(s) within which winegrowers are located.

Possibly the most related stream of writing related to competence innovation is writing on collaboration and cooperation in wine clusters and networks that focuses on the flows of information between firms (Aylward, 2002; 2005; 2006; Aylward and Turpin, 2003; 2008; Chiffoleau, 2005; Chiffoleau et al., 2006; Cusmano, Morrison, and Rabelloti, 2008; Hall, 2014; Hira and Bwenge, 2011; Taplin and Breckenridge, 2008). The level of institutional support which is provided by regional and national governing bodies has also been recognized as serving to increase levels of collaboration and therefore knowledge exchange that can contribute to firm level innovations (Aylward, 2006; Guthey, 2008; Hira and Bwenge, 2011; Simpson, Bretherton, and de Vere, 2005), although regulatory demands can also impede relationship building (Malm, Gössling, and Hall, 2013).

The geographical proximity of members of wine clusters is another important factor for successful knowledge sharing between networks (Aylward, 2006; Gilinsky et al., 2008; Giuliani, Morrison, and Rabellotti, 2011), including specifically in relation to wine tourism (Hall, 2003; 2004; Hall et al., 1997). However, not all wineries work cooperatively even when co-located. Difficulties firms experience with innovations may also have repercussions throughout particular wine networks. For example, Mortensen and Marks (2003) observe that the failure of product innovations resulted in a loss of confidence among producers, which then went on to affect the rates at which future innovations were adopted by other wineries within their network. This observation supports the argument that innovation-related performance within a firm is dependent on the extent of the utilization of competences that occurs and how this is viewed by other members of the network (Bogner, Thomas, and McGee, 1999; Goh, 2000). Pike and Melewar (2006) note that the protection of business reputation and brand identity was paramount among network members as no one wanted to be associated with an innovation which had failed to succeed.

## Method

No prior studies specifically examine New Zealand wine industry or wine tourism innovation. Applying innovation measures as set out by the OECD (2005) to the New Zealand wine industry does provide an opportunity to benchmark attitudes towards innovation within the context of past innovation studies conducted within the New Zealand agricultural sector. The 2010 New Zealand National Wineries' Survey was designed to facilitate the collection of information about wine tourism in New Zealand from the wineries' perspective. The sample population was derived from all New Zealand wineries registered in *The 2009 Australian and New Zealand Wine Industry Directory* (Winetitles, 2009) and it was the third such national wine tourism survey to be undertaken as part of a longitudinal study of wine tourism in New Zealand.

### SURVEY DESIGN

Survey questions were based on the template provided by the two previous New Zealand National Wineries' Surveys (Hall and Johnson, 1998; Christensen, Hall, and Mitchell, 2004). A question regarding biosecurity was added to the second New Zealand National Wineries' Survey (Christensen, Hall, and Mitchell, 2004), and this was expanded out into a series of questions that make up a section dedicated solely to biosecurity issues in the 2010 New Zealand National Wineries' Survey. The determined stance of the current New Zealand wine industry towards sustainable practices as a form of innovation was introduced as a new section in the 2010 New Zealand National Wineries' Survey which utilized the framework of the OECD (2005) as a basis for the questions. In addition, questions based on those in the 'Innovation in New Zealand' survey (Statistics New Zealand, 2007), were used in order to provide a benchmark of the wine industry with other agricultural-based industries and the tourism sector. Modifications to questions were also based on the results of previous New Zealand wine tourism research (e.g. Christensen, Hall, and Mitchell, 2004; Hall and Johnson, 1998; Hall et al., 2000; Mitchell and Hall, 2001a; 2001b).

## SOURCE DATA

The 2010 survey utilized primary data obtained from participants who represent each of the 511 vineyards located within New Zealand as per publicly available winery listings published in *The 2009 Australian and New Zealand Wine Industry Directory* (Winetitles, 2009). They initially received the survey via email (491 wineries) or by post (20 wineries). Nearly all wineries are open to visitors either for cellar door sales or by appointment. Prior response rates to the 1997 survey amounted to 111 responses out of 270 producers, giving a response rate of 41.1 per cent (Hall and Johnson, 1998). The second survey conducted in 2003 achieved a response rate of 121 usable responses out of the 419 wineries surveyed, resulting in a response rate of 28.9 per cent, which compares very favourably to other business surveys conducted within the New Zealand wine industry (Christensen, Hall, and Mitchell, 2004).

## Findings

The results illustrate levels of innovation within the New Zealand wine industry, and are compared, where possible, with the benchmark provided by the average overall 2007, 2009, 2011 and 2013 New Zealand innovation levels and New Zealand agricultural sector innovation levels from the same timeframe as that reported in the biannual *Innovation in New Zealand* studies (Statistics New Zealand, 2007; 2009; 2012; 2013). New Zealand wine industry figures are also compared where possible to the average overall 2009, 2011 and 2013 New Zealand innovation levels and New Zealand agricultural sector innovation levels as reported in 'Innovation in New Zealand' studies (Statistics New Zealand, 2007; 2009; 2012; 2013).

## INTRODUCTION OF INNOVATIONS

The first set of questions on innovation asked respondents whether they had introduced any innovations over the two financial years prior to 2009. Results indicate that 67 per cent of respondents had not introduced any new or improved goods or services over this period, while the remaining 33 per cent stated that their vineyards had made changes to previously existing goods or services on offer (Figure 12.2). This figure is just over twice the New Zealand agricultural innovation average recorded in 2007 (16 per cent), and is also higher than the overall 2007 New Zealand innovation average of 23 per cent (Statistics New Zealand, 2007). Only 22.3 per cent of respondents reported that they had introduced new or significantly improved operational processes, which also includes sustainable production methods. A total of 39.8 per cent of wineries had decided to implement new or significantly improved organizational or managerial processes in their businesses. This figure is much higher than the 2007 New Zealand agricultural innovation average of 15 per cent, as well as the overall 2007 New Zealand innovation average of 27 per cent (Statistics New Zealand, 2007). The highest degree of innovation occurred in the implementation of new or significantly improved sales or marketing methods (43.7 per cent), many of which appeared geared towards wine tourism.

Figures 12.3, 12.4 and 12.5 compare the 2010 survey figures to the New Zealand national and agricultural averages for 2009, 2011 and 2013 respectively across various categories of innovation. This illustrates that changes occurred within this period with a drop in the New Zealand agricultural average across all categories, while the national innovation average remained relatively stable.

## SALES FROM AND IMPROVEMENTS MADE TO GOODS OR SERVICES

New or significantly improved goods or services were reported by 37.9 per cent of respondents as having had no effect on sales in 2010 (Table 12.1). This figure is over twice the 2007–2013 New Zealand agricultural innovation averages and also the New Zealand innovation averages for this same period (Statistics New Zealand, 2007; 2009; 2012; 2013). Despite the emphasis given to networks and cooperation in much of the wine tourism literature (see above), only 8.7 per cent of wineries had opted to develop new or significantly improved goods or services in partnership with other businesses (Table 12.2). The figure of 30.1 per cent for respondents who had actually developed new or significantly improved goods or services themselves also falls well below the

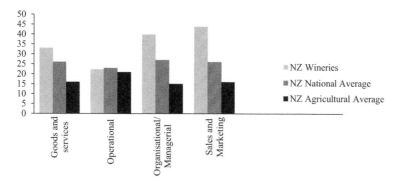

**Figure 12.2    Introduction of innovations over the two financial years prior to 2007**

*Sources*: Statistics New Zealand, 2007; authors' results.

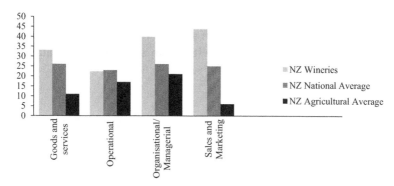

**Figure 12.3    Introduction of innovations over the two financial years prior to 2009**

*Sources*: Statistics New Zealand, 2009; authors' results.

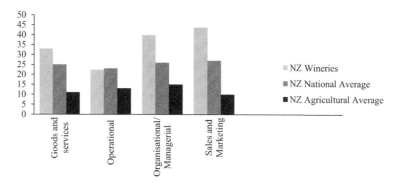

**Figure 12.4    Introduction of innovations over the two financial years prior to 2011**

*Sources*: Statistics New Zealand, 2012; authors' results.

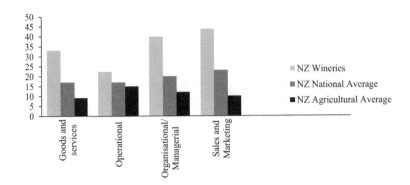

**Figure 12.5    Introduction of innovations over the two financial years prior to 2013**

*Sources*: Statistics New Zealand, 2013; authors' results.

**Table 12.1    Percentage of sales from significantly improved goods or services (compared with innovation in New Zealand agriculture 2007–2013)**

| Category | # 2010 survey | per cent of sales in 2010 | NZ National average 2007 | NZ Agricultural average 2007 | NZ National average 2009 | NZ Agricultural average 2009 | NZ National average 2011 | NZ Agricultural average 2011 | NZ National average 2013 | NZ Agricultural average 2013 |
|---|---|---|---|---|---|---|---|---|---|---|
|  |  | % | % | % | % | % | % | % | % | % |
| Zero | 39 | 37.9 | 2.0 | 15.0 | 3.0 | 0 | 17.0 | 18.0 | 6.0 | 0 |
| 10% or less | 14 | 13.6 | 41.0 | 42.0 | 51.0 | 66.0 | 48.0 | 46.0 | 46.0 | 72.0 |
| 20% or less | 6 | 5.8 | 21.0 | 24.0 | 20.0 | 21.0 | 33.0 | 31.0 | 33.0 | 24.0 |
| 30% or less | 8 | 7.8 | 17.0 | 15.0 | 13.0 | 13.0 | 0 | 0 | 11.0 | 0 |
| 40% or less | 0 | 0 | 0.0 | 0 | 2.0 | 0 | 0 | 0 | 0 | 0 |
| 41%– 100% | 2 | 1.9 | 1.0 | 0 | 2.0 | 0 | 2.0 | 0 | 2.0 | 0 |
| Don't know | 34 | 33.0 | 9.0 | 8.0 | 9.0 | 0 | 0 | 5.0 | 2.0 | 4.0 |

*Sources*: Statistics New Zealand, 2007; 2009; 2012, 2013; authors' results.

Table 12.2    Significantly improved goods or services (compared with the New Zealand national averages 2007–2011)

| Method used to make improvement | Yes | No | NZ National average 2007 | NZ National average 2009 | NZ National average 2011 |
|---|---|---|---|---|---|
| Developed by this business | % 30.1 | % 69.9 | % 56.0 | % 58.0 | % 59.0 |
| Developed by this business in partnership with others | 8.7 | 91.3 | 27.0 | 27.0 | 25.0 |
| Obtained from others and significant improvements made by your business | 1.9 | 98.1 | 17.0 | 17.0 | 15.0 |
| Obtained from others and NO significant improvements made by your business | 100 | 0 | 19.0 | 15.0 | 19.0 |

Sources: Statistics New Zealand, 2007; 2009; 2012; authors' results.

national innovation averages (Statistics New Zealand, 2007; 2009; 2012). Few wineries had obtained any new or significantly improved goods or services from others and then implemented changes themselves. All wineries stated that if they had obtained new or significantly improved goods or services from others, then once these were implemented no further improvements were undertaken.

## IMPROVEMENTS MADE TO OPERATIONAL, ORGANIZATIONAL AND MANAGERIAL PROCESSES

Of those wineries that had opted to introduce new or significantly improved operational processes (Table 12.3), 17.5 per cent of businesses had developed their own innovations, which is well below the 2007–2011 New Zealand innovation averages. Reports from 5.8 per cent of wineries stated that these significantly improved operational processes had been developed in partnership with others and 2.9 per cent reported that they had developed significantly improved operational processes obtained from other businesses. Reluctance to implement or adopt new or significantly improved operational processes once again touches on the unwillingness of some wineries to engage in collaboration and cooperation within existing clusters and networks. Significantly improved organizational and managerial processes (Table 12.4) were developed by 30.1 per cent of those surveyed, while 9.7 per cent stated that they developed these processes in partnership with other businesses. These results are well under half of those recorded for the 2007–2011 New Zealand innovation averages in these areas.

**Table 12.3    Significantly improved operational processes**

| Method used to make improvement | Yes | No | NZ National average 2007 | NZ National average 2009 | NZ National average 2011 |
|---|---|---|---|---|---|
| | % | % | % | % | % |
| Developed by this business | 17.5 | 82.5 | 62.0 | 56.0 | 57.0 |
| Developed by this business in partnership with others | 5.8 | 94.2 | 24.0 | 23.0 | 26.0 |
| Obtained from others and significant improvements made by your business | 2.9 | 97.1 | 17.0 | 24.0 | 25.0 |
| Obtained from others and no significant improvements made by your business | 1.0 | 99.0 | 18.0 | 7.0 | 7.0 |

*Sources*: Statistics New Zealand, 2007; 2009; 2012; authors' results.

**Table 12.4    Significantly improved organizational and managerial processes**

| Method used to make improvement | Yes | No | NZ National average 2007 | NZ National average 2009 | NZ National average 2011 |
|---|---|---|---|---|---|
| | % | % | % | % | % |
| Developed by this business | 30.1 | 69.9 | 68.0 | 66.0 | 74.0 |
| Developed by this business in partnership with others | 9.7 | 90.3 | 24.0 | 23.0 | 20.0 |
| Obtained from others and significant improvements made by your business | 4.9 | 95.1 | 15.0 | 13.0 | 12.0 |
| Obtained from others and NO significant improvements made by your business | 4.9 | 95.1 | 14.0 | 8.0 | 7.0 |

*Sources*: Statistics New Zealand; 2007; 2009; 2012; authors' results.

## IMPROVEMENTS MADE TO SALES AND MARKETING METHODS

Significantly improved sales and marketing methods (Table 12.5) were reported as having being developed by 35 per cent of wineries, which is well below the 2007–2011 New Zealand innovation averages. 13.6 per cent indicated that these methods were developed in partnership with other businesses, which in comparison rated at 36 per cent for the 2007 New Zealand innovation average (Statistics New Zealand, 2007), 35 per cent in 2009 (Statistics New Zealand, 2009), and 37 per cent in 2011 (Statistics New Zealand, 2012). Only 8.7 per cent stated that they had obtained improved sales and marketing methods from other businesses. This is low compared to the 2007–2011 New Zealand innovation averages.

Table 12.5    Significantly improved sales and marketing methods (compared with the New Zealand national innovation averages 2007–2011)

| Method used to make improvement | Yes | No | NZ national average 2007 | NZ national average 2009 | NZ national average 2011 |
|---|---|---|---|---|---|
| Developed by this business | %<br>35.0 | %<br>65.0 | %<br>52.0 | %<br>62.0 | %<br>55.0 |
| Developed by this business in partnership with others | 13.6 | 86.4 | 36.0 | 35.0 | 37.0 |
| Obtained from others and significant improvements made by your business | 8.7 | 91.3 | 15.0 | 13.0 | 15.0 |
| Obtained from others and NO significant improvements made by your business | 3.9 | 96.1 | 14.0 | 8.0 | 19.0 |

*Sources*: Statistics New Zealand, 2007; 2009; 2012; authors' results.

## REASONS FOR INNOVATION

Varied reasons were given for innovation (Table 12.6), with the need to establish or exploit new market opportunities given as the main reason (52.4 per cent). This was well above the 2007 New Zealand innovation average of 38 per cent and the New Zealand agricultural sector average of 32 per cent (Statistics New Zealand, 2007). Desire to increase market share and reduce costs ranked second equal, followed by the need to reduce environmental impacts (47.6 per cent). The ranking of the latter is especially interesting, given the emphasis provided in New Zealand on sustainable winegrowing. Improvements to productivity

Table 12.6   Reasons for innovation

| Reason | Yes % | No % | Don't know % | NZ national average 2007 % | NZ agricultural average 2007 % | NZ national Average 2009 % | NZ agricultural average 2009 % | NZ national average 2011 % | NZ agricultural average 2011 % | NZ national average 2013 % | NZ agricultural average 2013 % |
|---|---|---|---|---|---|---|---|---|---|---|---|
| To increase productivity | 45.6 | 28.2 | 26.2 | 66.0 | 64.0 | 88.0 | 90.0 | 81.0 | 78.0 | 83.0 | 82.0 |
| To increase revenue | 41.7 | 31.1 | 27.2 | 66.0 | 64.0 | 87.0 | 88.0 | 85.0 | 87.0 | 74.0 | 74.0 |
| To reduce costs | 50.5 | 22.3 | 27.2 | 71.0 | 28.0 | 76.0 | 80.0 | 86.0 | 91.0 | 68.0 | 64.0 |
| To increase responsiveness to customers | 45.6 | 26.2 | 28.2 | 59.0 | 51.0 | 34.0 | 19.0 | 45.0 | 48.0 | 29.0 | 15.0 |
| To increase market share | 50.5 | 20.4 | 29.1 | 68.0 | 45.0 | 38.0 | 38.0 | 44.0 | 46.0 | 33.0 | 29.0 |
| To establish or exploit new market opportunities | 52.4 | 24.3 | 23.3 | 38.0 | 32.0 | 38.0 | 38.0 | 36.0 | 52.0 | 31.0 | 26.0 |
| To improve work safety standards | 23.3 | 43.7 | 33.0 | 24.0 | 26.0 | 57.0 | 57.0 | 50.0 | 45.0 | 53.0 | 43.0 |
| To reduce energy consumption | 35.0 | 35.0 | 30.1 | 26.0 | 17.0 | 30.0 | 30.0 | 33.0 | 35.0 | 25.0 | 26.0 |
| To reduce environmental impact | 47.6 | 27.2 | 25.2 | 33.0 | 18.0 | 49.0 | 56.0 | 38.0 | 38.0 | 46.0 | 53.0 |
| To replace goods and services being phased out | 5.8 | 63.1 | 31.1 | 26.0 | 35.0 | 15.0 | 14.0 | 22.0 | 23.0 | 18.0 | 22.0 |

*Sources:* Statistics New Zealand, 2007; 2009; 2012; 2013; authors' results.

and the creation of an increased responsiveness to customers both ranked third equal at 45.6 per cent. Other notable mentions were to increase productivity (41.7 per cent) and to reduce energy consumption (35 per cent). Reducing energy consumption was an area where New Zealand wineries really stood out against the 2007 New Zealand innovation average which was only 26 per cent (Statistics New Zealand, 2007) and the agricultural sector average, which was less than half that of the 35 per cent reported by wineries at 17 per cent (Statistics New Zealand, 2007).

## SOURCES OF IDEAS AND INFORMATION FOR INNOVATION

Sources of ideas and information for innovation (Table 12.7) primarily came from existing staff (52.4 per cent) or competitors and other businesses within the wine industry (33 per cent). New staff (32 per cent) and suggestions from customers (31.1 per cent) were also cited as important, while ideas and information from books, journals, patent disclosures and the Internet are also a resource (29.1 per cent). It is of interest that Crown Research Institutes (government research bodies) and government agencies both rated poorly as sources, whereas in other rural tourism businesses they had been perceived as significant sources of independent information with respect to climate change adaptation and mitigation (Hall, 2006). The winegrowers' responses show substantial variation from the New Zealand innovation surveys, with wineries consistently falling below national averages on sourcing ideas. These findings also support the notion that there is a distinct lack of institutional support currently available to New Zealand wineries specifically designed to encourage innovation, or alternatively, a lack of willingness from winegrowers to access or accept such expertise. Competences for innovation are also internally grounded. Nevertheless, external competences and institutional support has been noted as an important factor in improving levels of innovation in winegrowers (Simpson, Bretherton, and De Vere, 2005; Aylward, 2006; Guthey, 2008; Hira and Bwenge, 2011).

## ACTIVITIES TO SUPPORT INNOVATION

There was a relative lack of activities undertaken to support innovation among respondents. When compared against the 2007, 2009 and 2011 New Zealand innovation averages (Table 12.8), the main activities listed that were carried out in support of innovation were the acquisition of new computer hardware or software and the design of product labelling, which were both at 18.4 per cent, with the acquisition of new computer hardware or software well below the 2007 national averages. The figures reported for design tended to reflect these averages:

**Table 12.7**     Sources of ideas and information for innovation

| Source | Yes | No | Don't know | NZ national average 2007 | NZ national average 2009 | NZ national average 2011 | NZ national average 2013 |
|---|---|---|---|---|---|---|---|
| New staff (appointed in the last 2 years) | % | % | % | % | % | % | % |
| | 32.0 | 64.1 | 3.9 | 51.0 | 54.0 | 44.0 | 50.0 |
| Existing staff | 52.4 | 45.6 | 1.9 | 70.0 | 74.0 | 69.0 | 72.0 |
| Other businesses within the business group (e.g. subsidiaries or parent companies) | 14.6 | 82.5 | 2.9 | 31.0 | 54.0 | 31.0 | 45.0 |
| Customers | 31.1 | 65.0 | 3.9 | 57.0 | 61.0 | 54.0 | 26.0 |
| Suppliers | 30.1 | 68.0 | 1.9 | 47.0 | 50.0 | 41.0 | 42.0 |
| Competitors and other businesses from the same industry | 33.0 | 63.1 | 3.9 | 45.0 | 46.0 | 69.0 | N/A |
| Businesses from other industries (not including customers or suppliers) | 20.4 | 74.8 | 4.9 | 22.0 | 45.0 | 23.0 | N/A |
| Professional advisors, consultants, banks or accountants | 27.2 | 68.9 | 3.9 | 44.0 | 47.0 | 55.0 | 63.0 |
| Books, journals, patent disclosures or the Internet | 29.1 | 65.0 | 5.8 | 41.0 | 44.0 | 51.0 | 52.0 |
| Wine shows, festivals or conferences | 22.3 | 71.8 | 5.8 | 46.0 | 44.0 | 36.0 | 48.0 |
| Industry or employer organizations | 19.4 | 74.8 | 5.8 | 30.0 | 28.0 | 50.0 | 37.0 |
| Universities or polytechnics | 11.7 | 83.5 | 4.9 | 9.0 | 8.0 | 20.0 | 14.0 |
| Crown Research institutes, other research institutes or associations | 6.8 | 88.3 | 4.9 | 7.0 | 6.0 | 34.0 | 20.0 |
| Government agencies | 7.8 | 86.4 | 5.8 | 13.0 | 11.0 | 22.0 | 5.0 |

*Sources*: Statistics New Zealand, 2007; 2009; 2012; 2013; authors' results.

**Table 12.8  Activities to support innovation (compared with the New Zealand national averages 2007–2013)**

| Activity | Done to support innovation % | Done, though not to support innovation % | Not Done % | Don't know % | Done to support innovation (NZ average 2007) | Done, though not to support innovation (NZ average 2007) | Done to support innovation (NZ average 2009) | Done, though not to support innovation (NZ average 2009) | Done to support innovation (NZ average 2011) | Done, though not to support innovation (NZ average 2011) | Done to support innovation (NZ average 2013) | Done, though not to support innovation (NZ average 2013) |
|---|---|---|---|---|---|---|---|---|---|---|---|---|
| Introduce a new variety of grape | 16.5 | 1.9 | 62.1 | 19.4 | — | — | — | — | — | — | — | — |
| Use of new viticultural techniques | 16.5 | 13.6 | 45.6 | 24.3 | — | — | — | — | — | — | — | — |
| Acquire new machinery and equipment | 15.5 | 12.6 | 52.4 | 19.4 | 29.0 | 38.0 | 19.0 | N/A | 16.0 | 34.0 | 16.0 | 31.0 |
| Acquire new computer hardware and software | 18.4 | 20.4 | 45.6 | 15.5 | 38.0 | 46.0 | 19.0 | N/A | 22.0 | 21.0 | 21.0 | 42.0 |
| Acquire other knowledge | 13.6 | 6.8 | 64.1 | 15.5 | 14.0 | 6.0 | 12.0 | N/A | 7.0 | 6.0 | 7.0 | 7.0 |
| Implement new business strategies or techniques | 16.5 | 10.7 | 48.5 | 24.3 | 35.0 | 16.0 | 19.0 | N/A | 16.0 | 12.0 | 15.0 | 20.0 |
| Implement organizational restructuring | 7.8 | 7.8 | 53.4 | 31.1 | 22.0 | 11.0 | 12.0 | N/A | 11.0 | 8.0 | 10.0 | 19.0 |
| Design* | 18.4 | 7.8 | 44.7 | 29.1 | 17.0 | 5.0 | 3.0 | N/A | 9.0 | 2.0 | 9.0 | 5.0 |
| Market the introduction of new goods and services | 15.5 | 3.9 | 50.5 | 30.1 | 33.0 | 13.0 | 7.0 | N/A | 15.0 | 13.0 | 14.0 | 13.0 |
| Market research | 9.7 | 11.7 | 47.6 | 31.1 | 20.0 | 10.0 | 5.0 | N/A | 9.0 | 3.0 | 9.0 | 10.0 |
| Significant changes to marketing strategies | 14.6 | 12.6 | 44.7 | 28.2 | 17.0 | 8.0 | 8.0 | N/A | 8.0 | 9.0 | 9.0 | 10.0 |
| Employee training | 13.6 | 20.4 | 38.8 | 27.2 | 38.0 | 26.0 | 24.0 | N/A | 21.0 | 56.0 | 21.0 | 50.0 |

*For example, graphic design on labelling of bottles.
*Sources:* Statistics New Zealand, 2007; 2009; 2012; 2013; authors' results.

17 per cent of activities in this area undertaken to support innovation and seven per cent were not. The introduction of new varieties of grapes and viticultural techniques were both reported as being undertaken by only 16.5 per cent of those who were surveyed. Marketing the introduction of new goods and services (15.5 per cent) along with the purchasing of new machinery and equipment (15.5 per cent) were noted as having been done to support innovation, but they still fell short of the 2007 New Zealand innovation averages by comparison (Statistics New Zealand, 2007). The pattern of these results when also compared to the 2009, 2011 and 2013 New Zealand innovation averages suggest some resistance from wineries towards activities supporting innovation.

## New Zealand Winegrowers' Participation in and Competences for Innovation

Winegrowing and its significant relationship to tourism at the cellar door presents a conundrum in seeking to understand the role of innovation. Visitors to the cellar door represents a significant external source of competence with respect to innovation, and although some wineries undoubtedly embrace the product and consumer knowledge that wine tourism brings, winegrowers in the main focus on internal innovation competences that are based on their existing staff. illustrates the relative contribution of internal and external competences to winegrower innovation in New Zealand.

Unless there was a proven track record for an innovative process which could enhance the managerial and organizational objectives of the wineries involved, or provide more efficient organizational and marketing objectives through product innovations (Hjalager, 2009), then New Zealand wineries appeared to adopt a cautious approach towards innovation, particularly in the adoption of sustainable methods of wine production. In great part this appears to be a function of the overreliance on internal competences, particularly the use of existing staff. In addition, it may also be a reflection of the fact that many winegrowers are small operations which do not have systems in place to transfer external competences and which are inherently cautious in their business strategies, as they cannot afford to make significant mistakes. Indeed, the results of the survey suggest that larger wineries, whether measured by number of full time, part time and casual workers, or by the amount of wine produced per annum, were more innovative than the smaller wineries that were surveyed. Nevertheless, the overriding impression from this survey is of a sector that, despite attention in the wine tourism literature to collaboration and networks, remains relatively insular and focused on internal competences with respect to innovation activities (Baird and Hall, 2013; Hall and Baird, 2014a).

|  | Internal Competencies | External Competencies |
|---|---|---|
| **Competence Enhancing Innovation** innovation that builds upon and reinforces existing knowledge and capacities | • **Existing staff**<br>• New staff<br>• Use of books, journals, patent disclosures or the Internet<br>• Other businesses within the business group | • Product knowledge derived from wine tourists<br>• Customers<br>• Suppliers<br>• Competitors and other wine businesses<br>• Universities<br>• Industry and employer organisations<br>• Crown Research Institutes, other research institutes, or associations<br>• Government agencies |
| **New Competence Innovation** Innovation that is based on competences new to the firm and requires it to reach beyond existing skills and knowledge | • **Some new staff**<br>• Use of books, journals, patent disclosures or the Internet<br>• Other businesses within the business group | • Consumer knowledge derived from wine tourists<br>• Businesses from other industries<br>• Professional advisors, consultants, banks and accountants<br>• Wine shows, festivals or conferences |

**Figure 12.6    Framing the relative contributions of internal and external innovation competences of New Zealand winegrowers**

*Sources*: The authors.

For those wineries that did innovate, the reasons were related to increasing productivity, reducing energy consumption, and reducing environmental impact (Baird and Hall, 2013). Indeed, the environmental and energy efforts of the winegrowers engaged in wine tourism were larger than those of other sectors of the New Zealand tourism industry (Hall, 2009) as well as New Zealand industry overall. In part, this may be explained as a response to the dictates of Wine New Zealand that winegrowers must be part of the sustainable winegrowing programme to be able to receive support for overseas marketing, however this is arguably an overly simplistic response, given that a number of winegrowers were already well engaged in developing sustainable practices long before the development of the nation-wide scheme (Baird and Hall, 2013). In fact, the virtually mandatory application of the scheme to New Zealand winegrowers has removed first-mover advantage with respect to the adoption of innovative sustainable practices and could arguably be interpreted as potentially a competence destroying change at the level of the firm, although possibly not with respect to the branding of New Zealand wine products where it can be regarded as a competence-enhancing change (Meyer, Brooks, and Goes, 1990). Indeed, the research conducted in this chapter begins to suggest a far more nuanced approach towards competence-based innovation in tourism, whereby it is not just a matter of recognizing firms' internal and external competences, important as that is, but also noting that firms are embedded within innovation networks at different levels, e.g. local, regional, national and international, together with different levels of connectivity, e.g. sectoral, spatial (Hall and Williams, 2008; Weidenfeld and Hall, 2014).

Gersick's (1991) argument: that a firm will refrain from an innovation associated with competence-destroying change if it causes the firm to innovate less effectively or have a weaker positioning in the future, and thereby lose its competitive advantage over rival firms, only makes sense in the absence of environmental conditions that are not, in effect, forced upon a firm. In the case of being able to market overseas under the Wine New Zealand umbrella, and thereby gain access to export, shows, and national branding opportunities, individual winegrowers are required to participate in the sustainable winegrowing programme (Hall and Baird, 2014b). Therefore, arguably only the very largest wine brands and/or those that are part of international companies with their own distribution channels, could afford not to participate in such schemes. Indeed, the implications of competence-destroying change, whether regulatory, technological, or socio-economic, needs to be better understood by firms, especially by those that are partially industrialized, as it would be logical to assume that changes in the environment of one sector that a firm is connected to may lead to new strategies in other sectors.

## Conclusion

Therefore a longer-term issue for the first wave of firms that embraced sustainable winegrowing will be: where do such businesses now focus their innovative efforts and seek to develop their competences? One response is clearly with respect to improving grape and wine quality. However, this has long been the dominant focus of winegrowers with respect to product improvement; it reflects the internal competences of many businesses in the sector and would not appear to offer significant opportunities for product differentiation. Instead, Prahalad and Hamels' (1994) insights that the more opportunities an environment presents, including those to harness the role of competence utilization in the context of innovation, the more will a firm select the environmental change that improves its position in relation to its competitors (Goh, 2000), resonates well with the partially industrialized nature of many tourism firms, including winegrowers. Arguably, the area of competence that appears to offer substantial benefit is with respect to the development of external competences and especially those provided by wine tourist and consumer contact whereby the focus shifts from an internal focus on the physical characteristics of wine to an external focus on the attributes and experiences that consumers and tourists associate with wine and wineries (Hall and Mitchell, 2008). If this is indeed the case one would expect that greater emphasis would be placed on marketing innovation over time, a situation that the present research potentially observes, although further survey iterations are required to confirm this.

The generally positive attitude of the New Zealand wine industry towards tourism does indicate that there is still unrealized potential within the industry, provided that it is both safeguarded against external threats and promoted correctly through the appropriate channels in order to assure future growth. Nevertheless, there appear to be significant barriers in the sector to embracing the external competences that can enable the increased knowledge and competence-sharing that need to occur so that the harsh lessons learned by overseas wine regions are not repeated in New Zealand.

## References

Argote, L., and Ingram, P. (2000). Knowledge transfer: A basis for competitive advantage in firms. *Organisational Behaviour and Human Decision Processes*, 82(1), 150–169.

Asheim, B., Boschma, R., and Cooke, P. (2011). Constructing regional advantage: Platform policies based on related variety and differentiated knowledge bases. *Regional Studies*, 45, 1–12.

Aylward, D.K. (2002). Diffusion of R&D within the Australian wine industry. *Prometheus*, 20(4), 351–366.

Aylward, D.K. (2004a). Working together: Innovation and export links within highly developed and embryonic wine clusters. *Strategic Change*, 13(8), 429–439.

Aylward, D.K. (2004b). A documentary of innovation support among new world wine industries. *Journal of Wine Research*, 14(1), 31–43.

Aylward, D.K. (2005). Innovation lock-in: Unlocking research and development path dependency in the Australian wine industry. *Strategic Change*, 15(7–8), 361–372.

Aylward, D.K. (2006). Global pipelines: Profiling successful SME exporters within the Australian wine industry. *International Journal of Technology, Policy and Management*, 6(1), 49–65.

Aylward, D.K., and Turpin, T. (2003). New wine in old bottles: A case study of innovation territories in 'new world' wine production. *International Journal of Innovation Management*, 7(4), 501–525.

Baird, T., and Hall, C.M. (2013). Sustainable winegrowing in New Zealand. In C.M. Hall and S. Gössling (eds), *Sustainable Culinary Systems: Local Foods, Innovation, and Tourism and Hospitality* (223–240), London: Routledge.

Baird, T., and Hall, C.M. (2014). Between the vines: Wine tourism in New Zealand. In P. Howland (ed.), *Social, Cultural and Economic Impacts of Wine in New Zealand* (191–207). London: Routledge.

Bogner, W.C., Thomas, H., and McGee, J. (1999). Competence and competitive advantage: Towards a dynamic model. *British Journal of Management*, 10(4), 275–290.

Brannon, D.L. and Wiklund, J. (2014). Tourism and business model innovation: The case of US wine makers. In G.A. Alsos, D. Eide, and E.L. Madsen (eds), *Handbook of Research on Innovation in Tourism Industries* (228–249). Cheltenham, UK: Edward Elgar.

Chiffoleau, Y. (2005). Learning about innovation through networks: The development of environment-friendly viticulture. *Technovation*, 25(10), 1193–1204.

Chiffoleau, Y., Dreyfus, F., Stofer, R. and Touzard, J. (2006). Networks, innovation and performance: Evidence from a cluster of wine cooperatives [Languedoc, South of France]. In K. Karantininis and J. Nelson (eds), *Vertical Markets and Cooperative Hierarchies* (37–61). Dordrecht, The Netherlands: Springer.

Christensen, D., Hall, C.M., and Mitchell, R. (2004). The 2003 New Zealand Wineries' Survey. In C. Cooper, C. Arcodia, D. Soinet and M. Whitford (eds), *Creating Tourism Knowledge, 14th International Research Conference of Australian University Tourism and Hospitality Education, Book of Abstracts*, February 10–13. Brisbane: University of Queensland.

Cusmano, L., Morrison, M., and Rabellotti R. (2008). Catching up trajectories in the wine sector: A comparative study of Chile, Italy, and South Africa. *World Development*, 38(11), 1588–1602.

Deloitte (2010). *Vintage 2009 New Zealand Wine Industry Benchmarking Survey*. Available at: http://www.deloitte.com/assets/Dcom-NewZealand/Local%20 Assets/Documents/Industries/Wine/nz_en_Vintage_2009.pdf [accessed 00 September 2015].

Doloreux, D., Chamberlin, T., and Ben Amor, S. (2013). Modes of innovation in the Canadian wine industry. *International Journal of Wine Business Research*, 25(1), 6–26.

Doloreux, D., and Lord-Tarte, E. (2013). The organisation of innovation in the wine industry: Open innovation, external sources of knowledge and proximity. *European Journal of Innovation Management*, 16(2), 171–189.

Ferreira, S.L., and Muller, R. (2013). Innovating the wine tourism product: Food-and-wine pairing in Stellenbosch wine routes. *African Journal for Physical Health Education, Recreation and Dance*, S3(19), 72–85.

Gersick, C. (1991). Revolutionary change theories: A multilevel exploration of the punctuated equilibrium paradigm. *Academy of Management Review*, 16(1), 10–36.

Gilinsky, A., Santini, C., Lazzeretti, L., and Eyler, R. (2008). Desperately seeking serendipity: Exploring the impact of country location on innovation in the wine industry. *International Journal of Wine Business Research*, 20(4), 302–320.

Giuliani, E., Morrison, A., and Rabellotti, R. (eds) (2011), *Innovation and Technological Catch-Up: The Changing Geography of Wine Production*, Aldershot: Edward Elgar.

Goh, A.L.S. (2000). A correlation-based impact analysis of competence utilization on innovation performance. *International Journal of Applied Entrepreneurship*, 1(3), 1–19.

Gössling, S. and Hall, C.M. (2013a). Sustainable culinary systems: An introduction. In C.M. Hall and S. Gössling (eds), *Sustainable Culinary Systems: Local Foods, Innovation, and Tourism and Hospitality* (3–44). Abingdon: Routledge.

Gössling, S. and Hall, C.M. (eds) (2013b). *Sustainable Culinary Systems: Local Foods, Innovation, and Tourism and Hospitality*. Abingdon: Routledge.

Guthey, G.T. (2008). Agro-industrial conventions: Some evidence from northern California's wine industry. *The Geographical Journal*, 174(2), 138–148.

Hall, C.M. (1996). Wine tourism in New Zealand. In G. Kearsley (ed.) *Proceedings of Tourism Down Under II: A Tourism Research Conference*. Dunedin: University of Otago, Centre for Tourism,

Hall, C.M. (2003). Wine and food tourism networks: A comparative study. In K. Pavlovich and M. Akoorie (eds), *Strategic Alliances and Collaborative Partnerships: A Case Book* (262–268). Palmerston North: Dunmore Press.

Hall, C.M. (2004). Small firms and wine and food tourism in New Zealand: Issues of collaboration, clusters and lifestyles. In R. Thomas (ed.), *Small Firms in Tourism: International Perspectives* (167–182). Oxford: Elsevier.

Hall, C.M. (2006). New Zealand tourism entrepreneur attitudes and behaviours with respect to climate change adaption and mitigation. *International Journal of Innovation and Sustainable Development*, 1(3), 229–237.

Hall, C.M. (2009). Innovation and tourism policy in Australia and New Zealand: Never the twain shall meet? *Journal of Policy Research in Tourism, Leisure and Events*, 1(1), 2–18.

Hall, C.M. (2012). Boosting food and tourism-related regional economic development. In OECD, *Food and the Tourism Experience: The OECD–Korea Workshop*, OECD Studies on Tourism (49–62). Paris: OECD Publishing.

Hall, C.M. (2014). The changing self-identity of English wine. In M. Harvey, L. White and W. Frost (eds), *Wine and Identity* (156–168). Abingdon: Routledge.

Hall, C.M., and Baird, T. (2014a). New Zealand wine and environmental sustainability. In P. Howland (ed.), *Social, Cultural and Economic Impacts of Wine in New Zealand* (58–70). Abingdon: Routledge.

Hall, C.M., and Baird, T. (2014b). Brand New Zealand wine: Architecture, positioning and vulnerability in the global marketplace. In P. Howland (ed.), *Social, Cultural and Economic Impacts of Wine in New Zealand* (105–119). Abingdon: Routledge.

Hall, C.M., Cambourne, B., Macionis, N., and Johnson, G. (1997). Wine tourism and network development in Australia and New Zealand: Review, establishment and prospects. *International Journal of Wine Marketing*, 9(2/3), 5–31.

Hall, C.M. and Gössling, S. (2013). Conclusion: Re-imagining sustainable culinary systems. In C.M. Hall and S. Gössling (eds), *Sustainable Culinary Systems: Local Foods, Innovation, and Tourism and Hospitality* (293–304). Abingdon: Routledge.

Hall, C.M., Heyworth, S., and Baird, T. (2014). Wine consumption and behaviour in New Zealand. In P. Howland (ed.), *Social, Cultural and Economic Impacts of Wine in New Zealand* (105–119). London: Routledge.

Hall, C.M., and Johnson, G. (1998). Wine and food tourism in New Zealand: Difficulties in the creation of sustainable tourism business networks. In D. Hall and L. O'Hanlon (eds), *Rural Tourism Management: Sustainable Options, Conference Proceedings* (21–38). Ayr: Scottish Agricultural College.

Hall, C.M., Johnson, G., and Mitchell, R. (2000). Wine tourism and regional development. In C.M. Hall, E. Sharples, B. Cambourne and N. Macionis (eds), *Wine Tourism Around the World* (196–225). Oxford: Butterworth-Heinemann.

Hall, C.M., Johnson, G., Cambourne, B., Macionis, N., Mitchell, R.D., and Sharples, E. (2000). Wine tourism: An introduction. In C.M. Hall, E. Sharples, B. Cambourne and N. Macionis (eds), *Wine Tourism Around the World* (1–23). Oxford: Butterworth Heinemann.

Hall, C.M., and Mitchell, R. (2005). Gastronomic tourism: Comparing food and wine tourism experiences. In M. Novelli (ed.), *Niche Tourism* (73–88). Oxford: Butterworth-Heinemann.

Hall, C.M., and Mitchell, R. (2008). *Wine Marketing: A Practical Guide*. Oxford: Butterworth-Heinemann.

Hall, C.M., Mitchell, R., and Sharples, E. (2003). Consuming places: The role of food, wine and tourism in regional development. In C.M. Hall, E. Sharples, R. Mitchell, B. Cambourne, and N. Macionis (eds), *Food Tourism Around the World* (25–29). Oxford: Butterworth-Heinemann.

Hall, C.M., and Page, S. (2010). The contribution of Neil Leiper to tourism studies. *Current Issues in Tourism*, 13, 299–309.

Hall, C.M., and Williams, A.M. (2008). *Tourism and Innovation*, London: Routledge.

Hira, A., and Bwenge, A.W. (2011). *The Wine Industry in British Columbia: Issues and Potential*. Available at: http://www.wine-economics.org/workingpapers/ AAWE_WP89.pdf [accessed 13 September 2015].

Hjalager, A.M. (2009). A review of innovation research in tourism. *Tourism Management*, 31(1), 1–12.

Leiper, N., Stear, L., Hing, N., and Firth, T. (2008). Partial industrialisation in tourism: A new model. *Current Issues in Tourism*, 11, 207–235.

Lenzi, C. (2013). Smart upgrading innovation strategies in a traditional industry: Evidence from the wine production in the province of Arezzo. *Regional Science Policy and Practice*, 5(4), 435–452.

Malm, K., Gössling, S. and Hall, C.M. (2013). Regulatory and institutional barriers to new business development: The case of Swedish wine tourism. In C.M. Hall and S. Gössling (eds), *Sustainable Culinary Systems: Local Foods, Innovation, and Tourism and Hospitality* (241–255), London: Routledge.

Meyer, A., Brooks, G., and Goes, J. (1990). Environmental jolts and industry revolutions: Organisational responses to discontinuous change. *Strategic Management Journal*, 25(3), 465–499.

Mitchell, R. and Hall, C.M. (2001a). Wine at home: Self ascribed wine knowledge and the wine behaviour of New Zealand winery visitors. *Australian and New Zealand Wine Industry Journal*, 16(6), 115–122.

Mitchell, R., and Hall, C.M. (2001b). Lifestyle behaviours of New Zealand winery visitors: Wine club activities, wine cellars and place of purchase. *International Journal of Wine Marketing*, 13(3), 82–93.

Mitchell, R. and Hall, C.M. (2003). Consuming tourists: Food tourism consumer behaviour. In C.M. Hall, E. Sharples, R. Mitchell, B. Cambourne and N. Macionis (eds), *Food Tourism Around the World: Development, Management and Markets* (60–80). Oxford: Butterworth-Heinemann.

Mitchell, R. and Hall, C.M. (2004). The post-visit consumer behaviour of New Zealand winery visitors. *Journal of Wine Research*, 15(1), 39–49.

Mitchell, R., and Hall, C.M. (2006). Wine tourism research: The state of play. *Tourism Review International*, 9(4), 307–332.

Mortensen, W.J., and Marks, B. (2003). The failure of a wine closure innovation: A strategic marketing analysis. Available at: http://academyofwinebusiness. com/wp-content/uploads/2010/05/File-008.pdf [accessed 13 September 2015].

Mowery, D.C., Oxley, J.E., and Silverman, B.S. (1996). Strategic alliances and inter-firm knowledge transfer. *Strategic Management Journal*, 17(S2), 77–91.

Nambisan, S. (2013). Industry technical committees, technological distance, and innovation performance. *Research Policy*, 42(4), 928–940.

New Zealand Wine (2014). *Annual Report 2014*. Available at: http://www.nzwine.com/assets/sm/upload/b5/2j/rr/2n/NZW%20AR%202014_web.pdf [accessed 13 September 2015].

OECD (2005). *Oslo Manual: Guidelines for Collecting and Interpreting Innovation Data*. 3rd Edition. OECD – Organisation for European Co-operation and Development/Eurostat: Statistical Office of the European Communities. Paris: OECD.

Ohmart, C. (2008). Innovative outreach increases adoption of sustainable winegrowing practices in Lodi region. *California Agriculture*, 62(4), 142–147.

Olavarría, J., García, M., Moreno, Y., and Mosalvez, C. (2006). Characterization and technological performance in two clusters wine: Colchagua and Maule valleys. Talca: Universidad de Talca.

Pike, W., and Melewar, T. (2006). The demise of independent wine production in France: A marketing challenge? *International Journal of Wine Marketing*, 18(3), 183–203.

Prahalad, C.K., and Hamel, G. (1994). Strategy as a field of study: Why search for a new paradigm? *Strategic Management Journal*, 15(2), 5–16.

Preston-Whyte, R. (2000). Wine routes in South Africa. In C.M. Hall, E. Sharples, B. Cambourne and N. Macionis (eds), *Wine Tourism Around the World* (102–115). Oxford: Butterworth-Heinemann.

Simpson, K., Bretherton, P., and de Vere, G. (2005). Lifestyle market segmentation, small business entrepreneurs, and the New Zealand wine tourism industry. *Journal of Quality Assurance in Hospitality and Tourism*, 5(2), 157–188.

Statistics New Zealand. (2007). *Innovation in New Zealand 2007*. Available at: http://www.stats.govt.nz/browse_for_stats/businesses/business_growth_and_innovation/innovation-in-new-zealand-2007.aspx [accessed 13 September 2015]

Statistics New Zealand. (2009). *Innovation in New Zealand 2009*. Available at: http://www.stats.govt.nz/browse_for_stats/businesses/business_growth_and_innovation/innovation-in-new-zealand-2009.aspx [accessed 13 September 2015].

Statistics New Zealand. (2012). *Innovation in New Zealand 2011*. Retrieved from http:// www.stats.govt.nz/.../innovation-in-new-zealand-2011.aspx

Statistics New Zealand (2013). *Innovation in New Zealand 2013*. Available at: http://www.stats.govt.nz/browse_for_stats/businesses/business_growth_and_innovation/innovation-in-new-zealand-2013-tables.aspx [accessed 13 September 2015].

Sustainable Winegrowing New Zealand (SNWZ) (2010). *About Sustainable Winegrowing NewZealand: What We Do*. Retrieved from http://wineinf.nzwine.com/swnzabout.asp

Taplin, I.M., and Breckenridge, R.S. (2008). Large firms, legitimation and industry identity: The growth of the North Carolina wine industry. *The Social Science Journal*, 45, 352–360.

Tourism New Zealand (2014). Tourism profile: Special Interest – Wine Tourism. Available at: http://www.tourismnewzealand.com/media/1132209/wine-tourism-profile.pdf [accessed 00 September 2015].

Weidenfeld, A., and Hall, C.M. (2014). Tourism in the development of regional and sectoral innovation systems. In A. Lew, C.M. Hall and A. Williams (eds), *The Wiley Blackwell Companion to Tourism* (578–588). Oxford: Wiley-Blackwell.

Winetitles (2009). *The Australian and New Zealand Wine Industry Directory*. Adelaide: Hartley Higgins.

Winetitles (2014). *The Australian and New Zealand Wine Industry Directory*. Adelaide: Hartley Higgins.

# Chapter 13

# The Margaret River Wine Region: Analysing Key Resources as a Basis for a Competitive Wellness Tourism Destination

CHRISTOF PFORR, CORNELIA VOIGT and CORNELIA LOCHER

This chapter examines Western Australia's wellness tourism industry in the context of the broader debates on the development, management and success of wellness tourism destinations. It draws on the findings of a multidisciplinary body of new research, utilizing a novel framework to assess wellness tourism destination competitiveness. In light of this, the chapter makes a special study of the wellness tourism sector in the Margaret River Wine Region of Western Australia by assessing the relevance of eight categories of core resources and competencies derived from this framework, which are considered to be crucial for its competitiveness.

## Australia's Wellness Tourism Industry

While global tourism has resumed growth since 2009, maturing growth rates in many regions and an extreme diversification in tourism products and services have made competitiveness a critical issue in the tourism industry. Tourism growth coupled with the behaviour of increasingly informed, quality-conscious tourists – who often express their feelings in a volatile manner – have caused management at many destinations to rethink their competitiveness. An analysis of destination competitiveness has become recognized as a key tool in the long-term positioning and strategic planning of destinations. The latest development since Porter (1990) introduced the notion of competitiveness to assess and compare countries, regions and locations, is that the notion of destination competitiveness has become not only important to the industry but also the major focus of tourism research.

In this light, this chapter examines Western Australia's wellness tourism industry in the context of the broader debates on the development, management and success of wellness tourism destinations. Drawing on the findings of a multidisciplinary body of new research, a novel framework is utilized to assess wellness tourism destination competitiveness. This chapter makes a special study of the wellness tourism sector in the Margaret River Wine Region of Western Australia by assessing the relevance of eight categories of core resources and competencies derived from this framework, which are considered to be crucial for its competitiveness.

## Destination Competitiveness

The concept of destination competitiveness appears to be straightforward. It is linked to 'the ability of a destination to successfully attract tourists over time in a marketplace where numerous other destinations are competing for the same or similar target markets' (Prideaux, Berbigier and Thompson, 2014: 58). However, the complexity of the concept becomes evident when reviewing the literature on determinants of destination competitiveness and destination competitiveness models (e.g., Crouch, 2010; Dwyer and Kim, 2003; Enright and Newton, 2005; Hassan, 2000; Prideaux, Berbigier, and Thompson, 2014; Ritchie and Crouch, 2003). Recently, Voigt and Pforr (2014) proposed a framework of wellness tourism destination competitiveness, particularly building on Ritchie and Crouch's (2003) comprehensive model. The aim of this framework was to depict the major dimensions of wellness destination competitiveness. While this framework may be applicable to tourism destinations in general, it highlights areas that wellness tourism case studies have shown to be critical to the success of the wellness tourism destination. Taking all models together, it is clear that of yet there is no commonly agreed definition or established set of attributes of destination competitiveness. Nevertheless, it is also noticeable that there are similarities. For instance, many models include strategic destination management, tourism policy and industry structural factors, as well as the endowments or resources of the destination, as key factors for competitiveness.

Some of the literature cited above directly or indirectly suggests a *resource-based* view as the basis of destination competitiveness. Accordingly, destinations can be viewed as bundles of resources (Ryan, 2002). The following literature review predominantly concentrates on resources which constitute the main focus of this chapter.

In the context of wellness tourism, resources have been referred to as 'competencies' (Pechlaner, Reuter, and Bachinger, 2014), 'assets' (Smith and Puczkó, 2009) and 'substance' (Hjalager, 2011). Dwyer and Kim (2003) differentiate *endowed* (i.e., intrinsic to a destination) and *created* (i.e., man-made) resources. Importantly, a destination's resources constitute *comparative advantages*, and a *competitive advantage* is about utilizing those resources effectively in the long term (Ritchie and Crouch, 2003). Accordingly, destinations with an abundance of wellness tourism resources may not be competitive because a wellness tourism vision, strategy and comprehensive 'product' based on these resources has not been developed and/or brought to appropriate target markets. Destination management organizations (DMOs) are seen as key players in strategic tourism development and competitive long-term survival of a destination. Destination managers can exert little control over the availability of endowed resources, however on the positive side these are hard to imitate and tend to be place-specific. On the other hand, destination managers are able to innovatively develop created resources to add value to the attractiveness of a destination; these however, may then be much more easily copied by competing destinations.

The wellness tourism destination competitiveness framework (Voigt and Pforr, 2014) proposes eight different types or categories of wellness tourism resources, the first four constituting endowed resources and the latter created resources. The eight categories are depicted in Figure 13.1 and are briefly explained below.

1.  *Natural resources* (e.g., water, the climate, raw materials such as plants, clay and mud): First, in wellness tourism, many of the natural resources are perceived to have inherent therapeutic qualities. Some of these qualities can be exactly specified and certified, such as air quality or certain minerals in the water. Also, environmental psychology proposes that particular aesthetic geographical features may contribute to the wellbeing of wellness tourists. Second, natural resources are used in cosmetic products, natural medicine, or as building materials for place-specific architecture, which ties in with the next category of wellness tourism resources.

2.  *Cultural, historical and spiritual resources*: In many regions wellness tourism has a rich and sometimes ancient history. Resources of this type include material wellness-related architecture and heritage (e.g., the Turkish hammam, the Finnish sauna, the German 'Kur' park), as well as cultural and spiritual customs and rituals.

3.  *Complementary and alternative medicine (CAM)*: Wellness tourism draws heavily on CAM. There is an immense variety of CAM modalities and entire alternative medical systems from non-Western (e.g., Traditional Chinese Medicine (TCM), Ayurveda) and

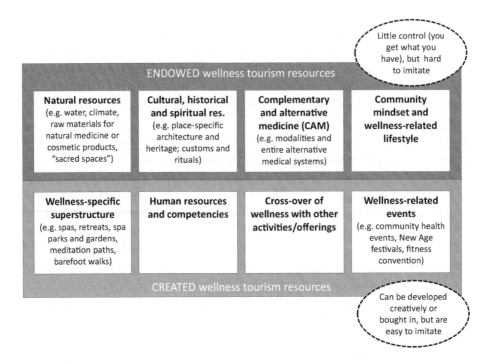

**Figure 13.1     Eight categories of wellness tourism resources**
*Source*: The authors.

Western cultures (e.g. homeopathy, naturopathy), typically closely tied to certain regions.

4.    *Community mindset and wellness-related lifestyle*: Wellness tourism case studies (Wray and Weiler, 2014) have shown that communities with wellness-related values such as an alternative, health-conscious lifestyle and environmental activism not only safeguard natural and cultural resources essential for the wellness tourism product but also attract wellness tourists with congruent values.

5.    *Wellness-specific superstructure*: This category of created wellness tourism resources consists of wellness tourism-related superstructure. 'Superstructure' is a term coined by Ritchie and Crouch (2003) and refers to facilities specifically built for tourists like hotels or restaurants. Accordingly, wellness tourism superstructure has been specifically built for wellness tourists. Different classifications of such superstructures can be found in the literature; especially relevant for destinations outside Europe may be Voigt's (2014) classification of three core wellness tourism provider types, namely beauty spas, lifestyle resorts and spiritual

retreats. Perhaps more so than in other tourism contexts, wellness-specific superstructure is a key ingredient in the mix of resources at the destination, as many providers offer programmes where the guests never leave the property and do not engage in other touristic activities at the destination (Voigt, 2010). Many wellness tourism destinations host a cluster of wellness tourism providers; however, in some cases a single provider has become so well known that it has become quasi synonymous with the destination.

6.     *Human resources and competencies*: Qualified, competent and friendly staff is one of the most important factors determining the success of a wellness tourism business and so also for the entire destination. This is also because contacts between employees and wellness tourists can be characterized as intimate and personal – more so than in many other tourism contexts. Human resources appear to be a scarce and thus especially valuable resource category, as the wellness industry currently suffers from high staff turnover rates, labour shortage and sometimes obscure qualifications schemes.

7.     *Crossover of wellness with other products or tourism activities*: A current existing example of crossover products concerns the spa sector, where spa-visiting may be complemented with other luxury tourism activities such as spa and skiing, or spa and wineries (e.g. vinotherapy). Food (especially wholesome approaches such as slow food or organic produce) also often features in wellness tourism crossover products. There are also examples where not only different tourism sectors but also different industries (e.g. hospitality and health care) collaborate in developing innovative wellness tourism destinations.

8.     *Wellness-related events*: At the present time there seem to be few examples of wellness-related events through which a wellness destination has achieved a competitive advantage. However, wellness-related events such as New Age festivals, slow food festivals and fitness conventions can augment other wellness resources of a destination.

As has been briefly explained, having diverse wellness resources at a destination does not make this destination competitive. There seems to be general agreement in the tourism literature that strategic management of destinations must involve *sustainable* resource development (e.g. Ritchie and Crouch, 2003) to ensure their long-term competitiveness. As other models, Voigt and Pforr's (2014) framework interlaces destination competitiveness with sustainability. Wellness, as a health paradigm, postulates health as a broad, positive and multidimensional concept that includes environmental and social dimensions (Voigt, 2014). It follows that sustainability should be the guiding management philosophy for all stakeholders developing wellness tourism destinations and should permeate all levels of policy and all business practices. As an ultimate sign of the success of a competitive wellness tourism destination, the adopted framework suggests the dual outcome of providing 'unique authentic and sustainable wellness tourism experiences', as well as 'actual health benefits for tourists and residents' (Voigt and Pforr, 2014: 301). The tourism sector that purposely 'sells' wellness] has not only to take the individual well-being of wellness tourists into account but also the well-being of the host population (see also above resource category 4). While there are examples that show that wellness businesses, DMOs and to some extent even entire stakeholder networks take sustainability into account, as yet there seem to be very few destinations where health benefits of guests or hosts are strategically assessed and evaluated.

The framework of wellness tourism competitiveness does not only contain a resource-based approach. Perhaps more than other models it emphasizes *collaborative destination governance*. A destination can also be understood as a complex network consisting of interdependent private and public stakeholders (Baggio, Scott, and Cooper, 2010). Understanding destinations as bundles of resources and as a network is not mutually exclusive but complementary. Ideally, a tight collaborative network of stakeholders shares and coordinates resources, knowledge and competencies in a manner that creates a competitive advantage over other destinations (e.g. Pechlaner, Fischer, and Hamman, 2008). This may be even more important in wellness tourism, where stakeholders from different industry sectors could collaborate to develop innovative products (i.e., tourism and hospitality and the alternative or mainstream health care sectors). However, a recent review on the issue of collaboration in wellness tourism destinations illustrated that there is often little collaboration between major groups of stakeholders and that wellness development was either impeded or failed entirely (Voigt and Laing, 2014). Providing leadership and facilitating collaboration often falls to DMOs. Nevertheless, there are examples of successful wellness tourism destinations which enjoy little support from DMOs. In some cases wellness tourism providers have also bypassed the DMO and built marketing alliances to attract wellness tourists to their destination.

In the following, some of these issues are explored in more detail in the context of the Margaret River Wine Region in Western Australia, the case study area selected to apply Voigt and Pforr's (2014) wellness tourism destination competitiveness model.

## The Case of the Margaret River Wine Region

To better reflect different visitor experiences, Western Australia (WA) is divided into five tourism regions (Figure 13.2): 'Australia's Coral Coast', 'Australia's Golden Outback', 'Experience Perth', 'Australia's North West', and 'Australia's South West' (Pforr, 2007). These regions currently cater for the state's thriving tourism industry; in 2014 they attracted 807,000 international, 1.2 million national and 6.1 million local visitors respectively (Tourism Western Australia, 2014a). The Australia's South West tourism region ranks as the second most visited (22 per cent) behind the Experience Perth tourism region (62 per cent), which includes the state capital, Perth. In 2014 Australia's South West attracted 2.3 million visitors, 89 per cent of them from intrastate. Of those, 65 per cent originated from Perth, taking advantage of the region's close proximity (approximately 300 kilometres) and convenient access via a newly built dual carriageway (Tourism WA, 2014a; Augusta Margaret River Tourism Association (AMRTA), 2014). For logistical and administrative reasons and also in an effort to maximize marketing synergies Australia's South West is further divided into five sub-regions (Figure 13.2), known as 'Geographe Bay', 'Blackwood River Valley', 'Southern Forests', 'Great Southern' and the 'Margaret River Wine Region', the latter being the particular focus of this case study. It stretches from Cape Leeuwin, the most south-westerly point of Australia, and the adjacent town Augusta to the towns Dunsborough and Yallingup at the northern end of the cape. The township of Margaret River, with its estimated population of about 12,000 residents, is centrally located within the Margaret River Wine Region (Figure 13.3).

With annual visitor numbers of 857,000 (Tourism Australia, 2015), the case study area is a very popular tourist destination for locals, interstate and international visitors alike, providing four of the five iconic experiences promoted for the state by Tourism Western Australia, the WA government's lead tourism agency. In the region 'where rolling vineyards sit against a backdrop of ocean and forest' (Tourism Western Australia, 2015), these include marine and coastal experiences, outback and adventure, food and wine, forest and wild flowers, as well as people and lifestyle experiences (Tourism Western Australia, 2005).

As an internationally renowned surfer destination with 138 kilometres of spectacular coastline, more than 70 surf breaks and numerous pristine beaches, as well as a wealth of marine life, exceptional marine and coastal experiences are an obvious tourism drawcard for the region (AMRTA, 2015b). It is also known as a food and wine destination, increasingly so even beyond state and national boarders (Mitchell, Charters, and Albrecht, 2012), thus offering another of the state's iconic experiences. With over 5,000 hectares of vineyards and 150

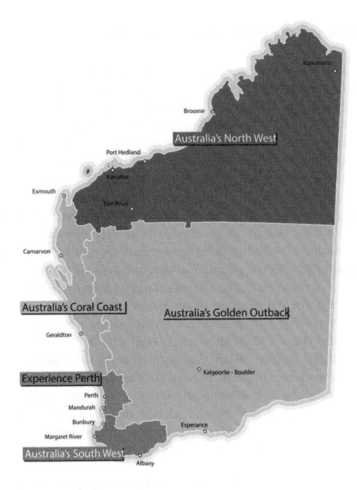

**Figure 13.2    Western Australia's five tourism zones**
*Source*: Tourism Western Australia, 2014b.

wine producers (Margaret River Wine Association, 2015), a major industry in the Margaret River Wine Region, as the name suggests, is viticulture, but farming of sheep, beef and dairy cattle, as well as fishing and horticulture, also serve as economic cornerstones. In particular, the growth of the wine industry since the late 1960s has facilitated the development of associated businesses concentrating on food, such as a range of different restaurants, a chocolate and a cheese factory, a brewery and other value-added products (Mitchell, Charters, and Albrecht, 2012). These feature prominently in the region's marketing, emphasizing that

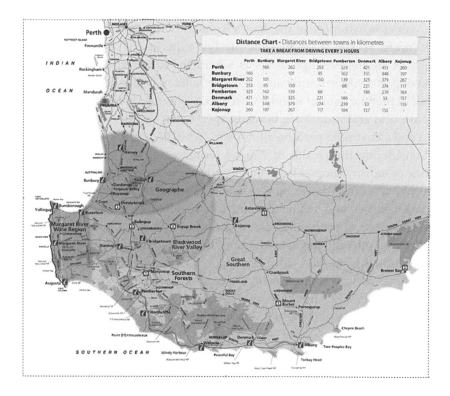

| Distance Chart - Distances between towns in kilometres |
| TAKE A BREAK FROM DRIVING EVERY 2 HOURS |

| | Perth | Bunbury | Margaret River | Bridgetown | Pemberton | Denmark | Albany | Kojonup |
|---|---|---|---|---|---|---|---|---|
| Perth | - | 166 | 262 | 253 | 323 | 421 | 413 | 260 |
| Bunbury | 166 | - | 101 | 95 | 162 | 331 | 348 | 197 |
| Margaret River | 262 | 101 | - | 150 | 139 | 325 | 379 | 267 |
| Bridgetown | 253 | 95 | 150 | - | 68 | 221 | 274 | 117 |
| Pemberton | 323 | 162 | 139 | 68 | - | 186 | 239 | 184 |
| Denmark | 421 | 331 | 325 | 221 | 186 | - | 53 | 157 |
| Albany | 413 | 348 | 379 | 274 | 239 | 53 | - | 155 |
| Kojonup | 260 | 197 | 267 | 117 | 184 | 157 | 155 | - |

**Figure 13.3   Australia's South West (including the Margaret River Wine Region)**

*Source*: Australia's South West, 2013: 5.

> *already renowned for its fine wines and perfect waves, the Margaret River Region is now capturing the world's attention for its food. From handmade chocolate and artisan cheese to super-healthy grass-fed beef and heirloom organic fruit and vegetables, the delicious produce from this beautiful region is ripe for discovery. (AMRTA, 2015a: 2)*

Based on high-quality local produce and boutique food outlets, the region is promoted as a destination for romantic and intimate escapes only a short drive away from the hustles and bustles of Perth and its about 2 million residents. Marketing images of the region thus include indulging in luxury, enjoying high-quality food and wine experiences, evoking feelings of happiness and relaxation.

Boasting large areas of old-growth forest with a large number of walking trails, such as the karri forests of the Leeuwin–Naturaliste National Park, and being renowned for its easygoing, alternative people and lifestyle, the region also caters for two more of the state's iconic experiences, 'forest and seasonal wildflowers' as well as 'people and lifestyle experiences'. Both are influential aspects of its tourism appeal, as is succinctly summarized in the region's marketing as 'Western Australia's premier holiday region [that] is an enticing mosaic of pristine natural wonders, premium wineries, fine restaurants, world-class arts and crafts, dazzling beaches, spectacular forests, warm and friendly locals and a charming persona all its own' (AMRTA, 2015c).

Considering the wealth of natural resources, from rich marine life and pristine costal environments to old-growth forests, the Margaret River region is an obvious nature-based tourism destination and its Mediterranean climate, unspoilt beaches and nationally and internationally renowned surf breaks provide ample opportunities for a thriving 'sea, sand and surf' holiday experience. Aptly, the Augusta Margaret River Tourism Association (AMRTA, 2014) identifies in its 2014–2015 Destination Marketing Plan and Strategy the beauty of its natural environment, the region's wine industry, local boutique food producers and markets, and an engaged and innovative creative community as some of the region's core strengths.

Health and wellness are seen by the Regional Tourism Association as emerging tourism sectors (AMRTA, 2014), which is very plausible as the case study area features many of the basic elements required to support a thriving wellness tourism destination. Already in the 1990s Weiler and Hall (1992) identified suitable natural resources, qualified health professionals and attractive scenery as key characteristics of a successful wellness destination. As is discussed later, all of these basic requirements are met in the case-study region. However, with the framework of wellness tourism destination competitiveness developed by Voigt and Pforr (2014) additional characteristics have been identified, which help foster the development of a successful wellness tourism destination. The eight categories of wellness tourism resources (Figure 13.1) as the essential basis of this larger framework are the major focus of this case study. Other attributes of wellness tourism destination competitiveness are briefly discussed, but it is beyond the scope of this chapter to analyse all attributes of the framework in detail. At the end of the chapter the analysis of resources and some other factors identify areas where future development efforts could be directed in an attempt to provide the best conditions for a thriving wellness tourism industry.

## NATURAL RESOURCES

'The Margaret River Region is world famous for its tall karri forests, pristine beaches, wonderful wildlife, spectacular landscapes, peaceful walk trails and epic surf breaks, so get amongst it all and get back to nature!' (AMRTA, 2015d). As is succinctly highlighted in this marketing piece, the Margaret River Wine Region offers without any doubt a wealth of natural resources that can support the promotion and development of wellness tourism. Experiencing nature in distinction from the stress often associated with modern living in urban settings has long been acknowledged as having beneficial health effects (Hughes, 2014) and thus provides the foundation for the association of natural resources and wellness tourism.

In this respect the case study region features an abundance of natural resources that can be integrated into an overall wellness experience, including flourishing and protected forests, pristine beaches with a variety of marine life, wild flowers (in season), a clean air environment and even distinct seasons with pleasant summer temperatures and cooler winters. Thus it can easily cater for those who prefer coastal environments, as well as those who seek forest or rural settings to wind down and refresh mentally and physically at different times in the year. Just one example in this context is the popular Cape Naturaliste to Cape Leeuwin walking trail. With its unique and varied flora and fauna and spectacular scenery, it transverses 135 kilometres of the coastal stretch of the case-study area. Though very popular (McCormack, 2010), it is still a way to experience solitude and a sense of discovery and as such can contribute to a feeling of wellbeing.

## CULTURAL, HISTORICAL AND SPIRITUAL RESOURCES

The case study region is also rich in Aboriginal and European settler history, both of which have left their mark on the region's tourism products and services. The Wardandi people, constituting the local indigenous community, refer to the region's central waterway, the Margaret River, as *Wooditchup*, which was named after the magic man 'Wooditch'. *They proudly highlight the* long and continued connection to their land. Archaeological evidence points to human activity in the area dating back up 48,000 years, making Devil's Lair cave, for example, which is situated at the southern end of the cape, one of the oldest sites of human settlement in the country (South West Aboriginal Land and Sea Council, 2015). Current tourism marketing for the region includes reference to the Wardandi people's 'deep affinity with the sea and land' and highlights that 'their culture is as rich and varied as the land itself' (AMRTA, 2015e: 20). European settlement of the area, on the other hand, is dated to 1857 with the establishment of Ellensbrook homestead by the Bussell family (Augusta Margaret River Mail, 2013). Today managed by the National Trust, the historic home and its picnic grounds are a popular destination for tourists to the region.

Of relevance to the Margaret River Wine Region as a developing wellness tourism destination have been some unique indigenous products and experiences that have helped to set the region apart from other wellness destinations. Among them, Moondance Lodge, established in 2004 in a tranquil bushland setting south of Yallingup, was the first major wellness retreat in the area. Offering experiences like 'digeridoo meditation, tribal bushwalks, dreamtime story telling and sacred women's time' it set a strong focus on the healing power of indigenous spirituality and thrived to offer authentic Aboriginal wellness experiences (Voigt et al., 2010: 185). This concept, unique to the region, was rewarded with a range of acclaims, including the 2005 Condé Nast Traveller Hot New Hotel and the 2005 Luxury Travel awards, the 2004 WA New Tourism Development Award, and the 2008 AHA Award for WA's Best Tourism Initiative. The Retreat was in operation for only five years, but it nonetheless illustrated that such an integrated approach to wellness, which incorporates aspects of local culture and spirituality, can form the basis of a successful wellness tourism business. Though on a much smaller scale, a similar concept is currently offered by the Wardan Aboriginal Cultural Centre located near Yallingup with its Bush Story Trail offering an insight into local bush tucker and traditional medicinal plants (Wardan Aboriginal Centre, 2010) and thus a glimpse into alternative healing practices.

## COMPLEMENTARY AND ALTERNATIVE MEDICINE

Only about 5,000 people currently live in the Margaret River township and about 12,000 in the Augusta Margaret River Shire (Australia's South West, 2015). Considering these low population numbers it is surprising to see how many health and wellness businesses offer their products and services to locals and visitors throughout Margaret River, Busselton, Dunsborough, Yallingup and the surrounding areas. According to the region's latest wellness directory (Wellness Margaret River, 2014) five day spas, eight beauty therapy businesses, four fitness establishments, twelve massage and body work specialists, four health clinics offering a wide spectrum of services ranging from skin treatments to breathing retraining, six specialist counsellors, eight businesses offering natural and holistic therapies and three specializing in pregnancy and lactation are currently in operation within the region. Although some overlaps in these categories exist, as some offer services within a number of categories, this is still an impressive number for such a small community and emphasizes the strong wellness focus within the region.

## POSITIVE COMMUNITY ATTITUDES TOWARDS WELLNESS-RELATED LIFESTYLE

The presence of this vast array of health and wellness focused businesses is not only a result of high demand for such experiences from visitors to the area and its growing reputation as a wellness tourism destination but also a reflection of the local community's positive attitudes towards wellness products and services. As Voigt et al. (2010: 184) argue, 'health and wellness opportunities are central to the unique lifestyle and its "alternative image" for many residents in the Margaret River region'.

It can be speculated that in particular those who settled in the region in the 1960s searching for surf and an alternative lifestyle have left a strong stamp on the community; like Byron Bay, Margaret River was 'one of the original hippie surf hangouts' (Australia Travel Market, 2015). They established a strong community presence, put a focus on environmentally sustainable practices, established alternative art and crafts shops and introduced the region's typical mud brick and rammed earth building style (Augusta Margaret River Tourism Association, 2013). Likeminded people continue to be attracted to the region with its 'hippy flair' and its alternative lifestyle, communes and community gardens.

The intersection between food and wellness tourism finds its expression in the growing popularity of food tours, healthy cooking classes or farm-to-table experiences that resonate with the sustainability aspects of wellbeing. In this light, the weekly Margaret River Farmers' Market represents a cornerstone of the region's sustainable food and wine movement that is well integrated with the local alternative lifestyle community and its wellness focus (AMRTA, 2015a).

## HUMAN RESOURCES AND COMPETENCIES

The previously mentioned complementary and alternative medicine products and services are well represented in the region. They are offered by a range of professionals like trained beauticians, accredited massage therapists and counsellors. Marketing their competence in health and wellness therapies, the Margaret River Wellness Centre (and the closely aligned Karrinyup Wellness Centre based in the Perth metropolitan area), for example, emphasizes its expertise in chiropractic, naturopathy, massage therapy and homoeopathics. As highlighted on its website, 'the desire to provide onsite the spectrum of services required to enable individuals to reach their optimum wellness potential was the catalyst for bringing together some of Perth's and Margaret River's finest natural health practitioners' (Margaret River Wellness Centre, 2015). The Centre also offers regular wellness workshops and a whole range of programmes targeting learning difficulties, weight loss, snoring, fertility, detoxification and energy restoration, as well as immune boost programmes. Moreover, the clinic also offers 'Corporate Performance Programs', running over three to twelve months, that are geared to assist employees to achieve a better balance physically (e.g. posture and biochemistry), as well as in their emotional state. The presence of six chiropractors, all with a number of university degrees, two qualified naturopaths and three remedial massage therapists is quite remarkable and thus illustrates the high demand for quality health and wellness products and services in the region.

Another wellness business, located in Yallingup, is Alchemy Body and Soul, which markets itself as 'the South West's most exclusive healing center' (Alchemy Body and Soul, 2015). It also offers a wide range of wellness products and services, ranging from massage and chiropractic treatments, Myopractic and Bowen Therapy to acupuncture, Reiki and energy healing. Next to promoting its retreat packages, regular classes and personal programmes, it also provides an opportunity to participate in myopractic training modules that are otherwise only offered in large metropolitan cities around Australia (e.g. Sydney, Brisbane, Perth). Though just an example for human resources and competencies, it illustrates the demand for and growing expertise in wellness products and services on offer in the case-study region.

As discussed in the literature review, in order to foster a successful wellness tourism industry in a regional context, the establishment of adequate communications networks and associated exchange of information and know-how transfer between the various stakeholders is seen as crucial. As is evident, for example, in joint marketing efforts via the Wellness Margaret River Directory and Website (Wellness Margaret River, 2014) which has been in operation since 2007, first collaborative activities among the range of wellness providers in the Margaret River region have already taken place over the past decade, providing a solid foundation for the future development of a much stronger, wider and denser network built on the region's endogenous wellness potential.

## WELLNESS-SPECIFIC SUPERSTRUCTURE

As previously mentioned, among a broad array of complementary and alternative medicine products and services the Margaret River Wine Region also hosts a number of facilities that are specifically geared towards wellness tourism such as beauty spas and lifestyle resorts and spiritual retreats. Developed in response to demand for wellness tourism products and services, they constitute the existing wellness specific superstructure in the case study region and thus play an important role in its current wellness tourism business and its continued future development.

Among the best-known wellness resorts in the region is Injidup Spa Retreat (Injidup Spa Retreat, 2015), located south of Yallingup at the northern end of the cape. It focuses on the higher end of the wellness tourism market, offering luxurious villa-style accommodation coupled with a range of spa experiences, including various beauty, massage and other body treatments. This concept was awarded by the readers of the Condé Nast Traveller Magazine in 2011, which ranked Injidup Spa tenth on a global list of best spa retreats (Condé Nast Traveller, 2011). Attracting a similar clientele, Bunker Bay Resort operated by Pullman Hotel and Resort Group and situated in one of the South West's most sought-after beach locations, offers its customers an opportunity to 'chill out with a sense of connectivity, calm and serenity'. Its spa facilities, where customers' 'wellness is nurtured to harmonize with [their] inner self, a place where care is personalized and life is celebrated', provide a range of beauty, body works and massage products and services similar to those offered by Injidup Spa Retreat (Pullman Bunker Bay Resort, 2015).

Living Synergy just outside the township of Dunsborough, on the other hand, takes a somewhat different approach. As a small lifestyle and spiritual retreat situated at the northern fringe of the case-study region, it markets itself as a place that assists its customers in 'getting their health and wellbeing back on track' by offering small-group, individualized immersion lifestyle retreats that offer nutritional coaching, massage therapy, yoga and meditation sessions in a 'nurturing home away from home' (Living Synergy, 2015).

Though the above are just a selection of wellness businesses that can be considered wellness tourism superstructure, they illustrate the solid foundation the case study area already has for the continued development of its wellness tourism industry.

### Wellness-related events

The case study area promotes itself as an event destination, highlighting in this context many of the characteristics that have been identified as cornerstones of its wellness tourism industry. 'With sumptuous wine, beer and food, stunning coastlines and magnificent beaches, an entrenched art and cultural scene, all wrapped up with a breathtaking Mediterranean climate and a huge choice of accommodation [...] the Margaret River region is the perfect place for events' (AMRTA, 2015f). However, referring to the 2014/2015 events calendar of the case-study area, wellness-specific events, at least in a narrow sense, appear to be missing from its schedule of tourism activities, which is somewhat surprising considering the importance of tourism to the region and also its growing reputation as a wellness destination. The relatively small size of the resident population can be assumed to be a significant contributor to this lack of specific wellness events, as there might not be resources in terms of manpower or financial and corporate sponsors readily available to support such an undertaking. This is not to say that large-scale events are not held in the region, in fact many of the annual events for which the Margaret River Wine Region is renown can be linked to health and wellness in a broader sense, including the annual Margaret River Fun Run, which has been hosted by the region for the past 18 years. On a much smaller scale and organized by some of its local wellness product and service providers, it is possible to participate in a number of wellness-focused retreats, as well as events such as traditional gong baths or a Gonh Sound journey based on ancient sacred sounds.

## Crossover with other events and activities

Facilitating the crossover between wellness tourism products and services and other sectors that have been identified as having the potential to further enhance the industry (and vice versa) stimulates innovation and new product development. Such a win–win collaboration can be identified for the case-study region with respect to its flourishing food and wine and also its nature-based and adventure tourism businesses, but possibly also the local timber industry. In this respect a number of successful crossover activities can be noted. Indeed, as Voigt et al. (2010: 178) highlighted a number of years ago, 'there is evidence of the way local products are being used in a complementary way to support wellness tourism, including olive oil, natural soap products and local produce such as cheese, chocolate, berries, olives, jams and condiments'.

The growing link between food, in particular sustainable food, and wellness has already been briefly discussed earlier. Quality local produce is indeed a very important cornerstone of the Margaret River Wine Region's tourism industry:

> From fresh local marron, organic vegetables and locally farmed meats to artisanal chocolate, nougat and hand-made ice cream, there is a wealth of culinary experiences to discover. The region is home to passionate and dynamic growers, chefs and producers – get amongst it by visiting a local farmers' market, take a tour of a kitchen garden, or do a cooking class to learn the process from paddock to plate! (AMRTA, 2015e: 11)

It follows that the region also lends itself to a much stronger promotion in the context of wellness tourism experiences. For example, initiatives like the Wholesome Life Retreat, offered at Smiths Beach Resort, one of the region's luxury self-contained accommodation providers, incorporates beachside fitness training and yoga coupled with live and raw food demonstrations supporting natural detox and eating options as well as an 'indulgent' tour to some of the area's organic food producers (Wholesome Live, 2015).

## Conclusion

The development of any region into a successful tourism destination, including a wellness tourism destination, poses challenges, particularly in the light of an ever more globalized world which offers consumers a wealth of often interchangeable experiences. Successful destination management therefore assists in the development of a unique and authentic destination profile, which provides the region with a competitive advantage (Sheldon and Park, 2009; Ritchie and Crouch, 2003). In the context of industrial districts and clusters (Porter 1990, 1998) it has been demonstrated that such a resource-based view by DMOs is advantageous as it gives due consideration to the destination's endogenous resources and competencies. On this basis a unique and hard to imitate wellness destination profile can be developed (Pforr, Hughes, Dawkins, and Gaunt, 2013; Pechlaner and Fischer, 2006; Haugland, Ness, Gronseth, and Aarsradt, 2011). However, these resources and competencies tend to spread across a wide range of stakeholders. Their active engagement and an effective coordination of their activities can be seen as another crucial aspect of successful wellness destination management, which thus needs to be built on strategic management, a resource-based approach as well as network and governance theory (Haugland, Ness, Gronseth, and Aarsradt, 2011; Denicolai, Cioccarelli, and Zucchella, 2010). Often called relational strategic destination management (Fischer, 2009), this approach enhances the core competencies of a particular regional setting (Bachinger, Pechlaner, and Widuckel, 2011; Pechlaner and Fischer, 2006), understood as 'the destination actors' collective ability to integrate, reconfigure, gain, and release distributed resources and competencies, and effectuate change' (Haugland, Ness, Gronseth, and Aarsradt, 2011: 273). In this context, the eight categories of wellness resources that form the basis of Voigt and Pforr's (2014) framework of wellness tourism destination competiveness have been analysed in relation to the Margaret River Wine Region.

In its current promotional material the Margaret River Wine Region already emphasizes many of the eight key resources that form the basis of Voigt and Pforr's (2014) framework. However, while already a key ingredient of the local wellness tourism industry, the case study area's natural assets could be even more strongly and more uniquely incorporated in its wellness products and services. A succinct example in this respect is the Samudra Yoga and Surf Retreat (Samudra, 2015) with its multi-modality Wellness Centre, located in the town of Dunsborough. It offers massage, musculoskeletal work and acupuncture, coupled with a range of yoga workshops. With its focus on blending surfing and wellness experiences, Samudra is tapping strongly into the region's wealth of natural resources, in particular its spectacular marine environment.

As has been identified in the preceding discussion, there is also still scope for further development, in particular in the area of wellness events and a stronger crossover with other sectors that could complement the existing wellness products and services. A specific 'Wellness Margaret River' weekend to showcase the region's diverse range of wellness experiences, similar to, for instance, the Florish Margaret River week that was held in October 2012 to highlight the region's biodiversity and natural beauty, or the annual Margaret River Gourmet Escape, marketed as 'an extraordinary festival of food and wine'[1] would greatly enhance the region's profile as a wellness tourism destination. Such an initiative showcasing a range of local wellness activities, workshops, presentations and displays would help attract new visitors, particularly from the Perth region, and could thus be an opportunity, especially for smaller operators, to showcase their business.

On the other hand, particularly the larger wellness operators in the region could benefit from more packaging initiatives, for example with accommodation and transport providers or tour operators and vice versa. At present, wellness products and services do not feature strongly in any of the inbound and wholesale packages, although in the light of an anticipated increasingly international market, specifically growth in the outbound China market based on recently introduced direct flight routes from China to Perth, such wellness packages would be beneficial for the region as a whole.

For continued future success, it will also be crucial to differentiate the wellness industry in the Margaret River Wine Region from its competitors elsewhere by providing wellness offerings within its unique context. A continued strong branding based on the region's endogenous potentials, in particular its nature-based wellness built on the region's rich natural resources and crossover products and services that draw on other key sectors that are well developed, such as its food and wine industry, could provide a significant competitive advantage.

However, a successful wellness tourism destination is also built on leadership. The steering of an increasingly complex network of wellness tourism stakeholders in the case study region requires effective and efficient network management. In this context, supported through an adequate government policy and planning framework, DMOs play a crucial role in developing and

---

1    See http://www.gourmetescape.com,

overseeing opportunities, providing leadership, bringing relevant network partners together and enhancing the relationships among the key stakeholders from the private and the public sector. It is important that this process is 'owned' and driven by the local community to give them a say in the direction and extent the wellness tourism industry in the region will develop. In the case of the Margaret River Wine Region it appears that while many of the essential key resources of a successful wellness tourism destination are already present, the region's DMO has to date not fully accepted its crucial role in assisting the development of a competitive wellness tourism destination. There is a need to fully amalgamate the available resources into a coherent wellness tourism destination image and to bundle them to form the basis of destination-specific wellness products and services. It can be argued that Wellness Margaret River, a marketing initiative driven by local wellness providers, has meanwhile stepped into this role and has tried to act as a platform that brings together and promotes the various wellness products and services that are available in the case study region.

To conclude, as assessed in this chapter using Voigt and Pforr's (2014) framework of wellness tourism destination competitiveness, the Margaret River Wine Region features many of the attributes identified in this model and is thus well placed to be developed into a competitive wellness tourism destination, in particular if some of the shortcomings identified in this analysis can be addressed.

## References

Alchemy Body and Soul (2015). Available at: http://www.alchemybodyandsoul.com/

AMRTA see Augusta Margaret River Tourism Association

Augusta Margaret River Mail (2013). *100 years of Margaret River: Timeline*, 7 February.

Augusta Margaret River Tourism Association (AMRTA) (2013). *Margaret River. com. Inspirational Stories 2013. Jewel of One of Lonely Planet's Top 10 Regions.* Available at: http://www.margaretriver.com/guide.pdf

Augusta Margaret River Tourism Association (AMRTA) (2014). *AMRTA Destination Marketing Plan and Strategy, 1 July 2014–30 June 2015.* Available at: http://corporate.margaretriver.com/wp-content/uploads/2014/09/AMRTA-Destination-Marketing-Strategy-Plan-2014–15.pdf

Augusta Margaret River Tourism Association (AMRTA) (2015a). *The Margaret River Region. Inspirational Food and Wine Journeys.* Available at: http://www.

margaretriver.com/uploads/file_library/file/32/Margaret_River_Region_-_Food_and_Wine_Journeys.pdf

Augusta Margaret River Tourism Association (AMRTA) (2015b). *Sun, Sea and Surf*. Available at: http://www.margaretriver.com/experiences/12

Augusta Margaret River Tourism Association (AMRTA) (2015c). *Explore the Region*. Available at: http://www.margaretriver.com/regions/

Augusta Margaret River Tourism Association (AMRTA) (2015d). *Get Back to Nature*. Available at: http://www.margaretriver.com/experiences/4

Augusta Margaret River Tourism Association (AMRTA) (2015e). *The Margaret River Region Visitor Guide 2015*. Available at: http://www.margaretriver.com/uploads/file_library/file/51/The_Margaret_River_Region_Visitor_Guide_2015.pdf

Augusta Margaret River Tourism Association (AMRTA) (2015f). *Events*. Available at: http://www.margaretriver.com/what-to-do/events

Australia's South West (2013). *Your Holiday Guide to Australia's South West 2013/2014*. Bunbury: Australia's South West.

Australia's South West (2015). *Margaret River*. Available at: http://www.australiassouthwest.com/Explore_Australias_South_West/Margaret_River_Region/Margaret_River

Australia Travel Market (2015). *Margaret River*. Available at: http://www.australiatravelmarket.com/discover/western-australia/margaret-river.html

Bachinger, M., Pechlaner, H., and Widuckel, W. (2011). *Regionen und Netzwerke*. Berlin: Springer Verlag.

Baggio, R., Scott, N., and Cooper, C. (2010). Network science: A review focused on tourism. *Annals of Tourism Research*, 37: 802–827. doi: 10.1177/0047287515569777

Condé Nast Traveller (2011). The Readers' Spa Awards 2011. Available at: http://www.cntraveller.com/magazine/readers-spa-awards-2011/page/spa-retreats-overseas

Crouch, G.I. (2010). Destination competitiveness: An analysis of determinant attributes, *Journal of Travel Research*, 50: 27–45. doi: 10.1177/0047287510362776

Denicolai, S., Cioccarelli, G., and Zucchella, A. (2010). Resource-based local development and networked core-competencies for tourism excellence. *Tourism Management*, 31: 260–266. doi: 10.1016/j.tourman.2009.03.002

Dwyer, L., and Kim, C. (2003). Destination competitiveness: Determinants and indicators. *Current Issues in Tourism*, 6:369–414. doi:10.1080/13683500308667962

Enright, M.J., and Newton, J. (2005). Determinants of tourism destination competitiveness in Asia Pacific: Comprehensiveness and universality. *Journal of Travel Research*, 43: 339–350. doi: 10.1177/0047287505274647

Fischer, E. (2009). *Das kompetenzorientierte Management der touristischen Destination*. Wiesbaden: Gabler.

Hassan, S. (2000). Determinants of market competitiveness in an environmentally sustainable tourism industry. *Journal of Travel Research*, 38 (February), 239–245.

Haugland, S.A., Ness, H., Gronseth, B.-O., and Aarsradt, J. (2011). Development of tourism destinations: An integrated multilevel perspective. *Annals of Tourism Research*, 38: 268–290. doi: 10.1016/j.annals.2010.08.008.

Hjalager, A.-M. (2011). The invention of a Danish well-being tourism region: Strategy, substance, structure, and symbolic action. *Tourism Planning and Development*, 8: 51–67. doi: 10.1080/21568316.2011.554044

Hughes, M. (2014). Researching the links between parklands and health. In C. Voigt and C. Pforr (eds), *Wellness Tourism: A Destination Perspective* (147–160). Milton Park: Routledge.

Injidup Spa Retreat (2015). Available at: http://www.injidupsparetreat.com.au/

Living Synergy (2015). Available at: http://www.livingsynergy.com.au/home/

McCormack, J. (2010). Cape to Cape Track. *Australian Geographic*, 20 October. Available at: http://www.australiangeographic.com.au/travel/destinations/2010/10/cape-to-cape-track/

Margaret River Visitor Centre (2015). *Discovering the Region*. Available at: https://www.margaretriver.com/uploads/file_library/file/31/Margaret_River_Region_Map.pdf

Margaret River Wellness Centre (2015). Company Profile. Available at: http://www.wellness-centre.com.au/companyprofile.asp

Margaret River Wine Association (2015). *Our Industry*. Available at: http://margaretriverwine.info/region/our-industry/

Mitchell, R., Charters, S., and Albrecht, J.N. (2012). Cultural systems and the wine tourism product. *Annals of Tourism Research*, 39: 311–335. doi: 10.1016/j.annals.2011.05.002

Pechlaner, H., and Fischer, E. (2006). Alpine wellness: A resource-based view. *Tourism Recreation Research*, 31: 67–77. doi: 10.1080/02508281.2006.11081248

Pechlaner, H., Fischer, E., and Hamman, E.-M. (2008). Leadership and innovation process: Development of products and services based on core competencies. *Journal of Quality Assurance in Hospitality and Tourism*, 6: 31–57. doi: 10.1300/J162v06n03_03

Pechlaner, H., Reuter, C., and Bachinger, M. (2014). Identification and development of core competencies as a basis for regional development with special focus on health tourism. In C. Voigt and C. Pforr (eds). *Wellness Tourism: A Destination Perspective* (112–129). Milton Park: Routledge.

Pforr, C. (2007). realignment of regional tourism: The case of Western Australia. *International Journal of Tourism Policy*, 1(1): 33–44.

Pforr, C., Hughes, M., Dawkins, M., and Gaunt, E. (2013). Nature-based wellness tourism: The case of the Margaret River region in Western Australia.

In C. Voigt and C. Pforr (eds). *Wellness Tourism: A Destination Perspective* (176–187). New York: Routledge.

Porter, M.E. (1990). *The Competitive Advantage of Nations*. New York: The Free Press.

Porter, M.E. (1998). Clusters and the new economics of competition. *Harvard Business Review*, 76(6): 77–90.

Prideaux, B., Berbigier, D., and Thompson, M. (2014). Wellness tourism and destination competitiveness. In C. Voigt and C. Pforr (eds) *Wellness Tourism: A Destination Perspective* (45–60). Milton Park: Routledge.

Pullman Bunker Bay Resort (2015). Available at: http://www.pullmanhotels.com/gb/hotel-8775-pullman-bunker-bay-resort-margaret-river-region/index.shtml

Ritchie, J.R.B., and Crouch, G.I. (2003). *The Competitive Destination: A Sustainable Tourism Perspective*. Wallingford: CABI Publishing.

Ryan, C. (2002). Equity, management, power sharing and sustainability: Issues of the 'new tourism'. *Tourism Management*, 23: 17–26. doi: 10.1016/S0261–5177(01)00064–4

Samudra (2015). Available at: http://samudra.com.au/

Sheldon, P.J., and Park, S.-Y. (2009). Development of a sustainable wellness tourism destination. In R. Bushell and P.J. Sheldon (eds), *Wellness and Tourism* (99–113). New York: Cognizant.

Smith, M., and Puczkó, L. (2009). *Health and Wellness Tourism*. Oxford: Butterworth-Heinemann.

South West Aboriginal Land and Sea Council (2015). *Noongar Knowledge. Margaret River*. Available at: http://www.noongarculture.org.au/margaret-river/

Tourism Australia (2015). *Regional Tourism Profile for Australia's South West 2012/13*. Available at: http://www.tourism.australia.com/statistics/visitor-statistics.aspx

Tourism Western Australia (2005). *Tourism Western Australia Strategic Plan 2005–2010*. Perth: Tourism WA. Gold Coast: Sustainable Tourism CRC.

Tourism Western Australia (2014a). *Fast Facts Year Ending September 2014*. Perth: TWA.

Tourism Western Australia (2014b). *Tourism Western Australia*. Available at: http://www.tourism.wa.gov.au/Pages/welcome_to_tourism_western_australia.aspx

Tourism Western Australia (2015). *Where Rolling Vineyards Sit Against a Backdrop of Ocean and Forest*. Available at: http://www.westernaustralia.com/au/Destinations/Australias_South_West/Pages/Australias_South_West.aspx

Voigt, C. (2010). *Understanding Wellness Tourism: An Analysis of Benefits Sought, Health-promoting Behaviours and Positive Psychological Well-being*.

Unpublished thesis, University of South Australia. Voigt, C. (2014). Towards a conceptualisation of wellness tourism. In C. Voigt and C. Pforr (eds), *Wellness Tourism: A Destination Perspective* (19–44). Milton Park: Routledge.

Voigt, C., and Laing, J. (2014). An examination of the extent of collaboration between major wellness tourism stakeholders in Australia. In C. Voigt and C. Pforr (eds), *Wellness Tourism: A Destination Perspective* (63–77). Milton Park: Routledge.

Voigt, C., Laing, J., Wray, M., Grown, G., Howat, G., Weiler, B., and Trembath, R. (2010). *Health Tourism in Australia. Supply, Demand and Opportunities*. Gold Coast, Queensland: CRC for Sustainable Tourism pty Ltd.

Voigt, C., and Pforr, C. (2014). Concluding discussion: Implications for destination development and management. In C. Voigt and C. Pforr (eds), *Wellness Tourism: A Destination Perspective* (289–310). Milton Park: Routledge.

Wardan Aboriginal Centre (2010). *Cultural Activities. Bush Story Trail*. Available at: http://www.wardan.com.au/home.htm

Weiler, B., and Hall, C.M. (1992). *Special Interest Tourism*. London: Belhaven Books.

Wellness Margaret River (2014). *Cape to Cape Wellness. Health and Wellbeing*. Available at: http://www.wellnessmargaretriver.com.au/index.html

Wholesome Life (2015). Available at: http://www.wholesomelife.com.au/

Wray, M., and Weiler, B. (2014). Wellness tourism: The factors and processes that drive sustainable regional destinations. In C. Voigt and C. Pforr (eds), *Wellness Tourism: A Destination Perspective* (78–98). Milton Park: Routledge.

# Chapter 14

# Conclusion

ELISA INNERHOFER and HARALD PECHLANER

This volume is a collection of articles on innovation, resource-based strategic management approaches, and hospitality and tourism management concepts. It analyses successful innovation strategies by integrating the resource-based and the competence-based views and their advance into the dynamic capabilities approach and the relational view. As well as theoretical explanations and frameworks, the contributions give numerous practical examples and case studies.

The chapters collected in this volume together emphasize the wide range of innovations in tourism. Different processes through which individuals, companies and organizations manage changing market conditions and satisfy the changing needs of their customers are illustrated. These processes include the modification of existing products, the adaptation of outdated and unattractive products, and the development of new products or service offerings, as well as the introduction of new marketing activities, the use of new distribution methods and changes in the management and leadership of tourism businesses and organizations.

The case studies presented recognize resources and competences as crucial for differentiation and innovation development. The examples of resource and competence-based innovations in hospitality and tourism show that a resource-based strategic approach in the management of tourism businesses and destinations can lead to the development of successful innovations and, consequently, to improved competitiveness. The authors combine innovations in hospitality and tourism with the resource-based approach of strategic management and present cases of successful innovation development through competence and cooperative competence-building. However, although this volume focuses on resources and competences as sources of competitive advantages, it recognizes the importance of external factors and the local environment in which a firm or other organization is based. Environment, customers' needs and requirements, and competitive markets are subject to change. Exogenous conditions affect the performance of companies, as well as destinations, and their resource and competence base. From a theoretical point of view the chapters in this volume combine resource- and competence-based strategic management approaches in an exemplary manner.

In addition another important aspect is pointed out in several chapters: that innovation in tourism requires relationship-building, collaboration, and the ability of actors to cooperate and exchange their resources, competences and experiences. In order to develop tourism businesses and destinations and to offer innovative tourism products and services along the entire tourism value chain, the willingness of private and public service providers and organizations to cooperate and to share knowledge seems to be crucial. Company and organizational boundaries have to be spanned and knowledge-sharing routines, as well as networking capabilities, are key success factors. From a theoretical perspective, it is the relational view which analyses and explains the ability to collaborate and to build inter-organizational relationships. The approach explains in theoretical terms how inter-firm routines and processes may gain a company competitive advantage.

Most new product development research literature is based on manufacturing industries, while development and innovation processes in tourism businesses and destinations have been of little interest for a long time. Researchers have paid little attention to innovation competences and new product development in service industries in general and in tourism in particular. However, the ever more globalized world puts more and more pressure on destination authorities, marketing agencies in destinations and tourism businesses, and calls for innovations to satisfy changing customer needs and to respond to changing market conditions. The practical approach in the chapters collected in this volume shows that tourism businesses and destination managers are often ahead of researchers, and that even if they act in an ad hoc manner and without strategic planning, they do innovate (see, for example, Innerhofer, 2012). In order to further develop innovation activities, to enhance performance and to stay in line with market requirements, some authors elaborate on recommendations for managers and entrepreneurs in tourism.

Changing market conditions and trends pose several challenges for destinations and hospitality businesses. Globalization is one of the major trends. At the same time a growing desire and need for regionalization, locally incorporated networks and sustainability can be observed (Gatterer, Reiter, and Rützler, 2014; Wenzel, Kirig, and Rauch, 2009). In addition to regionalization, the increasing attention of different countries on the green economy and sustainable production and consumption patterns can be observed (see, for example, Wenzel, Kirig, and Rauch, 2009). Green products gain ground in the mass market, alternative mobility concepts are getting becoming crucial in urban development strategies; the organic segment in the food industry, as well as preferences for regional food products, continue to grow; and green investments are becoming increasingly popular (Bundesministerium für Bildung und Forschung, 2014). The authors of several chapters show how these trends and developments influence innovation development in tourism businesses and destinations. By analysing the Northern Black Forest, Bachinger and Rau (Chapter 3) found out that establishing green innovations in destinations hampered by a lack of knowledge among tourism businesses in natural resources and of customer expectations. Based on their study, Bachinger and Rau make recommendations for green entrepreneurship; and Pforr, Voigt, and Locher (Chapter 13) also emphasize the importance of regional products and sustainably produced food for the development of attractive tourism packages. Other authors, like Baird and Hall (Chapter 12), focus on destination-specific natural products such as wine as the basis for the development of specific tourism types (in that case, wine tourism).

These cases and the types of innovation described illustrate that a rethink is taking place in the tourism industry towards favouring sustainable tourism. In order to meet the objectives of the Rio+20 conference towards sustainable development and to implement the 10YFP [10-Year Framework of Programmes], Programme on Sustainable Tourism, managed by the UN World Tourism Organization (UNWTO), ideas for innovation in tourism have to consider different aspects of economic, environmental, and social sustainability. The 10YFP Programme on Sustainable Tourism (United Nations, 2015), catalyses changes in tourism operations and promotes transformation for sustainability through efficiency, innovation, and adaptability. The programme aims to integrate sustainable consumption and production (SCP) patterns in tourism-related policies and frameworks, fostering collaboration among stakeholders for the improvement of the tourism sector's SCP performance, promoting the application of guidelines and technical solutions to prevent and mitigate the impact of tourism and enhancing sustainable tourism investments (United Nations, 2015).

This volume may encourage the shift towards more sustainable development of the tourism sector. Through sustainable innovation in tourism design and operations, consumers may be sensitized and encouraged to demand more sustainable consumption and production patterns.

The editors believe that this volume can advance tourism literature by relating the field of innovation in tourism to the resource-based theory of strategic management by combining innovation in tourism with networking behaviour of actors within a destination and by illustrating the possibilities of cooperative competence-building and its importance for successful innovation development. Recommendations may be of interest for practitioners. However, the editors of this book are aware of the existence of certain limitations.

Recommendations made in its chapters may work in some tourism businesses and fail in others depending on the situational context. The combination of theoretical insights and practical examples given in the case studies enables this volume aims to reach a wide audience. It may serve professors, students and academics as a teaching and course book for innovation management, strategic innovation development, innovation in hospitality and tourism, and cooperative innovation development in destinations. It also targets researchers in the field of resource- and competence-based management and presents them with the science of tourism as a field for the application of resource-based management approaches. In addition, this volume is of interest to a practitioner audience. Practitioners from the hospitality and tourism industry can learn from different best practice examples and may gain inputs for the development of innovations.

The purpose of this book has been to make a contribution to the literature on innovation in tourism through the collection of studies on an international level. Destinations and tourism businesses all over the world have served as examples. The editors recommend that similar research has to be carried out, for which the limitations of the research presented in this volume highlight additional paths to explore.

## References

*Bundesministerium für Bildung und Forschung* (2014). Bonn: Forschungsagenda Green Economy.

Gatterer, H., Reiter, W., and Rützler, H. (2014). *Workbook Hotel der Zukunft 2014.* Wien: Zukunftsinstitut Österreich GmbH.

Innerhofer, E. (2012). *Strategische Innovationen in der Hotellerie. Eine ressourcenorientierte Fallstudienanalyse touristischer Dienstleistungsunternehmen.* Wiesbaden: Springer Gabler Verlag.

United Nations (2015). United Nations Environment Programme, Sustainable Tourism Programme. Nairobi: UNEP. [Online.] Available at: http://www. unep.org/10yfp/Programmes/ProgrammeConsultationandCurrentStatus/ Sustainabletourism/tabid/106269/Default.aspx [accessed 17 September, 2015].

Wenzel, E., Kirig, A., and Rauch, C. (2008). *Greenomics – Wie der grüne Lifestyle Märkte und Konsumenten verändert.* München: Redline Verlag.

Wenzel, E., Kirig, A., and Rauch, C. (2009). *Lohas. Bewusst grün – alles über die neuen Lebenswelten.* München: Redline Verlag.

# Index

For Product Safety Concerns and Information please contact our EU
representative GPSR@taylorandfrancis.com Taylor & Francis Verlag GmbH,
Kaufingerstraße 24, 80331 München, Germany


Printed and bound by CPI Group (UK) Ltd, Croydon, CR0 4YY
01/05/2025
01858383-0002